The Sum
of Trifles

For Moreland, Glenn, and Theo

Is sorrow not, one asks, the only thing
in the world people really possess?

—VLADIMIR NABOKOV, *Pnin*

Contents

The Sum
of Trifles

FIRST

Always Magic

Keep? Trash? Donate? Sell?

"Come in the house," my mother used to call, every time she heard me at the door. She'd emerge from the sanctuary of her book-filled office, burning cigarette in hand, to welcome me home. "I'm so glad to see you," she'd say, her voice loud if Daddy's jazz was bebopping forth from the den, quiet if he was napping back in the bedroom.

"Come in the house."

Now when I walk into the frigid side hall, there's only the crunch underfoot of the dried leaves my brother Moreland tracked in the last time he checked on the place. Dead bugs and mouse droppings litter the black-and-white vinyl floor, but nothing stirs when I flick on the fixture over the kitchen sink.

I flip the switches in the front hall, with its flocked yellow wallpaper and ornate gold mirror, reminiscent of a pagoda. I bump up the thermostat. The place is freezing, but even if it weren't, I'd keep my coat on. There's nowhere clean to set it down.

Dust is general all over the house. It's burning as the furnace lurches into action. Specks glitter in the afternoon sun slanting through the living room blinds, drawing bright lines on the gray-and-blue Chinese rug, twenty feet square. Dust coats the mahogany tea tables, the two-hundred-year-old writing desk from Massachusetts, my mother's small collection of Korean celadon vessels.

In the den, the brown sofa is covered by the rumpled bath towel Mom used as a slipcover. For a moment, I imagine everything as it used to be; I pretend that the towel is rucked because my mother has just roused herself to go find her cigarettes or answer the phone or make popcorn to share with my father while they watch a movie. Then I open the blinds, breaking my little spell. Here's the dust again—on Daddy's turntable and the long-necked African statue, on the abandoned wheelchairs and empty hospital bed, on the wide window ledge and its row of pottery in which dead moths are gradually turning to powder.

Reviewing art exhibitions for a local weekly in the late 1990s, I became fascinated by a show called *Material World*, a series of large photographs of families around the globe. Each family represented the statistical average for their country, in terms of size and household income; the photographer had posed the members in front of their dwelling, surrounded by all of their belongings. The inventories ranged from luxurious (Kuwaitis, four cars) to basic (Ethiopians, livestock, pots and baskets used for food preparation). Pictures taken in affluent places like Japan, Germany, and the United States showed profusions of furniture, clothes, electronics, toys, and decorative items.

What would a similar portrait of my parents, my brother, and me have looked like, back in the early 1980s when I was growing up in Greensboro, North Carolina? Four white people standing in front of a ranch-style brick house. My father, a tall, broad-shouldered, dark-haired man in a button-down shirt; my mother, a blue-eyed brunette in a silky blouse and patterned wrap skirt. My brother, a stringy freckled redhead, awkward in the coat and tie Mom has insisted on for the picture. She's still irritated because my father refused to dress up, and if you look carefully, you can see the mutual annoyance lingering in Daddy's set jaw, Mom's forced smile. And then there's me, the youngest and smallest, a sturdy, beaming, square-faced girl in a smock-front dress, white stockings, Mary Janes. All around us, spread beneath the tulip poplars Moreland and I climb when not wearing Sunday clothes, is a vast array of objects from other places and times, a collection nobody would expect to find in such a modest-looking house.

Imagining us posing for such a portrait, I laughed at how impossible it would be to drag out into the yard every single item my parents owned. Years later, in 2012, the idea no longer amused me. My parents had died within six months of each other, and it was time to sell their house. In the forty years they'd lived there, the square footage had grown to about three thousand, mimicking the national trend toward bigger houses. Mom had converted the garage to living space, then added a large back room to hold the remnants of the antiques shop they'd been forced to close when Daddy's health declined and it became clear he'd lose his feet to diabetes. Later, when Mom knew she was dying, she wrote instructions about where to sell certain antiques, but she wanted us to keep far more furniture than Moreland and I could use. We also needed to disperse several thousand books, including her extensive library on the decorative arts. Papers and memorabilia packed every closet and drawer, cabinet and shelf. Sorting through it and deciding what to do with each and every thing—not to mention rustling up the hands necessary to get it all out the door—presented a Herculean task.

Moreland and I never considered letting anybody else perform this daunting job for us. Dealing with stuff, especially old stuff, was the family business. For almost three decades, Tyler-Smith Antiques was a fixture in downtown Greensboro. Daddy kept shop in a rented, two-story yellow house on the corner of Smith and Simpson Streets, while Mom went on buying trips or traveled to set up her booth at antiques shows in Raleigh or Charlotte or Asheville. This arrangement suited them, as he was sedentary and depended on routine, and she liked to be out and about.

She enrolled first Moreland, then me, in a morning preschool at the Episcopal church down the street; afternoons we spent at the shop. Upstairs in the office, Daddy read the *Wall Street Journal* or wrote sales in his olive-green ledger, and Mom researched her latest finds. Downstairs, Moreland and I squabbled in the playroom, penned in by a wooden baby gate that pinched our fingers if we tried to escape. The worn scratchy carpet smelled of products used to brighten the shop's wares: Wright's silver polish, baby oil to clean lacquer, Old English to fill in scratches on furniture. We played amid a sea of toys and books as the radio hummed the hits: "Raindrops Keep Falling on My Head," and "Funkytown," and "Sexual Healing."

Merchandise arrived and departed in Mom's van, a matte-green 1970s camper stripped of its bunk and golden burlap curtains. She was always wrangling "stuff," as she liked to call it—buying, selling, moving, arranging, studying—all the while bemoaning that there was too much of it. "Stuff!" she'd say, shaking her head as though the idea disgusted her. And then, the next day, the next hour, she'd bring home yet another thing from a flea market or junk shop, pleased with herself for having paid much less than what she could get for it.

From her, I learned that knowledge, aside from its nobler qualities, can give you a financial advantage. But for her, the business was about much more than profit. She wasn't religious, yet she saw relics everywhere, often justifying a purchase by saying she'd felt compelled to "rescue" it from its abject surroundings, from the shop proprietor and the other customers too ignorant to see its value. She dealt in higher-end stuff, mostly eighteenth- and early nineteenth-century—you wouldn't find Coca-Cola signs or Mammy cookie jars or Depression glass at Tyler-Smith Antiques. When she spied a "true antique" sitting in a midden heap of modern junk, she couldn't just leave it sitting there—it was *too good*. How could she stop bringing things home when the world kept turning up its curious treasures to her?

Spend more than a second looking at a particular object in the shop, and my mother or father would explain what cultural developments in China or Germany had led to the object's manufacture. They'd hypothesize how the thing had made its way to North Carolina and who might have owned it. They'd demonstrate how the object was used or take it apart to reveal its construction. One of Mom's favorite moves was to pronounce it time to perform a "full rectal" on a table or chair. She'd then ask the stunned customer to help her flip the piece over so she could show them the joinery and look for secondary woods, cabinetmakers' marks, or evidence of repairs.

My favorite items had to do with daily living. I liked holding in my hand things people had used in an intimate way two hundred years ago: a silver snuffbox carried in a man's pocket, a wooden busk a fashionable woman inserted in her bodice to stiffen it, tongs to be heated in the fire, then used to curl someone's hair. At five years old, I delighted in demonstrating to customers the workings of an antique commode cabinet, always offering the revelation of the pot as a punchline: *It's a toilet!* These objects proved that people from the past were not made up like characters in books; they had been as real as I was, with physical bodies full of needs and desires.

Best to me were travel desks, boxes that opened to make a slanted surface for writing. One retained its original green felt and a frayed stub of ribbon that you gently pulled to lift the writing surface and access the compartment beneath, divided into sections to hold ink, pens, and penknives; seals, wax, and paper. The most elegant traveling desks sported dovetail joints, decorative inlay, and, if we were lucky, a key that still turned.

Already a reader and writer, I loved learning words for things now obsolete: *porringer, Betty lamp, sugar nippers, niddy noddy*. These strange objects taught me about the inevitability of change. Wicks and lamp oil are replaced by filaments, which are then replaced by CFLs. When sugar ceases to be shipped in cones, nippers are no long necessary.

As enamored as I was of certain things in the shop, I knew they weren't really ours. They might stay for years, or they might be sold tomorrow. They were like the animals a farmer raises for slaughter—best not to get too attached.

I also knew how important the stock was to our parents and couldn't help feeling a bit jealous of it. Once, a customer asked if it made my mother nervous to have us little children around so many precious antiques. As soon as Mom proudly said we'd never broken anything, my brother picked up a porcelain teacup and dropped it on the floor. "He looked me dead in the eye when he did it," she would always say later. "He knew exactly what he was doing." Once, after I'd been told not to, I stood in a chair and my foot went through the seat. I got a spanking and a lecture about the expense of repairing cane.

These two incidents became part of Mom's repertoire. When she repeated such stories, I knew the point was supposed to be that our stubbornness was funny. But to my tender, resentful ears, it sounded—for just a moment—as though she thought the antiques more worthy of protection than the children.

As soon as toddlers cotton on to the idea of ownership, they clutch everything in sight, repeating one word until it sounds like a mantra: *mine, mine.* Who can blame them? As children, we live in a world not built to our scale, and we naturally seek things to call our own. Our first possessions delight us because they are *intended for us,* unlike so much else in the house, all the forbidding and forbidden stuff we are told to leave alone because it's fragile, expensive, dangerous, or simply *not ours.*

My crib. At bedtime, my mother put me in it, filled it with toys and books, kissed me goodnight. The light on, I'd play happily, throwing out things as I tired of them, until the crib was empty and I finally went to sleep.

Teddy bear. Classic brown, stubby arms and legs, plastic eyes reflecting the light.

Fisher-Price record player. Red and white, with a compartment in the back for storing a handful of plastic discs. I fell asleep to "Twinkle, Twinkle, Little Star" as the humidifier purred and bubbled, pumping into the room a cool mist meant to appease my asthma.

Books: Little Golden, Richard Scarry, Mother Goose.

My soft doll with comedian Flip Wilson on one side and his alter ego Geraldine on the other. When you pulled the cord, Flip/Geraldine said things like they said on TV: "Oh yeah? And I'll punch you right in the fist with my face!" and "The devil made me buy this dress!"

A Victorian child's rocking chair with a finely caned seat I already knew enough to be afraid to sit in.

When I think of or see one of these objects now, it all comes back: the bear's fur soft beneath my sleepy touch, the plinky familiar music, the moist air easy to breathe, the reassuring light in the hall.

In 1953 psychoanalyst and pediatrician Donald Winnicott published a paper about what he called the "transitional object," or the "first 'not-me' possession." It's usually a stuffed toy or blanket to which children become extremely attached, something they can use to soothe themselves when their mothers are absent. This "not-me possession" is supposed to teach you that you don't always need your mother, that you can be separate.

The closest thing to a transitional object for me was a worn-out fitted sheet I insisted on keeping balled up in my bed. Falling asleep,

I liked to hold a corner of it, I liked to be sure part of my body was touching each of my stuffed animals. Anyone I didn't touch would feel left out and sad. When my mother finally threw out my tattered sheet, I cried. But I have no memory of carrying it or anything else with me when I stayed with my grandparents or, later, went to overnight camp. Had anybody tried to sell me then on the idea of the transitional object, I would have scoffed. What kind of dummy would fall for a stupid idea like that? A toy? Replace *my* mother?

I adored my mother. I wrote her love notes and sang songs in which the only word was *Mama*, chanted over and over. If she was going out, I wanted to go with her. If she left me with Daddy, I would cry, secretly, chokingly, trying to hide my misery because I suspected my tears would irritate him. I loved my mother's smell, her husky voice, her smoky kisses. I loved to nestle against her warmth. The font of all goodness—affection, food, books, laughter—she tended to my needs.

I took it for granted that I could keep forever anything—and anyone—I deemed important. Then, one day—I don't remember what happened to make me understand this so suddenly—I realized that my mother was bound, like every other person, to die.

How old are you when this awareness of death strikes? Four? Five? The shocking thought dropped at bedtime. Now I knew why I was afraid of the dark. I began to cry. I got up and headed toward the light in the hall, toward my mother.

At the threshold, I hesitated. My grandparents were visiting. All the adults were laughing in the den. What if they called me silly when I went to ask for reassurance? My fear verged on panic. It could not stand teasing; I couldn't risk it. Instead, I stood barefoot in the half-light, weeping desperately, just as I would thirty years later, when I learned my mother had lung cancer, and for a long time after that whatever anybody said to me was the wrong thing to say, because it couldn't change the fundamental truth that, sooner or later, everything, and everybody, must go.

My mother's office is the warmest room in the house on a winter day. It's not a large room, and three walls of built-in bookcases and cabinets packed tight with books and papers provide excellent insulation. Despite the bookcases' sour goldenrod color—further yellowed by nicotine—I envy this office, the sort of space Virginia Woolf famously wrote about: a room of one's own. In such a cocoon, I imagine, a writer might do the long, slow work of transforming her visions into their final form.

I sit at Mom's kneehole desk and survey the papers cluttering the surface: correspondence, bills, magazines, to-do lists. A firm believer in lists, Mom jotted them on torn envelopes or scrap paper. When something serious was afoot, though, and she needed to embark on heavy thinking, she'd say, "Get me a yellow legal pad." All of life's crises might be weathered with the aid of a yellow legal pad, a Co'-Cola, and a pack of 100s.

In this messy room, my mother made much of her living during her last twenty professional years. Clients hired her to value household antiques for insurance or estate purposes, or because they were divorcing and needed to divvy up the assets. Here at this desk she researched and wrote hundreds of appraisals. She saved copies of them all in the four tan file cabinets lined up under the double window that looks out, uninspiringly, onto the driveway. Stacks of files and magazines slide into each other atop the file cabinets. Though she tried occasionally to tidy, cleaning bored her, and her office always remained a sea of paper.

That it was a room for work—as much as the fact that his wheelchair couldn't fit through the narrow double doors—kept my father out. Work was an activity he preferred others to perform while he hovered nearby, suggesting how they might do it better.

Alone at her desk, my mother could do what she liked, e-mailing friends or talking for hours on the phone, smoking the air blue as she played computer solitaire late into the night.

When my son was in preschool, I hung out with my mom several times a week. Although we both worked—I was a freelance editor, she was still doing the occasional antiques appraisal—care-giving shaped our days. Sitting across this desk from each other, we planned errands and doctors' appointments, lunches and outings with my son and nephews to the children's museum or the science center. In the mornings, we kept quiet because Daddy got mad if he woke before noon; in the afternoons, we avoided interrupting his naps. Often Moreland came over after work; sometimes the children and our spouses joined us, sometimes our cousins, and we'd all get loud and funny over takeout and beer.

On quieter nights, Mom, Moreland, and I repaired here to this desk to research a recently bought antique, talking and laughing as we leafed through books and searched the internet. It was a room for learning, but not all the things we learned here were good. Here, in the days of the landline, Mom offered consolation to friends sharing troubling news: failures and rejections, betrayals and divorces, illnesses and deaths. Here, one October evening in 2006, Mom delivered to me her own bad news: a spot on her lung. For weeks, months, afterward, I struggled to make sense of what this news would mean for her, for me, for the rest of the family. We all depended on her; what would we do when she died?

Here I sit now, six years later, alone with her yellow legal pad. The unthinkable has happened. I'm not yet forty. Most of my friends can offer no advice because they haven't faced this dilemma yet. The house must be emptied, and I'm trying to figure out where the hell to begin.

My brother is my partner in this endeavor, but he's like Daddy, he'll put off an unpleasant task indefinitely. Me? I'm like Mom—I hate to have a problem weighing on me. I want to make it disappear as fast as I can. This impatience goes way back. Among my first toys was a wooden box with a red lid. Cut into the lid were holes through which to pass square, triangle, circle, rhombus. After a few frustrated attempts to line up the blocks with the holes, it occurred to me to simply open the lid and drop the blocks inside. Problem solved. Toy conquered.

But there's no workaround for the problem I'm facing now. A recent statistic claims that the average American household contains three hundred thousand items, and I fear my parents' house is above average. Everything here requires a decision my brother and I must make: Keep? Trash? Donate? Sell?

We've cleaned out plenty of houses. Before Moreland's children were born, he ran a tag-sale business, a side hustle to his day job as a university IT administrator. Occasionally, the client was downsizing to a smaller place, but the usual scenario was that an elderly person or couple moved to a nursing home or died, and their family hired Moreland to sort, price, and sell what they didn't want to keep, everything from prized parlor heirlooms to jars of rusty nails in the garage.

At a yard sale, people shop in the yard. At a tag sale, the public is allowed to wander through the rooms of the sellers' house. Items difficult to carry, such as a dining table or a set of china, bear a price tag with a tear-off portion for the customer to bring to the cashier table—hence, "tag sale." In my late teens and early twenties, I helped run my brother's cashier table on sale days. Dealing with customers sucked, but $10 an hour was good money.

Better to me than cashiering was what we called the gross sort, the initial step of emptying every hidey-hole in the sale house. Left alone in some stranger's kitchen or bedroom, I spread everything out, grouped similar items, and flagged for special consideration things that might bring a high price. I trashed what was too filthy or broken for anybody to give even a nickel for, and put aside what couldn't be offered at a tag sale: checkbooks, liquor, drugs. Pornography. Firearms. Gold teeth.

Performing the gross sort appealed to my general compulsion to impose order. As I worked, I discovered much that was interesting, and much that was not. Kitchen cabinets spilled the trendy gadgets of yesteryear: yogurt makers, cookie presses, ridged plastic pans for microwaving bacon. In every geriatric bathroom, an ancient enema kit lay in wait under the sink, its brittle rubber bulb and tubing coiled in the original box. What about the mid-twentieth century had chronically constipated an entire generation of affluent people? In desks and attics, I uncovered love letters and photographs, Purple Hearts and creepy dolls. The writer-voyeur in me loved being permitted to look so closely into other people's lives, yet it was also depressing to see, again and again, how the things that make up a home—a personal, intimate world—eventually become nothing more than the residue of a life spent.

In the tag-sale years, Mom was healthy and energetic. I never worried about having to clean out her house. Later, throughout my twenties and thirties, that house remained the constant toward which the vacillating needle of my home-seeking compass always pointed. Even when I was living someplace I liked better, arriving at my parents' meant coming home. It's crushing now to contemplate a future in which I can't come here and feel their presence.

Many people say food triggers their richest memories. Think of the often-cited Proustian madeleine: it is symbol, it is synecdoche, it is smell, it is taste, it is memory, it is thing. It is the hardest-working cookie in all of literature. What might mine be? Perhaps a Little Debbie Nutty Bar, the overly sweet taste of which summons my paternal grandmother's kitchen, where her green apple-shaped cookie jar sat on the counter next to one of her three televisions. We watched contestants spin the glittering wheel on *The Price Is Right* while we ate at the round table with its own spinning wheel, the lazy Susan that smoothly delivered napkins, salt and pepper, more supper. I haven't eaten a Nutty Bar in years. Yet whenever I go to the grocery store and see the yellow box, the red letters, and Little Debbie's smiling cheeks, I feel the sugar charge through my jaw. "It makes my teeth sing," my brother liked to say. One look at that box, and, à la Proust, I am transported.

But what I remember even better than the cookie itself is the clank of the jar lid, the whir of the spinning wheel. For me, it's objects, not food, that evoke the richest memories. Of the thousands of things I grew up knowing or own now, which is my madeleine? Which one would I single out above all others for its ability to trigger memories of my childhood, that time before the trouble of growing up and being a grown-up? I cannot choose. All my things mean something to me—each is a key that unlocks a memory or set of memories. No one of them is essential, but together they fill a cabinet of recollection I would hate to lose.

For solace, I turn to my most reliable balm: books. I hope the process of emptying the house will hurt less if I can frame it as an intellectual exercise.

I read about loss and grief, about executing estates, about decluttering and letting go of things that no longer serve you. In 2012, Marie Kondo's U.S. debut is still in the future, and anyway, whatever has to happen here goes way beyond "tidying up." I find few books that address the existential questions associated with relinquishing your parents' belongings.

Inertia isn't an option, though. The financial and psychological burdens of maintaining this house and its contents aren't sustainable. Moreland and I both agree that we need to move forward, but we feel a pressure to get rid of everything a certain way—the *right* way. We've been raised to pay attention not only to the monetary value of antiques and art but also to what such things signify about themselves, their owners, and the world in which they circulate. Our parents saw objects as repositories of historical and cultural knowledge; they admired beauty, form, sublimity. They collected much of what they owned with thoughtful intention, and for my brother and me, it would be profoundly disrespectful to be careless in putting asunder what they joined together.

In *The Year of Magical Thinking*, Joan Didion tells how she couldn't bear to get rid of her dead husband's shoes because he might return and need them. If I think the same—that my parents might come back—it's not conscious. The loss feels utterly final: I have no hope of seeing them again. My own magical thinking has to do with preserving a place imbued with their spirit. If their things don't remain where they gathered them, I worry, my parents' spirits will vanish. The whole collection is magic; to disturb it, blasphemous.

In stories, as in life, people lose objects, forget them, search for them, destroy them. A particular object can take on significance beyond its function or value. Think of the Moonstone, Rosebud, the Maltese falcon, the Holy Grail. Why do people fight and even die trying to secure these things? The writer Italo Calvino says, "Around the magic object there forms a kind of force field that is in fact the territory of the story itself. We might say that the magic object is an outward and visible sign that reveals the connection between people or between events."

Calvino points to the narrative significance of particular magic objects, but my mother and I found countless objects significant. When I recall her "rescuing" antiques, or my childhood conviction that stuffed animals had feelings, I realize that our notions verged on animism—the belief that everything in the world, animate or inanimate, possesses a spirit or a soul. Animism is a crucial part of many religious, cultural, and spiritual traditions. Christians and atheists alike have tended to dismiss this way of thinking as "primitive." Yet I'd guess that even those of us who consider ourselves too rational to ascribe souls to rocks or trees remain powerfully attached to certain personal possessions for reasons not wholly explainable. Sentimental, we say, but what do we mean? We mean the object has the power to evoke memory. But how?

Whatever we believe about the object, its importance lies in how it *connects* us to people and events, in how it figures in the story of our lives that we want to keep telling. Calvino puts it this way: "The moment an object appears in a narrative, it is charged with a special force and becomes like the pole of a magnetic field, a knot in the network of invisible relationships. The symbolism of an object may be more or less explicit, but it is always there. We might even say that in a narrative any object is always magic."

We start cleaning out the house shortly after our father's death in January 2012. We don't know yet that it won't be empty until the summer of 2014, when Moreland will move the last of Mom's books into storage. By the time the house is sold, no one will have lived in it for more than five years.

We begin by donating what we can of the medical equipment. We throw away the useless: our moldy baby carriage, dried-up toiletries, Daddy's stacks of newspapers. Each of us takes home the family pieces Mom listed as special bequests in a letter she typed after learning her cancer had metastasized: "Sorry I am not available to help you sort out my mess. I am trying to do a little now and it is much worse than if you are doing it for others." She signed off, "You are mine forever."

Moreland and I divide up the photographs. We sort the papers into two mounds, one to discard and one to look through more carefully. Moreland is constantly putting things off; I'm always insisting we press on. At least that's the way it seems to me. Sometimes when he drags his heels, I lose my temper. I holler, I cuss, I cry. He hangs his head, makes a faint apology or a joke. I berate him a little more, then relent. We find a way to laugh and move on. I can't stay mad at my brother because I know he's stretched as thin as I am, and anyway, I like how the cleanout is forcing us to spend time together. Gradually, it becomes obvious that his delay tactics and my git-'er-done attitude originate from the same grief. But we seldom discuss feeling sad or missing our parents, and once the house is empty, I suspect, we'll revert to our old ways, rarely hanging out with each other despite living half a mile apart.

As long as the bulk of the good stuff stays inside the house, with the big furniture where it's always sat, the process of sorting feels tolerable, the remembering enjoyable. But on the days leading up to the painful moments when things actually have to leave—when the auctioneers come to pack up antiques, or dozens of boxes of papers go to the shred truck—on those days, I suffer. I feel, viscerally, as though parts of my mother and father, and of myself, are being torn away. It's impossible to imagine what might replace them.

⌁

To endure this ordeal, I decide I must break my attachment to this house. I make notes on Mom's yellow pad. I want to be rational, orderly. I'm convinced that I must become cold to my parents' possessions so that I don't *mind* getting rid of them. If I can just rearrange my thinking, I'll stop experiencing all these objectionable human emotions that I love to read about but so despise feeling myself. Sadness. Regret. Longing. Grief. Panic. Despair.

Surely, any meaning I see in my parents' belongings must derive from an idea or belief originating out of my own mind and the culture in which I've been raised. That's logical. But it's also deeply uncomfortable to think that the meaning of my parents' belongings is changeable and, worse, now depends on me.

I work on my thinking. I read about aesthetics and philosophies of material culture. I learn words like *ontology* and *epistemology*, words having to do with how we make meaning, how we determine what is real. Although acquiring new words is a pleasure, such questions prove a bit too metaphysical for me. I'm a story person, not a philosopher. I *want* objects to have an inherent meaning— whether it's empirical or magical—a meaning that exists independent of my thoughts and feelings.

I find help in Sherry Turkle's introduction to her *Evocative Objects: Things We Think With*: "We find it familiar to consider objects as useful or aesthetic, as necessities or vain indulgences. We are on less familiar ground when we consider objects as companions to our emotional lives or as provocations to thought. The notion of evocative objects brings together these two less familiar ideas, underscoring *the inseparability of thought and feeling in our relationship to things*. We think with the objects we love; we love the objects we think with."

My italics: *"the inseparability of thought and feeling in our relationship to things."* My folks have left me no shortage of things to think with. The intellectual questions swirl even though my grief is appallingly fresh. At times, my effort to examine and challenge my beliefs about objects, to divorce my emotions from *these* objects, feels like a cruel assault I'm perpetrating on my own tender feelings. Is it so wrong to want my parents' things around me while I mourn? Furthermore, if objects have the power to connect me to people who are no longer here, then maybe they really do possess a kind of magic. And if they are magic, how dare I let them go?

Each month that goes by is costing us money: home insurance, repairs, lawn care. Relentless, I push Moreland back to the house, weekend after weekend. We sort, pack, discard. As objects depart, I'm unsettled, even ashamed, to realize how much my sense of myself is tied to what is perishable, temporary. The bounds of my selfhood wobble and shift; I'm uneasy. I don't yet understand that anybody going through this rite of passage must suffer a similar sense of dislocation.

We put off emptying Mom's office. I continue asking what it really means, all this *stuff*. Why did my parents collect these things, keep them so long, leave them behind? What will happen once I take an object to my own house and look at it outside the context in which I've always known it? Will it continue to carry the import my folks attached to it, or will its perceived value change as the object comes to seem more my possession than theirs? The things that are sold or given away—will I forget them and the memories they evoke? Will I regret their loss and yearn to have them back? Most important, since I can keep only a few things to remember my parents by, which ones should I choose? How many will be enough?

Jazz on School Nights

The enormous cube-like speakers are plywood, stained a dull walnut and faced with a wooden grid laid over a nubby, metallic-flecked fabric. Between the speakers sits a deep cabinet made of a glossy black laminate that must be the grandfather of countless IKEA products. The cabinet's wide, heavy top opens like a coffin lid to reveal wells designed to hold a turntable and dozens of albums.

Some of the albums, mostly jazz, I'll keep too. When my husband plays them, we can give talk a rest, let the music do its thing.

Now mid-century modern looks hip again, but back in the day, my mother thought Daddy's stereo ugly. At nine feet, it's as long as a sofa, and Mom resented that it ate up a wall where real furniture might have stood. She'd had little use for the friend who helped Daddy build it in the 1960s. Whenever this fellow came over, she complained, he and my dad liked to "smoke that old rope."

Mom's main objection to marijuana, best I could tell, was that it made people's conversation too stupid to bear. At the movie *The Doors*, when one stoned character admired the false profundity of another smoker's dope-riddled nonsense—*far out, man*—my mother broke from munching her popcorn to whisper, "That's why we couldn't stand the hippies."

Daddy's friend no longer came around. As for the stereo, Daddy tended to play it only when Mom went out in the evening to teach a class about antiques at the community college, talk to a women's club about porcelain, or lead a meeting of Parents for the Advancement of Gifted Education. I liked to perch on the edge of her bed and watch her dress for these evenings. She might choose a paisley wrap dress and knee-high brown leather boots. Or a tie-neck blouse worn with an A-line skirt, blazer, and slingback heels. She favored jewel colors—crimson, peacock blue, emerald green—and bold African- and Asian-influenced patterns. While she struggled into her pantyhose, I'd root around in her jewelry tray to find her favorites—gold clip earrings, scarab bracelet, cloisonné beads, a half-moon of beaten brass on a black silk cord. Once dressed, she'd step into the bathroom, whip a brush through her short dark hair, stub out her cigarette, swipe on her signature red lipstick, then dispatch me to hunt for her purse. These preparations were hasty, as she'd had to get supper on the table, and maybe squeeze in a quick fight with my father, so she was always running late.

Daddy never went to meetings. He loathed organized religion. He didn't join civic groups. He didn't volunteer. He never went out to have a drink with a buddy. The few friendships he'd made before my brother and I were born had expired. His main outings were to grocery stores, with list and clipped coupons tucked into his shirt pocket. He often took me along, and I was happy enough to bask in the air-conditioning while he instructed me about generics and the intricacies of unit pricing. Otherwise, he mostly sat at home, reading his newspapers, balancing his ledgers, smoking his pipe. You got the feeling that, like Garbo, he wanted to be alone.

On those nights when Mom went out, Daddy usually sat in the den after supper, watching a ball game or listening to the radio, and Moreland and I retreated to our bedrooms to read. But once in a blue moon, left to himself, Daddy stepped into the living room and switched on the lamps. Hearing his movements from my bedroom down the hall, I wondered what was up. We rarely used the living room unless we had company.

I can see myself now: I tiptoe along the hallway until Daddy's back is in view. He raises the stereo cabinet lid, then bends to open the small door hiding the amplifier and preamp. Sensing me behind him, he turns, sees me hesitating at the edge of the room, and beckons me to come closer. I stand obediently while he explains once again how the preamp has to warm up, how I must not touch the dials or push any buttons, because everything has to be done in a specific order, with the finesse only he possesses, or else the speakers will blow out—a catastrophe.

Never in a million years would I have the nerve to touch his stereo or anything else that belongs to him. I'm scared to anger anybody, but especially him.

"Do you know who Miles Davis is?"

I shake my head. Everything he says is a test for which I'm unprepared.

"Well, have a seat and you'll find out."

I perch on the wing chair nearest the hall, ready to slip away if his friendly mood downshifts. Daddy pushes the power button. Orange light glows behind the amplifier's numbers and dials, the speakers pop like kindling. Frowning, Daddy adjusts the knobs until the crackle abates. I watch as he flips through his albums. Their old-fashioned covers intrigue me—the fonts alternately comic and cool, the artwork either photographs or abstract geometric collages of contrasting colors: aqua and cherry, robin's egg and black, black and white. The photographs often feature a dark-skinned man in a suit coat, intensely blowing a horn or poised at a piano. Daddy calls these men Duke, Miles, Trane, Monk, Bird—as though they are old friends.

He selects an album, studies its cover for a moment, then reverently slides the vinyl LP out of its sleeve. You should always handle a record by the edges to avoid making fingerprints and scratches. I nod. No need to risk spoiling his good humor by telling him there are a few things even I know. He blows on the disc and places it on the turntable. He sweeps his blocky red duster out from the record's center hole to its edges, each stroke deliberate. Finally, he flips a lever, and with a click, the arm lifts, swings left, and hovers, teasing, before dropping the needle into a spinning groove.

Again the speakers pop and crackle. I brace myself. How will the music reveal its power this time? Will the opening notes blast, full of bombast and taunt? Or will they sidle up so quiet that I'll wonder for a minute if the music I'm hearing is real or only imagined?

Diabetic since childhood, Daddy was always cross in the mornings until he'd had his cereal and his insulin injection. I used to listen in the hall, out of his sight, tense as a rabbit. Was he still eating, or had he moved on to his shot? His legs were thin, and he jabbed the needle into his wiry thigh muscle with such force that his chair would often creak or scoot. When I heard that noise, I knew it would soon be safe, or safer, to approach.

Back then, I never thought of his diabetes as a disease or a marker of fragility. It awed me that he was tough enough to give himself a shot every day. Mom told Moreland and me to forgive Daddy's dark moods because he didn't "feel good," but I didn't believe that ought to excuse his temper, quick to fire up and slow to relent. That temper—combined with his looming height (6′3″) and the throbbing vein in his temple (a cliché, but in his case, real)—made him a frightening figure. It wasn't that he was physically abusive. Sure, he spanked or whipped us a few times for misbehaving, but that was common enough in the seventies. The main problem was that you never knew what might set him off.

Whereas my mother's rules for our conduct had mostly to do with manners and social niceties, my father was beleaguered by other anxieties. His rules were about process. My brother and I dreaded hearing him say, "I've got a little job for you," because it meant he'd spend the next hour instructing us in tedious detail how to accomplish a simple task like sweeping the driveway or folding newspapers. Invariably, we messed up and were elaborately chastised. I grew to fear making the slightest mistake. He was so easily irritated, all the time, by the littlest things—if we shuffled when we walked ("Pick up your feet!"), if we kicked the seat in the car ("Do it again and I'll spank you!"), if we were slow picking up sticks in the yard he was getting ready to mow ("Don't make an all-day job of it!")—and his reactions struck us as overblown and mean.

Moreland and I learned to stay out of his way as much as possible, but Mom didn't practice the same caution. Her morning interactions with Daddy often devolved into arguments that might be sustained or reprised throughout the day. Whether at work or at home, it was good sport to holler; they both loved to be right, and neither could resist saying something cruel, especially if it was clever. Seldom did they apologize or admit to being wrong. I'd listen from my room, petrified, outraged, pretty much always on my mother's side—even when it seemed to me that she was baiting him. Why didn't she just back off so the fight could end? At first he yelled just as much as she did, but the more cutting her words became, the less he could keep up. Eventually, language failed, as though his anger had strangled the voice right out of him. At that point, he'd go silent, fuming as she kept hurling her clever, hurtful words. Sometimes I felt sorry for him, even though whatever had started the whole thing was usually his fault.

On Saturdays, he went to the shop and Mom stayed home with us children. After breakfast, I'd read in my room, trying not to cross Daddy's path as he executed his morning routine. When I heard the front door close, finally, I ran to watch from the window until the back of his yellow Ford Fairmont station wagon disappeared from view. Now Moreland and I could turn on our radios and spread out our board games. I could stay as long as I liked in the bathroom.

Mom could talk on the phone or start a load of laundry. The three of us were free for a few hours to get on with the business of being ourselves without worrying about making Daddy mad.

Banh, buh, banh, buh, banh, buh, banh buh . . . *BANH BANH.*

"Miles would play with his back to the audience," Daddy says. Miles was fed up.

Banh, buh, banh, buh, banh, buh, banh buh . . . *SO WHAT?*

"Why was that?" I ask. Daddy explains about how black and white worked back then, how even great artists, when they toured the South, weren't permitted to eat or sleep in certain places. Why should a genius like Miles look out into the faces of people who were hungry for his music but wouldn't sit down to take a meal with him?

My father came from a different sort of family than my mother did. His mother, for whom I was named, was born in 1911 and grew up in Columbus, Georgia. To her friends she was "Jackie," but Moreland and I called her Mimi. She left school at fifteen to marry Theo, ten years older than herself. Later they moved to North Carolina and settled in Burlington, where Theo ran an electrical repair shop and she worked as a beautician. On my chest of drawers, I keep a credit-card-sized hand mirror with her advertisement printed on the back: "Jackie's Beauty Shop: If your hair is not becoming to you, you should be coming to us."

In photos from the 1930s and 1940s, Theo and Jackie are attractive and stylish, but they hadn't always been comfortably off. She was the eighth child of a seamstress and a man who, suffering some chronic ailment or disability, spent a lot of time laid up in the bed, unable to provide for the family. Theo's mother, widowed young, earned money going door to door with a whetstone, sharpening knives. It must have been a well-sharpened knife with which she ran off a short-term second husband. Cruel, stupid, or both, the man had put hot pepper in Theo's eye in order, he claimed, to flush out a cinder.

Driving through Columbus when my father was a boy, Theo pointed out house after house, saying he'd lived there, and there, and there.

"Why did you live so many places, Daddy?" my father asked.

The answer sounds like a punchline, but it wasn't: "We had to move every time the rent came due."

As a girl, I loved visiting my Mimi. We played a card game called Kings on the Corner, drank diet RC Cola and gambled for pennies, then went for walks around her neighborhood to keep our figures trim. In the afternoon, she painted my nails scarlet while we watched soap operas; after supper, to game-show applause and sitcom laugh tracks, she rolled my hair on pink foam curlers. The next morning, the bouncy curls I longed for were mine. I couldn't stop touching them; by lunchtime, my hair hung straight again. I relished these frivolities—mindless television, nail painting, hair rolling—so frowned upon at home. Mimi also taught me how to do practical things like sew and crochet, shuck corn and scrub whitewall tires. More activities that seemed exotic to me, as my mother took no interest in domestic matters beyond decorating.

Mom didn't think much of the decor in Mimi's house. At best, it was conventionally middle-class; at worst, tacky. Plush-covered blue loveseats faced off in the living room, surrounded by marble-topped occasional tables and insipid artwork. Mimi had worked the needlepoint seats of the dining chairs herself—bouquets on a burgundy ground—but other chairs were covered with easy-to-clean vinyl, including a revolving red one in which Moreland and I spun until dizzy, laughing as the room whizzed by. On the table by the front door, Dürer's hands sent up their eternal bronze prayers, while in the den the cuckoo clock ejected its occupant on the hour. The clock's noise and action both fascinated and unnerved me: that damn bird popped out so all-of-a-sudden! Beneath it sat a glass fishbowl full of matchbooks from restaurants and beach hotels in North Carolina, South Carolina, Florida, and—could it really have been?—Atlantic City.

None of this charmed my father, who expressed little affection for his hometown or his mother. Theo had died in a boating accident when Daddy was eleven, and within a couple of years Mimi married a pharmacist, also widowed, with three sons around my father's age. Daddy grew fond of them all, but he missed his father, and his inherent need for solitude must have been taxed by the acquisition of four new family members. By the end of high school in the late 1950s, he was finding life in segregated Burlington stultifying. Most of the people he knew were white, square, and content to stay that way, but Daddy was too hip for all that. He was turning on to jazz and interested in serious ideas—in philosophy, politics, art. Longing for bigger things, broader vistas, he left college to spend a few months in Washington, D.C., and New York City in 1959 and 1960. Whenever he mentioned his time in those big cities, which wasn't often, I gleaned that going away had been the great adventure of his life. When he played his records on that stereo, it must have all come back—the smoky clubs where couples danced close, buzzing to the music, invigorated by being so far from home.

Another record? Oh, this evening is really cooking. Daddy drops the needle. A few stray bits of dust make the speakers pop and hiss. I hold my breath. The stereo cabinet and speakers: a concert hall in three boxes. What's the show this time? Daddy knows, but I can only guess. A band, eyeing their leader for the cue? A horn player about to embark on a lonesome wail? A singer closing her eyes, gathering herself for the song ahead?

My dad and I wait together for the new music to slide or bebop or crash into the room . . .

Here it is! The beat vibrates through the floor into our tapping feet. We thrum with its energy, electrified by what we're hearing.

Daddy listens, is happy, and his rare happiness overjoys me. I bob my head and snap my fingers, imitating him. So giddy am I with his pleasure in the music that it becomes my pleasure, too.

We thrill not just to the music but to our transgression. We are breaking the rules together. I'm supposed to be brushing my teeth and going to bed, and he's playing records at a volume that negates all possibility of conversation, my mother's favorite medium. She's tone-deaf, as is Moreland. Music doesn't move them the same way it moves Daddy and me. We're restless souls, peas in a pod straining to burst open. Although I don't yet know how to say it, I feel in my yearning bones that sometimes a body needs an outlet for its feelings. Sometimes a body needs to move, to raise a ruckus. Sometimes a body just wants to tear the roof off a motherfucker.

~

Music moved me, but books . . . Books transported. When I sank into a fictional world, my restless mind found something on which to fix—a great relief.

In books I traveled the world, bounding through time and across geography to find other girls who had no use for society's expectations that we should be quiet and obedient, calm and unambitious. Biographies and memoirs taught me about extraordinary, courageous lives—Amelia Earhart, Harriet Tubman, Anne Frank— and I admired Jo March, Anne of Green Gables, Jane Eyre, and other literary girls who spoke truth to power, even when they knew they'd be punished for it. Curious to know how you got such courage, I didn't want merely to speak to power; I wanted to *be* the power. I loved reading about queens. Brainy polyglot Elizabeth I and long-reigning Victoria, ill-starred Mary Queen of Scots and Anne Boleyn. What regrettable cosmic mix-up had made me a lonesome jeans-wearing seventh grader in a boring American brick ranch house, when I was supposed to be a lonesome velvet-clad princess awaiting her crown in a damp, stony English castle?

Given my poor chances of becoming an actual queen, I pondered

what else I could be when I grew up. Moreland was already buying antique tools with his own money and selling them at the shop,
saving every penny that crossed his palm. My parents were proud
of him for following in their footsteps. Eager for their approval, I
tried to figure out what antiques I might like to buy and sell. Books?
Prints? I couldn't afford much—since I always blew my paltry allowance on chocolate, paperbacks, and earrings—and trying to convince customers to buy things seemed tiresome, as did scouring the
world for merchandise.

Alas, the only aspect of commerce that truly appealed to me was
writing out the price stickers and receipts. Eventually, I had to accept that dealing antiques just wasn't my thing.

Daddy seldom bought merchandise for the shop—that was Mom's
bailiwick—but when he did, it was usually furniture or pottery
devoid of ornament. At home, opposite their California king sat
a waist-high bookcase filled with Daddy's dusty hardbacks from
his college days—heavy, forbidding tomes of philosophy and history whose covers looked to me as outdated as his albums. Atop this
bookcase sat a trio of ancient Chinese bronzes; above them hung
three Japanese prints of birds biding time on delicate flowered
branches. Upon waking in the morning, Daddy liked to study the
bronzes' forms against the pale yellow wall, admiring how each outline was embraced by negative space. This one shelf he tried to keep
clear of clutter so that its minimalist arrangement remained pure:
three bronzes, three prints. Each distinct form uncrowded, solitary.

Listening to music together, we were alert not just to the notes
but to the silences between them. Long before I understood the different purposes and effects of pauses and gaps in written language,
I learned to listen for them in Daddy's music. Strong feeling could
nest inside those spaces, like beasts in a den. Inside every rest, anything might be waiting to come out.

One time when my father was dying—I say "one time" because he tried dying so many times—he was admitted to the palliative-care unit at Moses Cone Hospital. One evening, a classical guitarist played soothing tunes out in the hall. My father praised his skill, then directed my attention toward the ceiling, wanting me to identify a constellation of black dots he insisted were there.

Seven years later, I attend a classical guitar concert at my son's arts high school. As my son plays his solo, I stare into the stage lights, then shift my eyes away. Black dots appear in my field of vision.

Feeling left out of the family shop talk, I threw myself into the performing arts—dance, piano, singing, acting—and the expressive: drawing, painting, writing. Greensboro boasted two universities and a handful of colleges, as well as various civic arts groups, so cheap theater was plentiful. Mom and Daddy dragged us to children's plays, musicals, jazz concerts, the symphony, Shakespeare, opera, ballet—whatever was on. They took us to film screenings and art exhibits, lectures and readings. Moreland and I learned to sit without complaint through several hours of anything—an invaluable life skill.

Our parents didn't care if we were bored. They didn't worry if what we saw was over our heads or a little risqué. A modest child, I squirmed during a modern dance in which a barely clothed couple alternated between crumpling to the floor and dry-humping each other. How old was I? Ten? Twelve? Old enough to realize what the dancers were simulating, young enough to be shocked and embarrassed rather than titillated. Another night, a man in a thong capered about the stage bare-assed, the stage lights further sculpting the bulges and concavities of his muscled cheeks. Scandalous. *Sweet Bird of Youth*, with its culminating scene of castration, was a revelation—not in a good way—and the travails of stripper Gypsy Rose Lee brought me to tears.

Despite these occasional disturbing surprises—or maybe because of them—I loved the theater. Costumes, sets, movement, the scripted language: I was enraptured by how these elements came together to create a world and draw in the audience. Seduced, I wanted to become the seducer, to join in the making of magical worlds. My mother encouraged me, paying for ballet lessons, driving me to rehearsals for *The Nutcracker*, attending every performance of my high school plays.

When I realized I'd never be thin enough to be a dancer or pretty enough to be an actress, I hit on the idea of becoming a costume designer. So Mom bought me secondhand books about fashion history, and I pored over their pages until I knew the difference between farthingales and panniers, hoops and bustles. I sewed clothes for dolls I no longer played with, and spent hours drawing and coloring dresses.

Before I could read, my mother read to me: nursery rhymes, fairy tales, Beatrix Potter. All my first books are inscribed. *To Julia, From Mimi and Papa, 1974. To Julia, Love Aunt Greg, 1976. To Julia, Love Margaret. Love, Granny and Daddy-Jack. Love, Moreland. Love, Mama and Daddy.* Mom believed in the personalized inscription, that intimate gesture implying the receiver will keep the book always and never forget the thoughtful giver.

By age four, I could read by myself: Dr. Seuss, *The Cat in the Hat*. E. B. White, *Charlotte's Web*. Beverly Cleary, the Ramona books. My little library grew. By then I'd already internalized two enduring beliefs: (1) Books and love are intimately related. (2) A library is a thing worth building and keeping.

Thirty years on, I delighted in reading my tattered favorites to my young son. Every turn of a page revived an infant enchantment long buried; certain images prompted a feeling of reunion with long-lost friends. Among the most potent memory stirrers were Richard Scarry's cats and pigs, wolves and hippos and baboons, going about their busy, busy work of plumbing and brick laying, wrecking cars and spilling fruit and scratching their furry heads as busted fire hydrants jetted blue water into the sky. Watching my son pat the pictures as I read, I recalled my small self loving the same colorful pages, so full of words to learn to read: *egg*, *sock*, *wrench*, *chimney*.

By the time I started grade school, I scorned picture books as babyish. I was greedy for stories that wouldn't end too soon, fat novels and multivolume sagas. My mother kept me well supplied. At the public library branch near our house, she taught me to use the card catalog. The little drawers charmed me, as did the neat typed cards, edges softened by curious fingers. Mostly, though, I navigated the library by divination. I beelined to my favorite sections—fiction, biography—scanned the spines with my eyes and fingers, skimmed random pages to vet the prose. Then and now, I judged books by their covers. Who wants to read an ugly book?

At our school library, we were allowed scant time to browse, and more than once I was deemed too young to check out a particular book. Although I shied away from conflict, this gross curtailment of my civil liberties and insult to my intelligence enraged me, and whenever it happened, I set out to prove wrong the officious eighth-grader manning the circulation desk. I'd open a book and read aloud until they rolled their eyes and let me have it. Which is why, in fifth grade, I lugged home a massive biography of Eleanor Roosevelt, only to abandon it after reading an upsetting incident in which the child Eleanor overheard her own mother call her ugly.

Too bad she didn't have a mother like mine, who told me all the time how smart and beautiful I was. (I didn't believe her, but I liked that she said it.) When I complained that kids at school teased me for being bookish, she claimed they were just jealous. I shouldn't worry what they said, they were "limited" people who didn't have my "advantages." I knew she was wrong. Nobody was jealous of a nerdy girl like me, especially not kids who had multiple best friends, cool backpacks, and real Member's Only jackets. But her words consoled me anyway, because I was pretty sure I possessed one thing those kids didn't—a mom who was always on my side.

She bought me all the reading materials she could afford, to the point that my growing library took over my room. I crammed books into the shelves any way they'd fit and stacked them on the floor. Nothing was as exciting as a trip to the used bookstore or the days when teachers handed out the Scholastic book order form. I studied the colorful newsprint pages, then tried to convince my parents to buy three books so I could get a free poster of two puppies celebrating friendship or of a monkey who just couldn't face Mondays.

At ten, I ordered a paperback copy of *Gone with the Wind*. Blazoned on the red cover was the movie poster—Rhett looking like he's about to eat Scarlett alive, white-bosomed Scarlett looking as if there's nothing she'd like better. The day the book order was delivered to our classroom, I told my teacher I felt sick, and by the time Mom picked me up, I'd sunk deep into antebellum Georgia and knew I couldn't bear to return to school until I'd read the novel straight through. Over my school years, I'd perfected my act—just enough symptoms to stay home, not quite so sick as to prompt a visit to the doctor.

If a book really caught hold of me, I lost all sense of time and my surroundings. So when Moreland came home from school the next afternoon and yelled, "What's burning?" I hollered back, "Atlanta!"

No, he insisted, something really was burning. Dazed, I realized the smoke I'd been smelling was real. Mom had walked away from a skillet of sausage on the stove, and the grease had caught fire. My brother doused the flames with baking soda from a coffee can, a Cub Scout safety project that had been gathering dust atop the refrigerator. While he helped my mother open windows, I shut my door and returned to Atlanta.

I consumed the book as though it were a realistic depiction of history. The narrative's racism and classism echoed justifications I'd been hearing in North Carolina all my life; to me these social problems were mere background to what I was really interested in: Scarlett and her romantic problems. I saw in her character, as many people had, a fierce woman who craves love and independence, and her obsessive determination to obtain both appeared to me admirable, if tragic. (And it would be many years before I'd understand the scene depicted in that cover image as rapey rather than romantic.) So hungry was I for books depicting powerful women that it didn't occur to me to be troubled by how Scarlett and other white female characters to which I gravitated had such limited ways to access power—sex, trickery, and the abuse or exploitation of others less advantaged than themselves.

The subject of race in America interested me. Why did the white children and the black children at school keep more or less separate? Why were white people so mean to and about black people? How did black people live in their world apart?

Nobody at school guided me toward stories told from viewpoints other than those of privileged white people, but my parents did. I don't know if I read *I Know Why the Caged Bird Sings* before or after they took me to hear Maya Angelou speak at UNC Greensboro. During her talk, she told about Sojourner Truth giving her famous "Ain't I a Woman" speech at a women's rights conference in 1851. Hearing Angelou speak the words ascribed to Truth—*And ain't I a woman*—I wanted to know more about this history. I longed to understand how a person could be so brave in the face of injustice. I wanted to know where you got courage like that.

The silence at the end of the record is a lonesome sound. The circle goes round and round, nothing to hear but dust.

What joy to realize you have only to start over, or flip the disc, and the music will live again.

⌁

Side A: reading. Side B: writing. First came hours of make-believe, using dolls or cousins or obliging neighbor children as my fellow actors. Contemporary with these games were my earliest attempts at literary production: illustrated "novels" with construction-paper covers, store-bought blank books I filled with poems and stories. But it wasn't until I read Eudora Welty's "Why I Live at the P.O." at the age of twelve or thirteen that I seriously thought I might become a writer.

I'd never before read a story in which people talked pretty much how people talked in my everyday life. Even though Welty came from Mississippi and I lived in North Carolina (separated from her characters by a good fifty years), her fictional southern world seemed so familiar: the sarcasm, the word play, the eccentric behavior, the undercurrent of distress. I felt a kinship with the story's main character, Sister, because I recognized her frustration as a young woman trying to claim a sliver of space for herself. Reading Welty, it struck me for the first time that the people who wrote books could be real, living people who lived in ordinary places like Jackson or Greensboro. They didn't have to be from England or New England or from the nineteenth century. They could be from anywhere and they might be anyone—even me.

Inspired, I wrote a short story all in dialogue. A woman calls another woman and says she's sending home the body of a relative who's choked to death on an orange. The body is arriving on the train, C.O.D. The story was based on two tidbits from real life: a remark Mom overheard in a restaurant about a choking death, and my grandmother Mimi complaining about having to help foot the bill for burying an estranged alcoholic cousin whose common-law wife refused to bear the expenses. Trying to come up with a title for the story, I consulted a map and found Prosperity, a town in Florida, the state where our down-and-out cousin had lived. Benevolence was in Georgia, Mimi's home state. I called the story "From Prosperity to Benevolence." It tickled me how the title sounded so highfalutin compared with the story's vernacular dialogue. Already I loved the juxtaposition of high and low. That was how my mother talked, the way I was coming to use language myself, running the gamut from erudite to vulgar, taking pleasure in the full range of what English can do.

Mom pressed copies of my story on her friends and mailed it to her parents. Outwardly, my teen self professed embarrassment; inwardly, I basked in her approval. Within a few years I recognized that writing stories answered something in me that dancing, acting, drawing, or doing well in school couldn't touch. What it was, I didn't exactly know, but from then on, I was determined to be a writer.

Listening to jazz, Daddy communed with artists he admired, iconoclasts he would have liked to emulate. Their music was cerebral *and* emotional, an expression of longing and sadness, of anger and impatience and joy. It resonated with his own complicated feelings. In his last decade—as he lost his legs, his eyesight failed, and a sedentary existence became his fate rather than his choice—Daddy turned more and more to music. Many afternoons, he simply sat or lay still, eyes closed, listening; his body, for once, no encumbrance to his pleasure. Music was the one thing he could receive, as he received nothing else, in a spirit of true, pure love and gratitude.

Several years after my parents died, I walked into their house one day and was greeted by loud jazz emanating from the living room.

For a confused moment, I thought my father was home. Then I realized it was only the housepainters' radio, an accompaniment to their efforts, a small pleasure to mitigate the tedium of the afternoon.

<hr />

Ella and Basie. Sarah Vaughan. Louis Armstrong.

Sunny Side of the Street. April in Paris. When the Saints Go Marching In.

It's after nine o'clock, past my bedtime. We don't hear my mother come home.

She sets down her purse and dances one number with Daddy. I see how the music makes them like each other, see how the way they move together is their own thing, separate from me. Later, lying in bed, I still hear the trumpet wailing in my ears.

Records and books raise the dead. Sustain the living. Soothe sad men, and make busy women stop to dance. Writers, musicians, artists, performers. They are sinners and saints both. And oh, how I want to be in that number.

The House Beautiful . . . or the House Good Enough

A faint, uneven grid crisscrosses the eight panels. Likely the background was laid on in thin sheets of gold leaf, a treatment common in the production of folding screens like this, which are called *byobu* and have been made in Japan since the eighth century. At the far left, two women in billowing robes float over hills dotted with scrubby evergreens. One carries a small pine or cypress cutting on her open fan. At the far right sit two larger ladies, wearing layers of greens, blues, and a dark red between cinnabar and plum, nearly the same shade as the screen's lacquered frame. The ladies' lustrous black hair is so long that it would be underfoot if they were standing upright. One sits with her back turned, while the other looks out, a hand lifting the bottom of a bamboo blind held together with green ribbon tapes. Beside the faceless woman is a folding screen like mine—a screen within a screen—also gold, and decorated with pines.

A male figure approaches the screened women. At his back, in the picture's central foreground, rooflines jag down into clumps of treetops. The man's profile is rendered like the women's faces—generic, expressionless. The only distinguishing detail is his wispy beard. He sports a tall, phallic black hat that makes me laugh a little, thinking what men do to impress. Dominating the picture, he stands on steps whose angles look odd to eyes habituated to Western art's postmedieval vanishing point. The figures here are sized relative to their social importance, not the distance from which they're seen, and so the man, the highest-ranking character among the five, is the largest.

The images on my screen derive from *The Tale of Genji*, written in the eleventh century during the Heian period (794–1185). *Genji* runs to well over a thousand pages and is often called the first novel. Its author, now known as Murasaki Shikibu, or Lady Murasaki, was one of those rare, lucky girls in history; her father, a provincial governor, educated her almost as though she were the son he wished she'd been. At the Heian court, knowledge of Chinese language, literature, and culture was as essential as a classical education would later be to elite men in England and America. Lady Murasaki recounts in her diary how she outshone her brother at learning Chinese, despite having to listen to the lessons from behind a screen. (Girls and ladies in her society were nearly always shielded from male eyes.)

By the time she began writing her novel around the year 1001, she was a widow with a daughter. The recent development of two major writing systems had contributed to a burst of literary activity in Japan. Kanji, still in use today, is based on Chinese characters and consists of thousands of symbols that represent whole words. The other system, kana, was syllabic; it employed only forty-six symbols, each indicating a different sound, which made it easier to learn than kanji. For the first time, Japanese people could write in the vernacular. Heian court ladies wrote an elegant cursive form of kana called hiragana, or "woman's hand," and it's fitting that this script was probably used to write *Genji*, for fiction in those days was women's work, women's pleasure. Fiction was considered a lesser art than poetry (as was also long true in Western literary culture), and well-born men did not deign to write it. Nevertheless, the emperor himself enjoyed Lady Murasaki's writing and admired her scholarship; perhaps because of this, she gained a position as lady-in-waiting to one of his consorts.

The great achievement of *The Tale of Genji* is beyond question. The scholar Donald Keene calls it "a monument of world literature, the first novel of magnitude composed anywhere, a work that is at once distinctively Japanese and universally affecting." He likens it to other renowned works written in the vernacular: "It occupies in Japanese literature, the place of Shakespeare in English literature, of Dante in Italian literature, or of Cervantes in Spanish literature." In other words, *Genji* gave birth to its country's subsequent literature.

And yet, within Keene's fulsome praise and acknowledgment of the work's cultural importance, there lies an erasure of the woman who wrote it; she goes unnamed alongside the famous men. Rewording the sentence—*Murasaki Shikibu occupies in Japanese literature the place of Shakespeare in English*—wouldn't exactly solve the problem, as that's not her real name. Nobody actually *knows* her name. "Shikibu" refers to the government title of the writer's father; Murasaki is the novel's heroine, whom the young prince Genji sees when she's a child of ten and he's a young man of around eighteen.

In Genji's imperial court society, it's essential to display correct manners, to do everything in a particular style. To deviate from what is graceful and proper condemns a person to harsh judgment from spirits as well as people. To appease angry spirits, offenders must observe specific rituals of atonement. Attention must constantly be paid to the smallest details.

I am separated from the Heian imperial court by more than a millennium and half the world's distance. But its stringency feels familiar. Raised in the latter days of the mannered South, I was schooled daily, hourly—minutely—on the proper ways to speak, dress, eat, move, and sit. My parents told me what I ought to think about countless topics, which strikes me as ironic now, given how they railed against whatever they considered narrow minded. They were socially liberal Democrats who despised Republicans and religious zealots—"Christ-bitten" "holy rollers" and "Bible beaters"—who struck them as greedy, censorious, bigoted hypocrites, lacking both compassion and imagination. On the other side of the fence, my parents had limited patience with hippies, Moonies, and New Agers; these folks were naive and/or shiftless. Their pot-befuddled talk was boring, and their self-righteousness as dull as that of their conservative counterparts.

And yet, even as my folks condemned other ideologues' blind conformity and preached about the rewards and virtues of individualism, they demanded complete obedience at home. They held my brother and me to a high standard of behavior. My mother, for instance, deemed it *common* to chew gum or use a toothpick in public. These were things that a lady, especially, did not do, and I understood early on that it was my job to become a lady. A lady did not paint her fingernails, pierce her ears, or wear an anklet; a lady crossed her legs at the ankle, never the knee. A lady expected a gentleman to hold the door for her, to help her with her coat, to wait for her to be served first. These were manners, and if you learned them as a child, they'd be second nature to you as an adult.

Our posture required constant correction, as did our grammar. Out in the world, my mother warned, you'd be judged not only on how you spoke but your choice of topic. *Nice people* simply did not talk about certain things in front of people whose affiliations they didn't know: politics, race, religion, sex. (Also, my father added, ACC basketball.) It was inexcusable to use racist language, act superior, or talk down to those in service positions, but you shouldn't make trouble by calling out acquaintances or strangers when they did these things. Also déclassé was discussing how much money you'd spent on something, whether it was a bargain or an extravagance.

Gradually, I came to understand the distinctions my mother was making among "people without your advantages," "nice people," and the "nouveaux riches," who were "trying too hard." She was teaching me about the social divisions of money and class. Alert to all the signifiers, large and small, of those differences, she wanted to be sure that I learned them, too. It was important that I understand what the world—meaning, the white, middle- and upper-class world she knew best—was going to think about me if I wore too much makeup or said "Me and him are going to the store."

Fast-forward to me fussing at my son to wear a button-down instead of a T-shirt when we went to the theater or an upscale restaurant. Nice people do things a certain way, and doesn't he want people to think he's *nice?* Like my own mother and father, I've tended to parent with the volume turned up to eleven: small infractions incite big reactions. I'm stricter than they were about certain things and more lenient about others. So far, I've done little to inculcate in my son the aesthetic principles imparted to me throughout my childhood as sacred, empirical truths. Whether I ought to feel badly about this neglect, I don't know.

Here are the articles of faith my mother taught me about decorating a house:

When arranging objects, a symmetrical arrangement is most pleasing, but an asymmetrical arrangement is also pleasing, if well balanced.

Less is more. (But our family's less is still a lot.)

Good quality but a bit worn is better than new, shiny, and cheaply made.

Avoid "the furniture store." (Impossible on the page to invest this phrase with the scorn in my mother's voice. *The furniture store* to me sounded like what *Hell* must have sounded like to children of evangelicals.) Even if you have to spend more for a decent antique, at least you'll have a *real* piece of furniture.

Every room must contain something tall, something short, and something red.

Vary the vertical and the horizontal.

Never, ever catty-corner a large piece of furniture like a bed or a wardrobe.

Inexpensive things attractively arranged make a more pleasing environment than a lot of expensive things poorly arranged.

Simple and elegant is best, but a little fabulous here and there doesn't hurt either.

No matchy-matchy.

While you must put a lot of thought into the way you decorate a room, you don't want a room that looks tarted up or like you are trying too hard.

Having bad opinions on decorating is preferable to having no opinions at all. When a room looks terrible because it was purposely made to look that way, we don't admire the result, but we can respect the people who decorated it for at least having the guts to express themselves.

Above all else, a well-appointed room conveys a sense of ease. A successful room, like a successful person, is permitted to exhibit flare, even high drama or eccentricity, as long as it exudes confidence. There must be no hint of striving or trying to present a false image, of pretending to be what you're not.

Growing up, when my mother mocked pretentious errors of taste, I thought she was right to criticize. A person ought to be an individual and not conform to herd mentality; people ought not put such stock in showing off how much money they have. It didn't occur to me then that if you start out with little and then make some money, you might want brand-new possessions because you can, for the first time, actually afford them. You might want to enjoy them as evidence of how far you've come in the world. Nor did it occur to me that you might not care for antiques because, to your eyes, they represent the long-standing and exploitative wealth of a class of people you dislike or envy or resent, people who actively oppressed you and yours. And while I knew that I was being taught that striving for status and prioritizing money are not things that "nice" people do (or, rather, *appear* to do), it took a long time before I recognized the implication that "nice" people are those who have already "made it" in the world, preferably generations before, and that the things they own—their inherited furniture and old silver and family portraits—are the proof.

~~~~

My maternal grandfather, whom we children called Daddy-Jack, believed that beautiful things and beautiful people were inherently good, and ugly ones suspect. His aesthetic proclivities became apparent in childhood. In a letter unevenly penciled to Santa, he requests a tea set. Did his parents think it a peculiar choice for a boy growing up in rural North Carolina in the 1920s? No matter. Doubtless they bought it for him, as he was their only child, and wanted for nothing.

In adulthood he sold antiques out of the back room of a general store he kept for a time in the tiny town of Roxobel. I knew my grandfather as a bent, gray, thin-lipped man prone to leaving his hat behind in restaurants, but Jack Tyler in his prime was tall and dark haired, with big soulful eyes and exceedingly courtly manners. A neighbor once asked my grandmother if it made her nervous, going off to teach school each day and leaving her good-looking husband surrounded by housewives whose own men were at work farther afield.

"Until there's a whore in town who can discuss the eighteenth century," Granny is said to have replied, "I'm not worried."

When they married in 1941, Daddy-Jack was an officer in the navy, and the newlyweds moved from post to post. My mother liked sharing that she'd been conceived in Newport, Rhode Island, and born in Charleston, South Carolina, both cities important in the history of American decorative arts, both quite different from the places where her family had lived for generations. Northeastern North Carolina was, and is, a land of piney woods and murky swamps. Driving through, you pass field after field after field, and wonder if the view will ever change. Here, from the 1600s on, my ancestors acquired extensive property in the usual ways of colonizers—by grant of the British crown, by exploiting labor, by prospering in trade or planting, by inheritance, and by making advantageous marriages with rich ladies. Their lands were worked first by enslaved people and later by tenant farmers.

Like his forebears, Daddy-Jack derived income from land he didn't have to work himself, an advantage that freed him to pursue his own interests. Though he depended on that income, he styled himself a "gentleman farmer," an old term meaning a "man who farms mainly for pleasure rather than for profit." The gentleman farmer celebrates the Jeffersonian ideal of agriculture as a noble pursuit, but I suspect my grandfather took little interest in pest control and crop selection. Not scientific in the least, he enjoyed writing and drawing, and studied history and the decorative arts all his life. When he inherited his family home, Oaklana, built circa 1827, he set about decorating it with finer furniture and art than it had ever possessed, adding these to the heirlooms that were already there to create the most beautiful home he could afford.

By the time I was a teenager, I understood that my mother's people had once been wealthy in a way that my parents themselves were not, and in a way my father's family had never been. Having learned that wealth—even its afterglow—is meant to impress, I was duly impressed. I didn't really understand money, except that my parents fought about it because cash was often tight and they had different ideas of what constituted a necessity. A fervent belief in the power of compound interest may have been the closest thing Daddy had to a religion, while Mom didn't think money at all nice to talk about. She loathed my father's "petty economies" and obsessive ledger keeping, and warned me to avoid the sin of "poor-mouthing,"

which is to bemoan the cost of things or your own financial situation when, actually, you're doing fine.

We weren't rich, but we weren't poor either. Poor people in books starved; poor children at school smelled like pee. Neither of these conditions applied to me. I wore hand-me-downs from friends and older relatives but was given piano and ballet lessons. We never ate in fancy restaurants but often attended concerts and plays. Antiques filled our house, but we ate store-brand food and drove clunky cars. Daddy balked at paying for repairs or replacements, so our appliances seldom worked right. The clothes dryer tumbled but didn't get hot, the stove eye could boil but not simmer. This was no inconvenience to him, since he never did laundry or cooked, and the burden of managing a work-around fell to my mother and, later, to my brother and me.

I resented Daddy's iron thrift. I hated drawing on the back of old homework. Not until I was a teenager did I realize that his penny-pinching was part of a larger system of financial vigilance that benefited me. Mom had some money of her own, which paid for our camps and lessons, but it was Daddy's saving and investing of his modest funds that yielded enough (along with a scholarship and my grandparents' help) to send me to boarding school and then to college.

When I went off to Salem Academy for tenth grade, my father promised me a small monthly allowance. If I wanted more pocket money, I'd have to earn it during school vacations by babysitting and working in restaurants. Okay—fair enough, fine, whatever. I was just happy to be going away and wasn't sure why he thought I'd feel I needed more than what I was given.

I soon learned. It was a shock to see girls in my dorm sit at the payphone with their own credit cards, casually ordering hundreds of dollars' worth of clothes from J. Crew catalogs. When we went out to dinner on a Saturday night, and a friend nonchalantly paid for everybody at the table, I was floored. Where on earth did their parents get so much money? I had no real concept of what people did to accrue wealth or maintain it. All I had was an idea of what "rich" *looked like*: swank cars, lavish jewelry, elegant clothes. It looked like what I saw when I went home with school friends on weekends, or at the houses of country-club customers who bought antiques from my parents' shop. It looked like what Daddy-Jack and Granny had at Oaklana: a big two- or three-story house. Capacious rooms filled with polished dark furniture and Oriental rugs. Letter paper with your name engraved at the top. Oil paintings on the walls, silver on the table. A white family who knew how to use, properly, all those silver forks, spoons, and knives. And, even still in the late twentieth-century South, black people who did the jobs the white family didn't want to do.

Fukinuki yatai, or "blown-off roof," is the artistic convention, born in the Heian era, of depicting rooms so that the viewer can spy down into them to see what the people are doing.

At Oaklana, there were two beds in the Red Room upstairs. The grand mahogany four-poster with red-and-white hangings was wide enough for my mother, my aunt, and a grown cousin or two to lie on after a holiday meal. Happy to be shed of their heels and their men, they'd light cigarettes, pass the ashtray as they talked, then read themselves into an afternoon nap. My younger cousin Margaret and I eavesdropped from across the room, where we lay on a small, low bed, much less fancy, built long ago of eastern North Carolina pine by a man Daddy-Jack referred to as Carpenter Charles. Margaret and I spent many an un-air-conditioned summer night in that little bed, lulled toward sweaty sleep by the attic fan's oceanic roar. Only when the fan was off could we hear the intermittent rebukes of the electric bug zapper out back, glowing blue in the night. That buzzy death trap hung next to the old dairy, on the other side of which was a rusty iron bell atop a pole—if not the original bell rung to call workers out of the field and up to the big house, then one similar.

Playing at Oaklana as a child, the objects I encountered were, to me, just more old things like the antiques at home or at my parents' shop. I didn't understand that Carpenter Charles had been enslaved; I didn't yet associate the place I loved with anyone's pain or the institution of slavery. What I did understand was that the objects there meant more to us because of the family stories handed down along with them, and so, in a way, the objects themselves were family. Because of them, history was more tangible for me at Oaklana than anywhere else. History infused the beds, the wavy-paned windows, the pots our supper was cooked in, the photographs I passed on the way to the bathroom.

~~~~~

My folks talked about long-dead ancestors as though they'd just stepped out of the room. *Did you know Perry Cotten would refuse to go to Sunday meeting at the Baptist church with Celia Creesy? He'd wait outside in the carriage. Probably hungover from a card party the night before. He was a Deist, you see. She'd be just perfectly furious and would shake her fist at him through the back window of the church.*

What about that time Mr. Ed ran away when he was a boy to join the Confederate army? He only got as far as Mulberry Grove, just down the road.

And how about his wife, Martha Adelia? She lost part of her arm in a gristmill accident when she was a girl but could still sew and paint pictures. That's one of hers there on the wall in the dining room.

Stories breathed life into the house and connected me to my ancestors. Today, if you come to visit me and express the slightest interest, I'll be happy to tell you about the little girl in the portrait over the sideboard, or show you the stereo my dad built with a buddy in the 1960s, or the Chinese print my mom gave my husband, a delicately colored picture of a placid man and woman copulating while a handmaiden waits with a towel. Only recently did the embarrassing thought occur to me that guests might think these tours are about showing off. That's never been my conscious intention. For me, telling people about the things in my house is hospitality, a way of opening my home and myself to them. I tell my stories to invite others to tell theirs in return.

When my grandparents were driving around buying antiques in the mid-twentieth century, a prevalent decorating style was Colonial Revival, a movement that had begun a hundred years before. Think Chippendale and Queen Anne, Williamsburg and Paul Revere, Windsor chairs and braided rugs. At a higher-end furniture store in Richmond, Daddy-Jack and Granny bought "the Princess" (my mother) a reproduction tall-post bed, bowfront chest of drawers, and kneehole desk, no doubt thinking, "this will do until she's old enough to have the real thing." The early indoctrination worked: as an adult, my mother found eighteenth-century American furniture the most aesthetically pleasing. She brought my father along: "the proportions," he'd say, admiring, "the restraint."

As part of its backward glance, Colonial Revival included a fascination with what used to be called Orientalia. Delirious on morphine in his last days, Daddy-Jack muttered about a trunkload of Chinese export porcelain he needed to sell. Although Mom never traveled to Asia, she adored embroidered silks and glossy lacquer, woodblock prints and calligraphy, porcelain and metalwork. Consider this, she marveled: during the same dark ages when our pale, lumpish European ancestors were living in damp hovels, eating moldy onions and dubious animals skewered over open fires, the literate, refined artisans of China and Japan were producing countless beautiful things.

Mom bought the Genji screen from the brother of Phyllis Hawthorne, who'd been in the class of 1938 with my grandmother at UNC Chapel Hill. Phyllis was a great-granddaughter of the writer

Nathaniel Hawthorne; Granny descended from *Mayflower* passenger Stephen Hopkins. And so both counted among their ancestors early English settlers who established colonial centers at Plymouth, Salem, and Boston.

Elementary school tableaux represent the first British emigrants to North America as a cohesive group of "pilgrims" with shared aims. In reality, white America started out already divided. William Bradford led religious dissenters to the New World looking for a place where they could worship without persecution; men like Hopkins emigrated for sundry other reasons. None of them, apparently, used the term *pilgrim*, and *Mayflower* passengers are known in the history as either "saints" or "strangers." Relations between the groups grew fractious when the die-hard religious tried telling the less fanatical how to behave. The saints, for instance, did not observe Christmas as a holiday and took issue with the contingent of colonists who preferred getting drunk to working on December 25.

No matter which group you hail from, calling yourself a *Mayflower* descendant is supposed to sound elite. Lists of *Mayflower* descendants include people of great wealth and station, folks accomplished in the arts or intellectual pursuits, and quite a few U.S. presidents. But it is also true that current estimates suppose there to be 35 million *Mayflower* descendants worldwide, hardly a select number and one that is, naturally, growing all the time. Those of us who wish to be impressed with our DNA would do well to remember that we also share it with buffoons and chancers; among Hopkins's many descendants are Sarah Palin (who by one report has *five* *Mayflower* ancestors), while "saint" Bradford's descendants include Hugh Hefner.

Hopkins's own record is spotty. Before arriving in Plymouth, he'd survived a shipwreck off Barbados—an incident on which *The Tempest* is said to be based. Shakespeare's drunken butler Stephano may have been modeled on Hopkins, who was nearly executed for mutiny after he questioned the authority of the colonial governor. In 1630 he was cited for assault and for allowing his tavern patrons to drink to excess and play shuffleboard on Sundays. His contrarian tendencies have persisted down the generations, and my family tends to be more proud than ashamed to be lumped with the strangers. The saints seem no fun at all.

Readers of U.S. history know the colonists consolidated their power via land grabbing and genocide, trade and commerce, slaveholding and patriarchy, church and state. But they also did it—and we continue to do it still—through narrative. How many times did I hear, growing up, about yet another of Granny's ancestors—Jonathan Edwards, the theologian, minister, and writer who became president of Yale University. His sermons, including the famous "Sinners in the Hands of an Angry God," profoundly influenced early American Christianity. I also heard about her revolutionary relatives who participated in the Halifax Resolves but didn't know until I was grown that we were also at the Boston Tea Party. Heroic stories such as these were among the narratives told to me as examples of what fine, accomplished folks we were. That there's truth in these stories, I don't doubt. Many of our relations clearly possessed the propitious mixture of intelligence, opportunity, and nerve that is the recipe for becoming an honored public servant, a successful businessman, or a renowned thinker—even all three.

But families are complicated. At least one North Carolina kinsman, a Loyalist, went back to England to wait out the Revolution. Jonathan Edwards's grandson, my distant cousin Aaron Burr, fatally shot Alexander Hamilton before hightailing it west. I seldom heard their stories told in the family. Nor did I hear much about the depredations we surely visited upon Native Americans, or details about our participation in the slave trade.

Nearly all the family success stories centered on men, ascribing their achievements solely to their personal qualities and leaving out the women who enabled them. An exception was the story of a lady so wealthy she was nicknamed "the Spanish galleon." Heiresses were the channels through which affluence flowed from one man to another. They brought to their husbands the houses, land, money, and slaves accumulated by their fathers—one more reason why it was in the patriarchy's interest to control women.

Power follows money, or course, and strategic marriages helped maintain power by keeping it in the family, a treasured heirloom. An African American man who was paid to clean the small Episcopal church in Roxobel told me once, "This is where the rich people go. They pass around a gold plate and collect up the money, and then they pass it around again and take the money out." His was as accurate a summary of what transpires among the monied classes as any I've ever heard, though it leaves out how the money often is initially gathered—by exploiting the labor of the poor.

No matter how we try to shape our family narratives into stories that makes us proud, we cannot deny that guilt is part of our inheritance. It's unpleasant, even horrifying, to contemplate certain things our ancestors did. Nathaniel Hawthorne famously changed the spelling of his name to dissociate himself from his forebear Judge John Hathorne, who sentenced more than twenty people to death during the Salem witch trials. The bloody stain of that sin remained ineradicable for Hawthorne; it haunts his fiction. So too, for me, does the stain of slaveholding mark my mother's family.

At Oaklana, there were as many as forty-seven enslaved people living on the place at once, but that number is only the tip of the iceberg. How many thousands of souls did my ancestors on various branches of the family tree "own" between 1619 and 1863? I could spend years in archives and never be able to determine an exact number.

What I do know for certain is that my family owes to forced labor and its fruits much of what we've been able to become. It no longer escapes me that the beautiful things that fill our houses were provided by a financial success that long depended on our moral failure and the suffering of thousands of human beings. Behind the facade of the house beautiful lies a lot of ugliness.

Walls should be painted white.
    Nice writing paper is cream colored or white.
    Nice bed linens are white.
    Don't you want to be *nice?*

As we began cleaning out my parents' place, I figured that in order to accommodate the things they wanted me to have, I needed to buy what I thought of (even at forty) as "a grown-up house." I'd never before been able to afford such a house, and now, post-inheritance, I was wary of acquiring a property that would soon prove too expensive and cumbersome to maintain. Still, as Moreland and I muddled along, sorting Mom and Daddy's things, I kept finding myself going home, pouring a drink, and ogling houses on realtor.com. Scrolling through images of glossy hardwood floors and subway-tiled bathrooms, I sometimes wondered why I was so susceptible to the idea that I ought to buy a bigger house at this stage in my life. Surely it wasn't only because I wanted a place to put my parents' things.

    Part of me was disgusted with myself. How had I—a woman who refuses make-up and hair dye and hates shopping, a feminist eager to smash the patriarchy, a *writer*, for Christ's sake, a fucking *artist*—how had I swallowed the bougie notion that a large, tastefully decorated house is the ultimate sign of a woman's success? Where had this idea even come from? And why is it still so pervasive?

In *The Refinement of America*, Richard Bushman describes how, in affluent eighteenth-century households, the Mister controlled the money and made the furnishing decisions, choosing decor that advertised his worldly success and status as a gentleman. Not until the nineteenth century did the job of creating the house beautiful fall to the Missus. She was expected to keep an inviting, handsomely appointed home, clean and well aired, where a guest would receive a polite but warm reception, feast on a delicious meal, and enjoy delightful entertainment. This standard was neither easy nor cheap to maintain, and it was never realistic, derived as it was from European royal court culture. Still, as time went on, more Americans aspired to this standard, which influenced the way houses looked as well as the behavior of the people living in them.

Circa 1998: I'm helping my grandfather in the office/library at Oaklana. As we take down one set of worn but good-quality old curtains so that we can put up a slightly less threadbare set, he repeats the mantra that "shabby gentility" is preferable to ostentation.

By then, his family had been gentry for two hundred years. Their financial fortunes had fluctuated during times of upheaval— the Civil War, the Depression—but they never lost their position in their rural community. My grandparents were still living in the big house, still following what Bushman calls the "genteel code." They'd been bred to be "disciplined, deferential, spirited, polite, knowledgeable, forceful, graceful," though picturing my grandmother deferring to anyone is like imagining a grizzly bear waiting to eat until everyone else is served.

When my parents married in 1961, they received the usual silver, china, glassware, and table linens that middle- and upper-class people in those days thought a young couple must possess in order to entertain properly. A photograph shows the wedding gifts displayed for visitors to view: a row of ivy-garlanded silver trays lined up like shields on a Viking longship.

My mother barely used any of that stuff. She couldn't be bothered to haul it out of the cabinet, wash off the dust, then hand wash it all again after it had been used. There was no need, anyway. She seldom invited people to dinner—she was a miserable cook—and my father balked at buying frivolities like party crackers and wine to be enjoyed by people other than himself. Why then did she insist I register for gifts when I was getting ready to marry? I thought this activity embarrassingly mercenary and bourgeois; she countered that it was sensible.

Once I started opening the gifts, I saw her point. Many of the non-registry presents we got were pretty useless for two graduate students in a tiny apartment. One well-meaning person gave us a pair of reproduction Staffordshire dogs. In eighteenth- and nineteenth-century Britain, Staffordshire figurines of shepherds and shepherdesses, or lords and ladies on horseback, or animals, often came in pairs. People displayed them on either end of a fireplace mantel, one looking toward the other. Particularly popular were the spaniels, and that's what I received: foot-high brown-and-white dogs with imbecilic, misshapen eyes. What on earth was I going to do with them?

Cajoling, as she always did when I was even a little down, Mom said, "Oh, they're not that bad. They'll do until you can get the real thing."

I had to laugh. Did I really live in a world where the attainment of my maturity, of my ultimate womanhood, would be signaled by owning old, matching statues of inbred dogs? Said like that, of course, it's silly, but Mom's comment pointed to something real—the expectation that marriage is the trailhead for the path toward owning and inhabiting an ideal house. For her and many of the people she knew, that ideal house was decorated in the genteel American style, with "real" antiques, Oriental rugs, custom-made curtains, paintings and prints, porcelains and books. All tasteful, correct, and welcoming, exuding warmth and richness but not ostentation.

To attain a house beautiful is to have arrived.

When Glenn and I got out of graduate school, I knew, we'd have lots of debt and low-paying jobs. I'd inherit "nice" things eventually but not be able to afford to buy them myself. Nor would I want to. I wasn't going to display clichéd accoutrements like Staffordshire dogs, and I certainly wasn't going to serve my friends dinner on Royal Doulton plates. Like my mother, I wouldn't have household help around to iron table linen and polish silver, and I sure as hell wasn't going to do all that myself. In no way was I interested in becoming the sort of woman who thought such possessions important. And yet . . . I could feel the lure of wanting to create my own ideal house, just as my mother and grandparents had.

In her adult life, Mom had neither the money nor the motivation to keep a large house, but she'd been raised with that genteel standard, and part of her held on to it as the ideal. For her, Oaklana was always "down home," and the way things were done there was the right way.

I, too, find it easy to be nostalgic about Oaklana—about, among other things, the beautiful table set for Christmas dinner. Daddy-Jack would cut branches of holly and evergreens from the yard and arrange a centerpiece of greenery, fruit, and nuts. We'd dress the long, glossy table with white placemats and pressed damask napkins, silver flatware, heavy water goblets and wine glasses, and Granny's Wedgwood china with the blue-green band. The children's table, sensibly, was set with the everyday dishes. Once, when quite small, Moreland protested because his place setting wasn't the same as the adults'. My mother tried to quiet him, but Daddy-Jack crowed, delighted: "If the child wants a bread and butter plate, he shall have it!"

On Christmas Eve, we sang carols in the tiny candlelit wooden church, ate party sandwiches at a nearby house, then braved the cold to head back to Oaklana. Under threat that Santa wouldn't deliver if we didn't go to bed, Cousin Margaret and I lay chattering under moth-nibbled wool blankets. The grownups' revelry was our lullaby; we prayed their late-night foolishness didn't keep Santa away. Electric baseboard heaters ticked away the dragging minutes until sleep. In the morning, we lined up with our brothers in the front hall, barely able to contain our excitement about what lay behind the living-room door: dozens of presents under the tree, bulging stockings—an overwhelming abundance we still believed was the product of pure magic.

Later, we'd sit at the gorgeous table to eat the delicious food prepared in the days before by Annie Mae Walton, who worked as cook and housekeeper for my grandparents, and who lived a few miles down the road. We children called her Mae Mae, and loved her, but the whole setup of having a maid versus being a maid struck me as unfair. Every Christmas, she gave us children each a card with a dollar or two enclosed, and we'd give her chocolates or pink soaps from Woolworth's, molded to look like flowers or seashells.

After Daddy-Jack died, I opened a kitchen cabinet at Oaklana and found the Christmas menu taped inside the door. He'd written: *Turkey and gravy, ham, rice, stewed tomatoes, broccoli casserole, Parker house rolls, sweet potato pie.* As if we'd forget.

Part of me wants to set those beautiful tables for my son and friends, for myself, but I haven't forgotten the pressures underlying that standard, the harried hours preparing for those occasions, the tedious cleaning after the meals were demolished. Even with Annie Mae cooking, the women in the family spent hours washing, drying, sweeping, vacuuming. Picking meat from carcasses, coaxing stains out of linen. I could wax nostalgic about our female camaraderie, but the fact is, the work was exhausting. Better to tell you about the holiday when I railed at the unfairness of the boys not being made to help in the kitchen, how my aunts burst into shocked laughter when I declared that I might as well flop out a breast and wipe the counter down with it, since drudgery was what my female body was apparently built for.

Bushman writes of the 1700s: "While outwardly harmonious and kindly, genteel society was inwardly judgmental and censorious. . . . All that went into the grand performance was subject to criticism." More than two centuries later, it's still true: we women are still judged on our appearance, our temperaments, our children, our houses, our bodies. We're supposed to maintain these impeccably with no apparent effort. Most strangely, we're supposed to do it without appearing to *care* too much about doing it.

My family put their own intensely picky spin on these unattainable, contradictory expectations. They lavished admiration on what pleased them and excoriated what didn't. Hearing how they talked about people they found lacking, I tried never to do anything to provoke anyone to talk about me that way. Departing from their ideals of aesthetics, family, and womanhood—excuse me, *lady*hood— was something I knew they'd see as a grave act of disloyalty, and in my youth, I wasn't about to commit that cardinal sin. (At least, not where they could find out about it.)

But as I grew older, I tired of all those damn rules. As much as I loved my family and wanted to please them, I needed to find my own way. The perfect Christmas? The house beautiful? Why set myself up to fail? Why waste the time? There are too many places to go, too much writing to do.

If I have one rule now about furnishing a house, it's this: My house must contain books—lots of books. The rest is negotiable.

It's not that I don't admire form. It's not that form doesn't matter. But forms need not stay static. They can change frequency: go low, then high. Why not?

Motherless, widowed Murasaki brushed her lowly woman's hiragana on paper and brought to life the fair prince Genji and all his ladies. They have lived now for a thousand years.

At a time when anything serious ought to have been written in

Latin, Dante mourned in vernacular Italian the loss of his great love Beatrice, and drew a picture of Hell so enduringly harrowing that we consign our enemies to its circles still.

Shakespeare peppered his lovely iambs with rude locutions like "'ods bodkins." He invented hundreds of words and phrases we say daily without knowing from whence they came.

These writers worked in forms their contemporaries thought too low for art. But what they made has been so long loved that with our loving we have raised it high.

On any given day, my house is simply home, the place where everything is familiar. But when a guest comments on all my old things, I look at my home with different eyes. I remember that it's unusual for a writer and university lecturer to own so many antiques, and I find myself explaining about my parents, my family. I act as though none of it has been my doing, this putting together of a home that's attractive and comfortable, that reflects my personal history and taste.

Your personal aesthetic is a product of your experience: an expression of it, a reaction to it. You continue what someone else started, or you turn away from it. Or, like me, you do both.

I wonder what I'd choose for myself if I hadn't inherited all these things. If I had to start now with an empty house and the money to furnish and decorate it, I suspect the result wouldn't end up looking markedly different from my house now. After all, it's too late to undo my early training in decorative matters—I tend to prefer old things to new—and antiques have become so devalued that they're now more affordable than good-quality new furniture. I'd choose an eclectic mix of styles and periods; I'd go for darker wood over light; clean lines over rococo. I'd buy work by contemporary artists to mix in with old paintings and prints. The dishes would be pretty but utilitarian. Books, of course, lots and lots. In each room, per the rules I learned at my mother's knee, a mix of horizontal and vertical, hard and soft, vibrant and neutral. There must be symmetry and something red. And in my parlor, at least one picture that reminds me of my vocation, a picture that tells an old, golden story, written in a woman's hand.

LAST

The Art of Dying

Until I was a teenager, talk of the Mint Museum Show or the Extravaganza induced in me a mild dread. As these antiques shows approached, the impending rupture in the daily routine agitated my father, like a rat whose nest has been disturbed, but the possibility for extra profit also invigorated him. He quarreled with my mother about which merchandise might appeal most to buyers in Charlotte or Winston-Salem, and badgered her to remember receipts and record her mileage. The day before the show, they wrapped breakables in old newspaper and adult diapers, packed it all into banana boxes, then fussed about how to fit the boxes and furniture into the van. Moreland and I were drafted into the commotion—go get more paper, find me a dust rag, carry this, *carefully!*—and while I didn't relish the bossing, I was happy my parents thought me mature enough to be included in such an important task.

My grandmother's arrival tempered my sadness about my mother leaving. Having Mimi around meant eating spaghetti and watching Victor and Nikki make out on *The Young and the Restless*.

Temporarily liberated from domestic responsibility, Mom wallowed in the freedoms of a solo motel room—having the TV to herself, leaving a mess, nobody asking her to do a goddamn thing. (She brought home the little soaps for me, lover of the miniature.) Traveling alone, she could go out with her dealer friends for late-night drinks or dancing at gay clubs. Traveling with Daddy-Jack was a different story. Although married, a mother, and a business owner, she was still the "Princess," who needed a chaperone to approve her outfits and keep her safe when she went out at night. His oversight annoyed her, but she appreciated his intellectual companionship, his eye for aesthetics, his fatherly approval. It tickled her to watch the public encounter his mannered elegance. He was, like the wares he sold, the product of another time.

On setup day they unpacked, arranged the booth, then retired to their motel room to rest before the show's opening party. To pass the time during the lull, they moved the chairs and luggage racks into a more pleasing arrangement, did a crossword, smoked, napped. Refreshed, they changed into formal clothes, frantically searched for their misplaced keys, then headed to the party, where they mingled with dealer friends from up and down the East Coast, and met well-heeled locals who could afford the pricey ticket.

The sponsoring organization at one of these shows held a fund-raising auction at its opening party. Each dealer supplied an item, along with an entertaining story about it. The better the story (and the cocktails), the higher the bidding climbed, even for objects lacking monetary value or visual appeal. One year, my courtly grandfather put up for sale a white porcelain urinal bearing the logo of Boots, the British drugstore chain. Nobody wanted it, so it went back to Oaklana, where it sat in Daddy-Jack's bathroom until the day my mother removed it to hers. Now it occupies a high shelf across from my shower. Inside, folded lengthwise, an index card bears Daddy-Jack's writing:

This rare + unusual item was
purchased at B——— L———s
Antiques. The auctioneers discription was
as follows: a rare example
of an 18th century
ALADIN LAMP, possibly an original.

Oh, my grandfather—he of the flights of fancy, he of the misspellings. He imagined the auctioneer mistaking the urinal for an Aladdin lamp because of its long-necked shape. It's a high-low joke: a laugh about the ignorance of the untutored, meant to appeal to a group of connoisseurs who, like him, found it incongruous, even ridiculous, to connect a basic bodily function with antiques and wish fulfillment. That Daddy-Jack had this crude joke in him—he of coat and tie, he of butter knife and sugar shell, he of *thank you kindly* and *rsvp*—is proof that the most elegant among us are but bodies after all.

⌇⌇

When my father became wheelchair bound in the late 1990s, he refused to have a handicapped bathroom installed. One day, he maintained, he'd walk again, so what was the point? He didn't want the expense or the bother of having workers in the house. So my mother put a commode chair in his office, formerly my bedroom. Daddy stationed plastic urinals around the house wherever he hung out. We became accustomed to the presence of these bottles on the floor by his recliner in the den or a few feet away from the table where we gathered to eat. Several times a day Mom poured the pee into the nearest toilet, no doubt wishing as she sprayed Lysol that some sudden magic—a genie with three wishes to grant—might materialize and change her life.

She joked that when she died we ought to bury her with a urinal in her hand.

"You can put a daisy in it to be festive."

Often when I'd go to empty one, Daddy would protest that there was no need. He was the sort of person who saw the urinal as half empty, whereas I, apparently, saw it as half full.

KEEP:

"Boots" urinal, inspirer of silly jokes for three generations

When we are healthy and able bodied, our housekeeping and decor tend to reflect nonphysical aspects of our identity. We create spaces that feel cozy to ourselves or welcoming to guests. Or we stage our rooms to impress visitors. Or we keep our house in such disarray that nobody but us (and maybe not even us) can feel comfortable in it. We may go so far as to conceive of ourselves as having a particular decorating style, and we give that style a descriptive name—traditional, country, masculine, boho—or allude to it by era: Victorian, mid-century modern. Others of us don't have the inclination or confidence, time or money, to pursue a particular style; we just furnish with whatever comes to hand. Whatever our house looks like, though, a lot of us believe it says something important about our personalities.

When all is well—when we are well—we seldom display direct signifiers of our health status around the house. Maybe our yoga mat or running shoes sit by the front door, hoping, like the dog, to go out. We might keep our vitamins on the kitchen counter so we'll remember to swallow them. Next to these, the fruit bowl sits in plain view, reminding us that an apple a day . . . If we do contract a cold or stomach bug, the nightstand becomes littered for a few days with medicines, cough drops, crumpled tissues. But when we recover, we hide these things in cabinets again until the next time we need them.

What a different story our rooms tell when our health troubles turn chronic, then terminal. Mom used to make fun of families who put hospital beds in their dens. Then, in the fall of 2006, a chest X-ray revealed a mass, and she underwent surgery to remove part of her lung. Subsequent scans came back clean until eighteen months later, when we learned her cancer had returned. Soon wheelchairs and walkers sidelined her Chippendale and Queen Anne chairs, and she had to laugh at her own aesthetic comedown. Although sick, she still wanted to be part of things. She, too, wanted her bed in the den, in the middle of the action—or at least near the television.

Daddy's health problems upset me, but when Mom got sick, it was as though my body knew that the body that had birthed it was suffering, and it wanted to physically share the burden. I developed a hernia in the exact same spot where she'd had one years before. Just days after my hernia repair, Mom underwent surgery to remove a tumor from around her adrenal gland. This was after her cancer had metastasized, and while the prognosis wasn't good, the surgery went well. She was wheeled from post-op to a private room, where it soon became clear that the narcotics they'd given her were suppressing her breathing. Still on pain medication myself, I stood by her bed, watching the monitor. Whenever her respirations per minute got dangerously low, I'd say loudly, "Breathe, Mama! Breathe!" She wasn't really conscious, but she must have heard me, because for a minute, she'd breathe. Then the number would fall again, and I'd repeat: "Breathe." This went on for hours, until daylight broke. As far as I as concerned, we were one body, a body in pain, and we were going to pull thorough this ordeal together.

When I visited my parents in those days, a sticker on the side door was the first sign that things had gone awry: red line through a cigarette, oxygen in use. (Before Mom and Daddy quit, you could smell the smoke as soon as you opened that door.) Inside, prescription bottles, glucometer and blood sugar log, inhalers and nebulizer cluttered the kitchen table. Beside these, alert buttons kept company with lists of phone numbers, writ large. You might know the day of the week by checking to see which pillbox cells were empty: SMTWTFS. On the refrigerator, interspersed among family photos, cartoons, and children's drawings, hung warnings about falls and choking, and magnets bearing the contact information for doctors' offices and medical supply companies. Dietary reminders listed foods to be and not to be eaten; inside the fridge I found items from both columns, much of it spoiled and needing to be thrown out.

Even in her prime, my mother despised housekeeping. Now that she was ailing alongside my father, everything grew dirtier. Repairs, never a priority, were put off indefinitely. Clutter mounted, including Daddy's hoarded newspapers, a significant source of discord. They'd piled up during his hospital stays, a tangible representation of the days illness had stolen from him, and which he could never get back. Around the time of his first leg amputation in the early 2000s, he started sleeping past noon, then sat around in the same nylon pajamas he'd worn for a week. The only time he got dressed and left the house was when he had a medical appointment. He and Mom both denied that he was depressed.

After Mom recovered from her first surgery, the household had resumed revolving around Daddy: his regimen of insulin injections and mealtimes; his preferences regarding light, noise, temperature, company, music, and television programs; his obsessively particular procedures for accomplishing simple tasks. His daily routine and his belongings were the few things over which he had any control, and he raged if we moved his drinking glass or his scissors. He needed to know exactly where things were, and he didn't care who found his placement of them unsightly or inconvenient. He was compelled to mark his territory so that none of us forgot his suffering or his need to leverage it to get the upper hand—one of his few remaining means of dominating us.

Now, after Mom's second surgery, it became clear that she'd never again be able to take care of Daddy and the house. Moreland and I took turns staying overnight with him whenever she was in the hospital. We did the shopping and errands, took over the bill paying and appointment making. Our spouses, relatives, and friends helped, but we both had small children and jobs, and after months of juggling it all, we were exhausted.

As these terrible months went along, my compulsion to share Mom's suffering flared up as hypochondria, and the freelance work I was doing at the time compounded my nervousness. A university press sent a hefty manuscript about breast cancer, and I spent weeks editing with one hand as I frantically checked myself for lumps with the other. I tackled a manuscript about AA, and only beer took the edge off my worries about becoming an alcoholic. I edited on my laptop in doctors' offices and hospital waiting rooms, or sitting with Mom eating Cheetos as chemo dripped into the port embedded in her chest. Sickness so surrounded me that it became difficult to resist the idea that my own horrible fate was bound to present any minute.

The final straw: the press offered me a massive manuscript about cardiac disease. By then Daddy had undergone quintuple bypass surgery, suffered multiple heart attacks, had a pacemaker installed, and lost both legs to poor circulation. Anxious to preserve my sanity, I politely declined to edit any more health-related books.

Paid part-time caregivers filled the gaps for a time, but the expense was unsustainable and Daddy soon turned against the aides, his rudeness driving at least one to quit. Finally, in the spring of 2009, Moreland suggested we look at assisted-living facilities. The two of us were drinking beer in a steakhouse, having just left Daddy at the hospital after yet another "heart event." (These events always seemed to prompt us immediately to eat the least heart-healthy food we could find.) The idea of assisted living had never occurred to me, I suppose because our folks seemed too young—only in their sixties. I listened to my brother's plan as we tore into the onion rings. I thought, not for the first time, how smart he was. Here was a reasonable way to regain a little normality in our lives.

By the time I sank into bed that night, relief had collapsed into guilt. Shouldn't I be offering to take my parents into my home? Or to move in with them? They'd always cared for us so unstintingly, giving us their time and attention, scrimping and denying themselves for us. Shouldn't we return the favor instead of parking them in a sterile, depressing facility?

I wanted to care for them; really, I did. But I also desperately didn't want them staying in my house. I hadn't lived with them year-round since I was fourteen. I chafed under their authority then; now that I was thirty-six, a wife and a mother, they would flat-out drive me crazy. They thought the food I ate was weird, too healthy. I didn't like having the television on all evening. I didn't want wheelchairs scraping the paint off the doorframes, and how would we manage the urinals with two dogs around? My five-year-old son was noisy in the mornings; Mom and Daddy were bound to criticize my parenting. I didn't want to be around sickness all the time or be beholden to their schedules, and I certainly didn't want to revert to the role of full-time daughter, striving to please them twenty-four hours a day.

And what about my husband? What would having my parents in the house do to him, to us? Would we ever have sex again? Or even a private conversation?

As usual, I should have skipped the guilt. When I floated the idea of living together to my mother, she said she'd much rather go to a home. Many older people feel the same way. In *Being Mortal*, surgeon and author Atul Gawande reveals that older people in most modern societies *prefer* to live on their own. They don't want their children constantly judging their choices and telling them what to do all the time. Just like you, your parents want to feel as though they are independent, even if, paradoxically, it means they have to live in an institution.

Moreland and I found an assisted-living place my mother thought she could stand. Then the three of us discussed how to broach the subject with Daddy, who was temporarily in a nursing home, recuperating from a heart attack. Mom wasn't visiting him there because she was on yet another course of chemo and trying to avoid germs, so Moreland and I arranged to be at his side one evening when she called. Over the phone, she told Daddy she was too sick and tired to stay at home anymore, and that she'd chosen a nice place to live. Moreland and I could tell him all about it. She hoped he would go with her.

How smart she was. She made it sound like his ornery ass had a choice in the matter.

He said that sounded like a good plan. He'd go with her.

My brother and I left in a daze of relief. We'd prepared ourselves for a battle, and then it had been so easy. That Daddy was sharing a room with a delirious guy who yelled a lot surely made the prospect of any single room attractive. Still, it was so unlike him not to argue. Later, I realized Daddy must have convinced himself that the move was temporary, that they'd both regain their health and return home before long.

Mom was under no such illusion. Soon after the surgeon confirmed that the fuzzy white spot on her X-ray was concerning, she said to me, "I guess all I have left to teach you is how to die."

My good friend Nina was also a writer. Over dinner or walks around our neighborhoods, we talked about books and writing, parenting and daughtering. We talked about our mothers: each living with cancer, each facing her oncoming death with reflective, foul-mouthed grace, each continually surprising her family into seeing anew how the process of dying was part of living. We saw them not only as mothers but as our close friends and intellectual guides.

Nina understood, perhaps better than anyone else, exactly what I feared when I contemplated my mother's death: the loss of one of the few people who spoke my peculiar language, the person who'd taught me that language in the first place. Together, Nina and I discussed the magnitude of our looming loss—how it would rob us of the women who, loving us best, helped us try to make sense of the world and laughed with us when we failed. When our mothers were gone, we'd be forced to forge our own ways of making meaning. This new way might be informed and infused by what our mothers taught us, but it wouldn't include the reliable comfort of their immediate presence. Their voices would be gone, and Nina and I agreed that the prospect of that absence, that silence, terrified us.

Then, an awful twist: Nina was also sick—hers an aggressive form of breast cancer. Our walks became shorter and less frequent. Eventually, tumors encroached on her spine and hips, and she acquired a cane, decorated with a flower pattern. Strolls along the winding park path were no longer possible. She burrowed into writing, racing the clock to finish her manuscript. She drew closer to her family, but her curiosity to know about lives other than her own, whether through books or conversation, never diminished. So we managed to make time for the occasional boozy dinner, where we lingered over empty plates, laughing, not wanting the evening to end. Much of what we talked about, especially after her diagnosis, circled back to matters that found their way into her funny, thoughtful book, *The Bright Hour: A Memoir of Living and Dying*, published to acclaim several months after she died. Readers admire the humor and honesty with which Nina chronicled the experience of learning to attend to and cherish the everyday as you accept the ever presence of death in your life.

Immanence is the idea that God permeates, is manifested in, everything around us, all the time. Though I've long been sure that I don't believe in a being called God, the idea of immanence makes sense to me. And so I have to ask: If there is something saturating us and everything that surrounds us, what is that thing? Is *that* God? Is it Death? Certainly, that capital-D specter waits all the time for each of us, and thus is immanent, as well as imminent.

What if "God" and "Death" are just names for different ways of thinking about time and its effect on human beings—"God" suggesting what is permanent and connects us, "Death" what is temporary and separates us only for as long as we outlive those who have gone before? Defined that way, God becomes a concept I can get behind, and Death a thing I might, with practice, learn to fear less.

While it may feel like news when a person receives a terminal diagnosis, we know that the condition of dying is not new. It's always been happening. The diagnosis is just a lens that brings certain things into sharper focus, even as it blurs, then edges into obscurity, what is peripheral. The October the doctor removed part of my mother's lung, she declared she'd never seen the autumn leaves so beautiful. Their colors dazzled her. Now that her knowledge of her mortality had become particular, close up, rather than general and distant, she was seeing through changed eyes the world's terror and its beauty.

Our eyes hunger for beauty, out in the world and in our homes. But when our medical equipment becomes so necessary that it dominates the rooms in which we live, we're forced, as Nina was, as my mother was, to acknowledge what is easy to ignore when we're used to good health: we have bodies that require tending. Those bodies break down; we die sooner than we'd like. How will we spend the time as we wait? What will we choose to look upon as we and Death draw closer to one another?

Before cancer struck, Mom used to say she hoped to drop dead of a heart attack in her sleep, like Granny. If she wasn't that lucky and instead got sick, then we were to "get the feather pillow," to suffocate her out of her misery. As with many things she said, it was only partly a joke. She wanted no awareness that she was dying—no fear, no suffering, no final reckoning.

Centuries ago, good Christians considered a sudden demise undesirable because it left no time to prepare to meet God. According to one scholar, "in late medieval and early modern England a vast body of devotional literature known as the *ars moriendi*, the art of dying, taught people how to die well, since dying was seen as a test of both courage and virtue, and a good death might go some way to compensate for a less worthy life. The state of the individual's soul at the moment of death was deemed of vital importance, since there was an immediate divine judgement on each individual at death, making constant preparation essential." By daily prayer and right behavior, one tried to keep one's soul squeaky clean. I think of it as the spiritual equivalent of putting on clean underwear, just in case you're in an accident. It's the Boy Scout motto: *Be prepared.* Of course, repentant Christians are not the only believers who regard Death as but a doorway from this pain-filled, tainted world into a perfect, peaceful state. Many religious traditions envision earthly life as transitory, a mere way station on the journey to whatever comes next.

For a materialist, however, there is no afterlife. Death is the final moment. Fade to black; curtain down. Show's over.

Say *materialist* today and your listener likely won't think of a person who doesn't believe in an afterlife. Instead, they'll imagine somebody who believes that living well depends on monetary wealth and status, who values material objects over matters of the intellect or spirit. To call someone "materialistic" is an insult, an accusation of shallowness and greed. And yet our capitalist society depends on the continued exchange of money for goods, and tends to see as odd anybody who wants to step out of the chain of production and consumption.

My parents decried base materialism, a relation to objects that focuses on avarice, profit, and show. Their careers as antique dealers obviously relied on commerce, as well as understanding the monetary value placed on certain items at certain times. But they didn't consider their attachment to objects materialistic, because their interest was in old and/or handmade things—objects that, like bodies, became ever more unique as they accrued wear and tear, and singular histories. At work, at home, my parents used objects as a means to consider intellectual and spiritual questions—again, as sociologist Sherry Turkle puts it, as "objects we think with." Moving to assisted living, however, my parents were forced to give up being in daily relation with most of their possessions, and a significant number of things taking up space in their new rooms were blatant reminders of what they preferred not to think about—their decrepitude and their dependence.

Because there are such opposite possibilities for conceiving of death—either you go into a black hole or you pass into a plane of heightened, everlasting existence—any story of a death in Western society has the potential to be one of conversion. Will the dying embrace a religious view that includes an afterlife? Or will the dying simply expire, without epiphany?

Among the most famous literary explorations of this quandary is *The Death of Ivan Ilyich*. The title character, says Tolstoy's narrator, has had a past "most simple and ordinary and most terrible." Ivan Ilyich is an affluent lawyer and bureaucrat, what we'd call upper middle class, and he's had all the experiences a man of his ilk is expected to have: a good education, a few years of sowing his wild oats, marriage, two children, career promotions, and, ultimately, a house, filled with carved tables, knickknacks, and a pouf covered in pink cretonne. There have been setbacks along the way, but generally his progress toward a comfortable, self-satisfied existence has been unimpeded.

Then, one day, he falls and hurts his side. The pain goes away after a few days, he feels fine. Over time, though, the pain returns. He sickens. Doctors poke and prescribe, but they can't figure out what's wrong with him. Only forty-five, Ivan Ilyich becomes an invalid, a burden to his family. His wife, children, friends, and colleagues avoid him because they can't bear his suffering, can't bear to acknowledge the fact of death. They pretend it isn't happening, and while he hates their falsity, Ivan Ilyich cannot really believe it either—that he's dying. He alternates between black despair and impossible hope for a cure, and hates his wife for not understanding what he's going through. His only sources of comfort are his little son and his hearty young servant, Gerasim.

At first, Ivan Ilyich is embarrassed to need Gerasim's help using the commode, but gradually he becomes able to accept being cared for: "Gerasim did it easily, willingly, simply, and with a kindness that moved Ivan Ilyich." Critics often identify this character as a Tolstoyan peasant-saint figure, and Ivan Ilyich himself regards the younger man with a kind of awe, not quite understanding how he can stand to carry repulsive effluvia, to wrench his own body in order to provide comfort to another.

Reading the scenes in which this vigorous rustic matter-of-factly tends his patient, I think of the times my brother or I rolled a wooden massager over our mother's back as she sat on the toilet, miserable with narcotic-induced constipation. Or the time chemo made her itching feet and ankles peel, and I bathed them in a pink plastic tub, the translucent skin sloughing off in gray sheets that floated on the lukewarm water. Or when Moreland held a tea bag inside my father's mouth for an hour, trying to stanch the bleeding where a tooth had been pulled earlier that day. Or, I think of when, after another chemo, Mom developed a yeast infection all over her torso and thighs, and I helped her out of the slippery bath, then carefully dried her skin with a blow dryer and powdered the folds of her belly because any moisture left there would encourage the yeast to grow. It was the only time I cried in front of her when she was sick. I thought she was suffering too much in trying to get cured; she patiently assured me *she'd* decide when she'd endured enough.

Ivan Ilyich seems to think that because Gerasim does not *act* disgusted or discomfited, he must not *feel* disgust or discomfort. This strikes me as the thought-mistake of a man who has never nursed a sick person. Moreland and I weren't immune to being disgusted by our parents' bloody wounds or the fluids and smells emanating from their wrecked bodies. We didn't possess supernatural energy. Nor did we always perform these services with good humor. We were far, far from being saints. We took care of them simply because our mother, by word and deed, had taught us that when you love somebody, you show up when they need help, and you do what you can to ease their suffering. You hope that one day somebody will do the same for you. As Gerasim says, "We'll all die. Why not take the trouble?"

Gawande opens *Being Mortal* with a discussion of Tolstoy's story, pointing to how Gerasim's humane care for Ivan is at odds with modern medical interventions that prolong life without necessarily improving its quality. When making treatment decisions, Gawande recommends asking terminal patients the following: What is it you want to continue to be able to do for as long as you can do it? What are you willing to endure in order to be able to do that? Questions to which I would add, On what do you want to *look* as you move toward death?

I insisted my parents take separate rooms at the assisted-living facility, knowing how they'd fight if cooped up together. They were assigned to the same floor, my father to a large corner room at one end of a long hall, my mother to a smaller space nearer the opposite end. Each had their own bathroom and mini-fridge. Planning the move, Mom sketched the rooms on her yellow legal pad, accurately remembering, after only a brief tour, their approximate dimensions and the position of every door and window. Her uncanny ability to visualize how furniture might best be arranged in a room was a kind of genius, born out of her aesthetic sensibility, her visual memory, and an intuitive grasp of three-dimensional space. Without measuring, she could look at an empty spot and say what piece of available furniture would fit into it. Her unerring instincts in these matters prompted a family refrain. When facing a decorating problem, we ask, *What would Ridley do?*

Moving our parents into their rooms in "the home" resembled moving teenagers into a college dorm. We hung pictures and unpacked suitcases, we made a list for a Target run: soap dishes, coat hangers. Established residents opened their doors and cast curious, suspicious looks in our direction. A few stopped to welcome Mom and Daddy, blocking the path with wheelchair or walker, cupping their hands behind their ears to catch names they'd immediately forget.

After dinner the first night, it finally came time to leave our folks alone in their new place. I drove away exhausted, feeling the mixture of relief and terror that comes with the realization that your family, after much preparation, has rounded a turning point from which it will never go back.

I worried Mom would be dispirited by leaving her home and her beautiful things, but she continued to take what pleasures she could. Cigarettes and work, trips and flea markets, planting flowers in the yard—all that was over. But there could still be books and television and Hershey's miniatures. Grandchildren and children. Friends, which she'd also spent her lifetime collecting. Most of the time she was up for visitors, to whom she hospitably offered a Co'-Cola from her mini-fridge before getting down to the lively, always-interesting business of talking. Whenever there was a game night or holiday party at the home, she asked us to bring the kids. My son and two nephews, who ranged from five to eleven years old in those years, were often the only children present, and the residents greeted them like little celebrities, smiling as they reached out knobbed hands and sweatered arms, eager for handshakes and hugs. No doubt schedules and geographical distance prevented many families from attending; others probably just couldn't bear watching elderly people in various states of cognitive and physical incapacity don party hats or leis and bob their heads to loud, theme-related music. I didn't always want to go either, but I figured if it made my mother happy and occupied the kids, why not? It seemed the least I could do. After all, I could go home after an hour or two and down a glass (or two) of wine, whereas my parents were stuck there until they died or went somewhere even more depressing.

Mom had an easier time assimilating than Daddy, not just because she was more sociable but because the institutional setting reminded her of St. Mary's, the boarding school where, fifty years earlier, she'd made lifelong friends. In the late 1950s, they were teenagers in baby-doll pajamas, hair rolled on thick Kotex pads to set a big wave, making Saturday plans to get hamburgers and milkshakes at the Huddle House, or go to the picture show and dances with boys. Now they were women of a certain age who exchanged Christmas cards and emails about retirements and health scares, grandbabies and widowhood. From time to time, a classmate came to visit, and though they had little left in common, Mom remained fond of these women with whom she'd reveled in her first tastes of independence.

Now, despite the limitations forced upon her by illness and the facility's regulations, Mom welcomed another novel freedom: My father lived down the hall, and she no longer had to wait on him. She enjoyed having her own room, her own television, her own schedule. Although she worried she wasn't much fun to be around anymore, she quickly became beloved around the home. She was one of the few residents who was still "with it," and the younger staff members relished her wicked sense of humor. They frequented her room, eating the chocolates she offered and gossiping over her *Peo-*

ple magazines. She professed herself honored to be the only resident for whom two aides performed "Shitty Cookie," an original ditty about a sweet old lady who proffered treats with her unwashed hands.

Mom came to know all about the women who worked there. She remembered their children's names and special talents, their struggles with boyfriends and girlfriends and husbands, their arguments with coworkers, the other jobs they were working to support their families. Many of the carers were black or mixed race, and working class, while most of the residents they bathed, dressed, diapered, medicated, and fed were affluent, white, retired professionals or homemakers. When money or objects went missing from patients' rooms, fingers always pointed at aides first, even though certain residents were known to wander into other people's rooms and take things. Sometimes, one aide told Mom, people said disrespectful or racist things to her, but she tried not to mind because they were sick and pitiful.

Mom admired these women's fortitude and drive, and she was especially partial to the aides studying for a degree. Once, she insisted I go to the bank to withdraw a hundred dollars for an aide who couldn't afford the materials required for a community college course. Workers weren't permitted to accept monetary gifts from the residents, and she didn't want this young woman to get in trouble, so Mom instructed me to write out a promissory note on her yellow pad. She handed over the cash, the aide signed the paper, and I witnessed the transaction, all three of us silently understanding that the money need never be returned.

After the aide left, my mother turned to me and shook her head. "Imagine," she said, "if not having that little bit of money was what stood between you and a better life."

Rather than living in a well-appointed house in which medical equipment presented an intrusive, depressing reminder of illness and mortality, my mother now lived in a place where such apparatus were everywhere. Even the building itself might be called a piece of medical equipment, since its dedicated purpose was to give succor to the sick, addled, and dying. But amid and amongst that equipment, for a while and because she made it that way, my mother and her small room served as an oasis where people were glad to sit among her pretty things and enjoy the life she had left in her.

Meanwhile, the house stood waiting. My brother and I used it as storage space for our own spare belongings. The dust accumulated. Every time I opened the door and didn't hear my mother say, "Come in the house," my heart cracked a little more. The house packed with stuff was devoid of life, and whenever I went there, I couldn't help imagining the echo of the bare rooms once we'd cleaned them out. I dreaded the empty feeling that can come after having done one's duty, that dry thing that is supposed to be its own reward. When Mom and Daddy died, I believed, a chasm would open between me and my past. As their things went away, the chasm would grow wider, harder to bridge. What if, once they died and we got rid of their stuff, I could never find my parents again?

As much as I dreaded that emptiness, I craved it, too. I hungered for all the dying to be over. I felt a pressing restlessness to be done.

During my mother's last year, I reread *Ivan Ilyich* and was struck by how he acquires his injury: he falls from a stepladder while making sure a curtain is hanging to best effect, and a seemingly minor injury leads to his suffering and death. Mom in her youth loved Russian novels, but when I asked her if she'd read *Ivan Ilyich*, she couldn't recall. She'd have approved of Ivan's enthusiasm for decorating, whereas Tolstoy sees it as a manifestation of a crass materialism, just another way of keeping up with the Jonesevichs: "It was the same as with all people who are not exactly rich, but who want to resemble the rich, and for that reason only resemble each other: damasks, ebony, flowers, carpets, and bronzes, dark and gleaming—all that all people of a certain kind acquire in order to resemble all people of a certain kind." In Tolstoy's eyes, Ivan's decorating is mere bourgeois consumption, not the expression of an artistic impulse, and anyway, by the time he wrote this story, Tolstoy was deeply suspicious of artistic impulses.

Vladimir Nabokov tells us that "this story was written in March 1886, at a time when Tolstoy was nearly sixty and had firmly established the Tolstoyan fact that writing masterpieces of fiction was a sin. He had firmly made up his mind that if he would write anything, after the great sins of his middle years, *War and Peace* and *Anna Karenin*, it would be only in the way of simple tales for the people." (Would that I could commit such a "sin" as producing anything as magnificent as *Anna Karenina* or *War and Peace*.) Despite his zeal to renounce his sinful art, however, Tolstoy could not quite do it. According to Nabokov, *The Death of Ivan Ilyich* "is Tolstoy's most artistic, most perfect, and most sophisticated achievement."

Tolstoy lived another twenty-four years after writing the novella. While he continued to write books, he never again produced a major novel. In this last stage of his life, he condemned the material preoccupations of the rich. Encouraged by his disciples, he wanted to get rid of his private property and give "the people" the rights to the profits from his works. His long-suffering wife, Sophia, understandably fought against this plan. Having borne him thirteen children and copied his lengthy manuscripts by hand multiple times, she wanted her due. They quarreled bitterly, again and again, until finally the eighty-two-year-old writer ran away from home, seeking to die elsewhere. When he became too ill to proceed with his journey, he was put to bed in the stationmaster's house at the Astapovo train depot. Sophia rushed there, but he refused to see her. She watched him suffer through a window until, his death imminent, she was admitted into his room to say good-bye. The master's attempt to write his own last chapter had failed.

Talking with terminal patients, Gawande learned that the dying "want to share memories, pass on wisdoms and keepsakes, settle relationships, establish their legacies, make peace with God, and ensure that those who are left behind will be okay. They want to end their stories on their own terms." His findings confirm the centrality of narrative to the human experience. Stories are not beside the point; they *are* the point. And what matters most, for many, is how the story ends. People tend to judge as a failure any experience with an unfortunate ending, even if the experience has been mostly good up until that point. Gawande gives the example of how fans can enjoy watching a football game for three hours but then count the experience as bad if their team loses at the end—even though for most of the game they felt pleasure. This dissonance happens, he says, "because a football game is a story. And in stories, endings matter."

Ivan Ilyich suffers terribly for three days, howling in anguish, terrified to die. Only when he realizes that his suffering is making his family suffer—and that their misery will ease only if *he* accepts what's happening—only then does his fear of death abate:

> What death? There was no more fear because there was no more death.
> Instead of death there was light.

In the late spring of 2010, we realized that chemo's terrible side effects were likely to kill Mom before her cancer did. She decided to stop treatment and receive hospice care. Upon admission into the program, patients are assigned a social worker who liaises between patients, their families, hospice nurses, doctors, medical supply companies, and healthcare facilities. The social worker can coordinate volunteers to keep you company, or summon a priest or other religious functionary to provide spiritual guidance. When my mother looked askance at the prospect of being visited by a cleric, her social worker offered to set up a visit from a nondenominational minister.

"Oh, no," Mom burst out. "That's even worse! If *he* can't make up his friggin' mind, what the hell am I supposed to do?"

So, my mother's how-to-die lesson was not to be a religious one. No surprise there. She took us to the Episcopal church growing up but later told me she'd done it as a kind of inoculation against religion. For an intelligent person, she figured, familiarity with the church would breed contempt, and you'd learn to know better than to drink the Kool-Aid of belief. A person who grew up without any church at all was in danger of one day thinking that lack of religion was the cause of all their discontent and might become a fanatic. She put it this way: "I took you to church so you wouldn't grow up and become a Moonie because you thought religion was going to solve all your problems."

Nearly every religion preaches relinquishing one's worldly goods as part of the path to spiritual enlightenment. I've wondered whether my mother, forced by her move to become less attached to her possessions, experienced any change in her beliefs about the afterlife. I have to say I don't know. To this day, I have no clue where, if anywhere, she thought she was headed.

As she neared the end of her life, her approach to spiritual matters remained what it had always been: a deeply private matter, not to be discussed. I don't even know whether she believed in God or not. A pragmatic person, she was more interested in the development of moral conscience than in abstract ideas of a supreme being, and she considered reading Russian novels a better way to learn about human beings than studying psychology. She believed in the Bible as a historically important piece of literature full of weird, violent stories that gave Western society a common cultural ground. For her, the metaphorical was more to be admired than the literal, and thus the Bible did not *need* to be anything other than literature to be significant. She understood that, for human beings, few things are more meaningful than stories, and whether they are "true" or not is irrelevant to their power to make meaning.

Even before she got sick, whenever Mom decided to do something indulgent, she'd say, "What the hell, I'm only coming through here one time"—meaning through this earthly life, this vale of tears.

Two weeks before she dies, I'm away at a writers' conference in Tennessee. She tells me on the phone that she wakes up each morning still thinking about what her day holds—who's coming to visit or what she's reading. She thinks about that first, she says, and then she remembers she's sick and in a nursing home. She marvels at her own optimism, wondering how she stays so cheerful in the face of death.

Near the end of our conversation, she says, "I'll be glad to see you when you get home, but I want you to wring every bit of pleasure out of what you're doing right now."

Wring every bit of pleasure out of what you're doing right now. For her, every morning, there was a day ahead in which to read or tell a story, a day in which somebody was bound to do a crazy or funny thing, a day in which she could find a mystery to solve or a beauty to observe. Every day held the chance of pleasure, as well as the opportunity to enjoy it all over again, telling me about it.

Just after she moves in to the home, as she's lying in her adjustable bed, Mom looks up toward the ceiling and says, "I can't believe I'm going to die in a room without crown molding."

I laugh and think of Oscar Wilde who, dying in France in 1900, supposedly looked around his room and said, "My wallpaper and I are fighting a duel to the death. One or the other of us has to go."

We laugh, but it is not a trivial question. To what do we want to turn our eye when we are dying? What is the last thing we want to see?

We throw a fiftieth-anniversary party for Mom and Daddy in June 2011. Mom delights in drawing up the guest list and choosing her favorite foods for the menu—lamb, shrimp, strawberries. She asks us to find the decoration that adorned her wedding cake, and mine, and my brother's—the porcelain cupid, inscribed *Je t'enflame*, which so embarrassed her as a bride of nineteen. She tells me to bring her silver Tiffany cake knife, a wedding gift. I pin to her blouse a piece of nineteenth-century jewelry that came down in her family: a ladies' gold watch dangling from a red coral hand.

At the party, she and Daddy sit together in their wheelchairs and greet guests. Almost everyone Mom knows has been invited to this party: school friends and distant cousins, antique dealers and shop customers, yoga instructors, church members, caregivers. After a while, seeing her energy flag, I ask Mom if she wants to take a break in a quieter room.

"Oh, no," she says, gazing around at the many people she knows she's seeing for the last time. "I just want to look at all their faces."

In August, I go to the beach for a week with my husband and son. Thursday is gray and gloomy, and I think perhaps we should leave the next day, end our vacation early. I'm worried about my mother, I miss her. I talked to her on the phone a couple of days ago, but the connection was patchy and I was impatient to hang up. She'd been telling me about some gifts she ordered, bedsheets with animals on them for her grandchildren and, for me, a box of soaps. She didn't say it, but I knew what she was thinking: she wouldn't be around at Christmas and wanted to give us one last gift. She talked fondly of taking my brother and me to the beach when we were young, how much she'd enjoyed those trips. She hoped I was having a good time, and I pretended I was, not wanting to sadden her with the admission that I never felt like I was having a good time now that she was leaving me.

Before driving down to the shore, I'd gone to eat supper with her at the home. In the dining room, Mom introduced me to a woman with gray curls and a baffled expression, who smelled of pee and was too far gone in her dementia to converse.

"This is my sweet friend Anne," Mom said, reaching across the tablecloth for the woman's liver-spotted claw. For much of the meal, they held hands, even after Mom, overcome with pain, put her head down on the dining table and asked for a pill.

After I wheeled Mom back up to her room, I helped her use her nebulizer and arranged the items she wanted close by.

"You know I wouldn't go away tomorrow if I thought you weren't going to be here when I come home," I told her.

"Go," she said. "Don't worry. I'll be sitting right here when you get back."

Nearly a week later I wake at dawn on Friday morning. The bed is low on the floor, the window high on the wall. Through the glass all I see is sky. I watch the morning light rise and think of her. I feel but don't yet know for sure that at this very moment she's dying. She's sitting in her wheelchair, my brother dozing at her side, a decorating show playing on the television. The faces of her beloveds look down from the wall of photographs above her bed. If she glances up, she can see them. But for the absence of crown molding, a good death.

A Miniature for My Mother

KEEP:
Eighteenth-century mourning pin

Aside from a few patches of white where the color has scratched off, the brooch is in good condition—a tiny painting on ivory, set in a gold mount. No jewels. It has been well cared for. Painted on the ivory is a pale young man in black clothes leaning against a pedestal topped with an urn. Hair-thin lines make up his cravat, his face, the blades of grass at his feet, and the serifs of the pedestal's inscription: *Sacred be thy memory.* He leans on his right elbow, his head resting on his hand; his left arm hangs by his side, holding an open book. Over the tomb, there's a hint of tree branches, behind them blue sky. Around the edge of the pin, there are gold letters: Rebecca Wilkinson * nat * 7 May 1771 * OB: 23 JAN * 1793.

January 23—that's my mother's birthday, and the pin belonged to her. What was a sad day for young Rebecca's family in 1793 was presumably a happy one for my grandparents in 1942. My mother, named Margaret Ridley after her mother and called Ridley, was their first child, born premature and apparently not pretty, both facts my grandmother would mention in a letter she wrote to her in-laws shortly after the birth. In this letter, she instructs them not to make excuses to people about why she's had a baby in January when she was only just married in June. They are not to tell anybody she

90

fell off a ladder or slipped in the tub. My grandmother knows the truth—her baby was born early—and, anyway, it's nobody's business. I doubt anybody said a word. She was only twenty-four, but people already knew better than to mess with her.

⌒

My grandmother left the pin to my mother, and my mother bequeathed it to me. My guess is that Rebecca Wilkinson was connected to our Ridley ancestors in Southampton County, Virginia, but I don't know for sure. Born a subject of King George III, Rebecca died a citizen of the United States, not quite two months before the second inauguration of George Washington. Her short life bookended the American Revolution, and this pin commemorating her is a thing very much of its time. As we rumbled toward nationhood, colonial nobs and their ladies were gaga for small portraits mounted in silver or gold and worn as brooches, bracelets, or pendants. They commissioned these miniatures, also known as limnings, from professional painters who are now largely forgotten. Those artists whose names we do know—Benjamin West, John Singleton Copley, the Peales—are recognizable to us today only because they also rendered the larger-scale scenes and portraits we know from history books, like West's *The Death of General Wolfe* (1770) or Copley's portraits of Paul Revere, John Hancock, and Samuel Adams.

But making a fine miniature was no more "practice" for making a large oil painting than writing a short story is practice for writing a novel. They are different forms, each requiring particular skills. The limner had to cut the ivory, prepare its surface, and paint a tiny image with the aid of a small brush and magnifying glass. Anyone who tries watercolor, remembering it from childhood as a beginner's paint, will quickly discover how difficult it is to mix the pigment and water to achieve a consistency that gives the desired effect. Imagine the frustration of attempting to control such runny paint on a slick bit of ivory only a few inches in diameter, hoping to create a detailed likeness good enough to please someone who knows the sitter well, perhaps intimately. The result, done well, is irresistible—a portrait that is pretty, luminous if the ivory is thin, and eminently portable. A miniature fits in the palm of your hand; it may even be so small that you can conceal it within a fist. It can be worn secretly—tucked behind ruffles, into a pocket, or next to the breast—or it can be displayed, a sign to all the world that the wearer truly has it all: money *and* love.

But no. Not quite all. You or your beloved might not have health. Hence, the mourning miniature, which might not be a picture of the deceased but, instead, an allegorical scene of a mourner at a tomb. The iconography of these scenes is instantly recognizable; the details vary but slightly. Often there's a white woman in white neo-classical robes, offering flowers or laurels or simply her tears at a tomb inscribed with a name and date. The monument might be an obelisk or an urn on a pedestal, the lachrymose figure a man or child rather than a woman. Sometimes there's a dog, symbol of fidelity. Always there's a tree, an evergreen or a weeping willow, both symbolic of the Resurrection, of the life everlasting.

Something in me responds to a weeping tree, the weeping cherry most of all. I love the contrast between the sweet, cheerful pink and white flowers and the graceful downward droop of the branches—in full display the tree appears both riotously joyous and deeply sad. To stand underneath, or inside, the branches of a weeping cherry in bloom is to stand in a magic world. It isn't cool and hidden like the dark world inside a magnolia; rather, it is a world at once shaded and bright, with a view to the outside that's always changing as the branches sway and wave and tremble with every breath of the air.

What if, I wonder, my mother had died in the era of the mourning miniature? What if she'd died at Oaklana in August 1811 rather than August 2011? Would her death have seemed more private?

Would that more death-accepting era have afforded me more time and space to mourn?

In 1811 there's no air-conditioning and no television to take our minds off things. No assisted-living facility, no paid health aides, but we are wealthy enough to own slaves, and one of them, a woman, has been helping in the sick room. This "servant," as enslaved people were euphemistically known in the South in those days, has carried away pots of effluvia, and brought water and food for me to eat.

When the figure of this "servant" appears in my imagined scene, I pause. I have to acknowledge the disturbing continuity between present and past. For too long, poor women of color have been forced to do the difficult, often thankless work of tending sick and dying white people, and it's troubling that—for all my family's professed progressivism, for all our society's many changes—we have not come further, as a family or a society, in two hundred years. I'm reminded that, for those who can afford it, even our most intimate family moments play out in ways that depend on the inequitable racial and class structures underlying every aspect of the world we live and die in.

The plantation culture of white dominance is not what I'm yearning to recapture as I imagine my mother dying at Oaklana in the nineteenth century. So why am I painting a different death for her, in that time and place, with different witnesses?

Because I wish I'd been beside her at the end, as I'd always intended to be. I mourn the lost, last opportunity for proximity, intimacy. I wanted to hold her hand as her circle closed, and to me, it seems our parting might have been more tolerable in a quieter era. No beeping machines, no strangers interrupting our leave-taking with forms to sign. No undertakers apologetically scurrying her body out of the building because the sight of it might unsettle her neighbors. Nobody pretending that death doesn't live always just around the corner. An era in which people made beautiful memento mori like the pin I inherited, and kept those mementos close.

As long as I'm imagining her death in a different time, why not put her dying privately at home instead of as a resident, really a paying customer, in "the home." One way to talk about dying is to say someone is *going home*. When religious people use that phrase, they're talking about heaven, but when Mom said it, she meant returning to Oaklana, to family. Obviously, her new death scene must play out there, in that old yellow house surrounded by ancient oaks.

And so, Oaklana, August 1811: Mama is past eating. She has spent the night hot and restless, moving from chair to bed and back, unable to get comfortable. Moreland and I have not offered to pray with her. Even in 1811, religion is not where she seeks solace. Instead, I've been reading aloud the poem she's requested to be read at her graveside, Andrew Marvell's "To His Coy Mistress." It's the one that begins, "Had we but world enough and time . . ."

Toward dawn, I fall asleep, and when I wake, I see my mother slumped in her chair in a new, awkward way. The enslaved woman, my brother, and I lift my mother's body and lay it on the bed. Later, I'll remove her rings and put them away for safekeeping, but for now, while the woman cleans urine from the chair, I hold my mother's still-soft hand and marvel at how the light has gone out of her face. I have no idea where she has gone.

On August 19, 1811, I help wash my mother's body and dress her for the grave. I cut locks of her hair to give to family and friends. I put on a black dress. For at least six months, maybe longer, I will wear only black. Then I may change to lilac or gray. The mirrors in the house will be covered with black cloth; her portrait will be draped with it. I will write my letters on paper with a black border. For months, I will attend no parties, neither will I throw them. Tomorrow, a black wreath or banner of black crape will be hung on the front door to tell anybody who comes by that ours is a house in mourning.

From ancient times forward, in every corner of the world, funeral and mourning practices have involved the preparation of the corpse, the selection of food and objects to be buried or burned with the dead, the donning of black or white or purple or red garments, the shearing of hair (either the corpse's or the mourners'), and the creation and giving out of memorial jewelry or keepsakes. All over the world, death demands ceremony—a wake, a funeral, a secular service—followed by a reception or feast, burial or cremation, and last, but never least, the division of the deceased's property. All of these customs remain with us in America in the twenty-first century except for the signaling of our bereavement by adorning or altering our bodies.

I find this omission curious. After all, it's not as though we have abandoned the idea of ceremonial clothing. We still dress up our babies for baptisms, our children for first Communions and Bar or Bat Mitzvahs, our teens for proms and graduations and debutante balls, our young (and not so young) for weddings. Give us a special occasion, and we are more than willing to invest in costly, elaborate clothes that custom dictates we wear only once. Often these are exaggerated, hyperbolic garments, made longer, bigger, shinier than our everyday clothes in order to show how important we are at a particular transitional moment in our lives. They are clothes for a special day, and we love choosing and wearing them.

But here in America, the corpse, which we may or may not see, is usually dressed in sedate Sunday best, as are those who attend the funeral. We may or may not wear black, on the funeral day or any other. And even if we have been robbed of our husband, our mother, our best friend, our child, we are expected, in the baffling days that follow, to put on our regular clothes and go around in the world wearing no outward sign that we have recently borne a terrible loss.

When my mother was preparing to follow my father to assisted living in 2009, I helped her decide which clothes and accessories to take. As she sorted through her brightly colored silk and chiffon scarves, she hit on a large square of net, edged with black ribbon—a widow's veil.

"I'll never get to wear it," she said, purposely making her voice sound wistful, as though widowhood had been something she'd hoped to experience. A joke, like most jokes, with a nut of truth at its center. She'd already decided that my father would outlive her, and as usual, she was right.

Queen Victoria lost her mother in March 1861 and her husband, Prince Albert, in December that same year. Afterward, she secluded herself in her various palaces as much as she could, wearing mourning for the next forty years until her own death in 1901. She is often pictured wearing a veil of black or white with a Mary Stuart cap, peaked at the front, a style that had been popular for widows since the sixteenth century. Though Victoria observed mourning far longer than required—about two and a half years would have been recommended for a widow at that time, three months for a widower—hers was but an extreme expression of what her era thought appropriate. While the elaborate rules of Victorian mourning rituals could produce a lot of anxiety and expense, I suspect most people found that wearing mourning helped. Clad in a black dress and unpolished jet jewelry, you didn't have to continually explain yourself. Everybody knew as soon as they saw you that you were in a state of sorrow, longing for the one who'd been taken away, and they didn't try to buck you up. Maybe they even treated you more gently.

In the university library on a May day, the year after my mother's death, I'm looking for a book on mourning dress when my roving eye catches sight of a worn spine: *The Fashion System* by Roland Barthes. Barthes, the philosopher and literary theorist, writing about *fashion*?

I skim the introduction and learn that in this book Barthes examines the linguistic signals we assign to objects that are already signaling to us visually; that is, he studies the words fashion magazines use to describe clothes. Now I begin to see. He was a semiotician, after all, an interpreter of signs, and clothes are among the most common signs we use to project who we are to other people. We make assumptions about people based on how they dress, and they, in turn, make assumptions about us. I find his endeavor fascinating, and yet a quick glance through the book shows me that there's no way I'm going to read it. A PhD dropout and a long-time copyeditor of academic books, I can read literary theory, but it's not the lens through which I prefer to study literature, much less the world. I prefer—I want and need—stories.

But I have a fondness for Barthes because of his book about photography, *Camera Lucida*, and the posthumously published collection *Mourning Diary*, a compilation of notes he made in the months after his mother's death. In the early days of my own mourning, I read Meghan O'Rourke's *The Long Goodbye* and Robin Romm's *The Mercy Papers* and Cheryl Strayed's bestseller *Wild*. Each tells a compelling story; each expresses realities of mother loss that I, too, was experiencing. But it was Barthes's *Mourning Diary*, each brief note just a few lines on an otherwise empty page, that I kept returning to. He says so much that is true about being bereft that it's difficult for me to choose only a few representative quotes. I'd rather put the whole book into your hands and say, *This is what losing her was like for me.*

On November 2, 1977, only a week after his mother's death, he writes: "What's remarkable about these notes is a devastated subject being the victim of *presence of mind.*"

Here is a thinker being chopped down, day after day, by his overwhelming feelings and yet, at the same time, watching himself, recording, analyzing. He is at once observer and observed. He asks not simply "What am I feeling?," but "What am I thinking about what I'm feeling?" And then, "What should I think about the thoughts I'm having about my feelings?"

The problem of not knowing where feeling ought to stop and thought to begin is familiar to me, as is the problem of being the sort of person who searches desperately to find the line over which you can step out of the uncomfortable territory of feeling and into the more solid-seeming realm of thought. I have often wondered: When does the habit of analysis become a liability rather than a gift?

On November 10, Barthes wrote:

> Embarrassed and almost guilty because sometimes I feel that my mourning is merely a susceptibility to emotion. But all my life haven't I been just that: *moved?*

It's been little more than two weeks and already he's *embarrassed* about his feelings. But I get it. After my mother died, I also felt humiliated by my emotions, seeing my extreme grief as just another way in which I, a flawed, weak person, was indulging my penchant for the hyperbolic. After all, her death had been long expected. I saw myself as helpless, overly dramatic, excessive, and was so sure that others would see me that way that I often avoided people altogether.

And then there's this entry from October 31: "Sometimes, very briefly, a blank moment—a kind of numbness—which is not a moment of forgetfulness. This terrifies me."

Oh, yes. Numbness. That, too.

Black is not a color but the absence of it, as any child who has recently been taught this fact will smugly tell you. The absence of color in the mourner's life is precisely the idea that mourning dress conveys. The color, and the light that enables us to see it—both have washed out to sea with the beloved, and the mourner is left on the shifting sands, watching the water swell and dip, waiting for them to return.

When we lose somebody we love, we want to put on the proverbial sackcloth and ashes because colors seem too gaudy. We the grieving look at the cheerful people, wandering around in their yellow shirts, laughing and eating things, and think: How can you? How can you *enjoy* anything, when my beloved is gone?

After my mother died, everything that once had given me pleasure no longer did. Food, books, movies, art, clothes, travel: I had lost my capacity for savoring any of it. Having always been a person with strong appetites, this worried me, but what worried me even more was that I took so little pleasure in my friends, my husband, my child. I became panicky if they weren't around, but I took almost no satisfaction in their actual company. That wasn't their fault. It was just that they weren't my mother, and she was what—who—I wanted. I didn't confess this feeling to anyone because it seemed so selfish, so embarrassingly infantile.

~

When I was growing up, Mom liked to agitate people by doing things they didn't expect a middle-aged white lady to do. Once when I brought a friend home from boarding school, Mama opened the door, cigarette dangling from her lips, and said, "Welcome to hell." For many years, I watched her raise her fist alongside her head in greeting before I understood she was throwing the Black Power salute. When she and I went to meet with our Episcopal priest a few months before I was to be married, she expressed her disappointment that we couldn't use the 1928 *Book of Common Prayer*. When the priest asked what was wrong with the revised version, she said, "They've de-balled the language, Jim."

About social interactions, she used to say, "Give them no quarter, and they will play." By this, she meant that you shouldn't dumb yourself down or curb your language just to fit in with people. If your conversation partners were unnerved by you or couldn't keep up, that was their problem. If they were game, though, everybody would have a wonderful time. My mother was fun to talk with, but she could wear you out. Her talk could be exhausting, both for the sheer amount of information, such as when she discussed Chinese porcelain or eighteenth-century cabinetmakers, and the vehemence of her invective, as when she excoriated Republicans or her sister's ex-husbands.

The flip side of that intensity was her wonderful enthusiasm, not only for what she'd seen or read but for *you*, what you were doing or interested in. When I was in a performance, she'd bring a dozen friends and relatives to watch and applaud. Always she brought a gift—flowers or, more often, a pertinent book, inscribed for the occasion. I still have a Christmas tree ornament she gave me one of the years I danced in *The Nutcracker*, as well as a print of Shakespeare's Viola that she had framed when I was a college freshman and played that character in *Twelfth Night*. She did the same for Moreland, our cousins, the children of her friends. Always she showed up—and brought a present that was in accord with your interests. She loved to see a young person get excited about something, whether it was art or Russia or woodworking, the trumpet or killer bees. She hated people to be "blasé." Better to risk embarrassment by being too eager, too interested, than to bore yourself and everyone around you. Better to overdo than to underdo.

When she died, I didn't collapse. I was able, along with my brother, to take care of the funeral, the memorial service, the estate paperwork, and, of course, our father, who would die not quite six months later, ostensibly of pneumonia but mostly of a broken heart.

I returned to working and socializing, but I didn't feel like myself. Anything that didn't relate to my parents, especially my mother, seemed difficult and pointless, and it was hard for me to concentrate even on reading. The world was full of flavors I couldn't taste, colors I couldn't see, music I couldn't hear. I wondered, with a mounting sense of panic as the months wore on and the first-year mark passed and then the second, if it would always be this way: me outside the gate, peering through the bars at the beautiful, fragrant garden everyone else knew how to enjoy.

Nowadays, the term *grief* has mostly replaced *mourning*. When your loved one dies, you can attend grief counseling or go to a grief support group or read a self-help book or blog. Grief is regarded as a normal condition that, with the right tools and attitude, can be, if not totally overcome, then at least managed and lived with, like diabetes or hypertension. Everybody agrees that grieving is an ordinary thing we all do—like eating or drinking alcohol or procrastinating—but it's possible to take it too far, do it too much. If your grief doesn't ease after six months, if it debilitates you and takes over your life, then it can be diagnosed as "complicated grief," and insurance may cover your therapy, which may or may not include prescription medication.

To *grieve* has two meanings: (1) to express hurt feelings, and (2) to bring a complaint. A grievance is angry; it demands to be addressed and requires a lot of paperwork. It can be about anything. But mourning is particular; it is the act of sorrowing over a death. It is feeling sad about the loss of someone who will never be restored to you, no matter how much paperwork you do or how many pills you take.

Roland Barthes, on November 30, 1977: "Don't say *Mourning*. It's too psychoanalytic. I'm not *mourning*. I'm suffering."

Oh, the sadness will come and go, friends would tell me. Over time, the waves of grief will occur less often and will become less intense. They'll stop knocking you down. I had to believe they knew what they were talking about. After all, they had lost parents, children. Finally, nearly two years after my mother's death, alarmed by what my suffering was doing to me and my family, I began seeing a therapist for the first time in my life. She had lots of questions for me, but I really only had one for her: When would I beat this thing called grief?

When Mama was sick, she sometimes would look the oncologist dead in the eye (in her tellings of her own stories, she always looked people "dead in the eye" or "right in the face") and demand to know how long she had to live. Months? Years? How many?

What could he say? He didn't know, and it would have been irresponsible of him to pretend that he did. Yet I understood her need to know. Any plan is better than no plan, she used to advise us. You can always change the plan, but you need to have one.

I wanted a timeline. I wanted a plan. I wanted a form on which to pin and drape my mourning. Gradually, I came to understand that I would have to make it myself.

Had my mother fallen ill in 1806 instead of 2006, everybody doubtless would have counseled me to pray. In those days, I'd have witnessed many more deaths by the time I was in my thirties, including those of siblings, friends, and my own children. I might already have been wearing mourning for someone else when my mother died. Of course, had it been 1806, there would have been no X-rays to show the spot on her lung, no surgeries to remove masses, no chemotherapy to give her a few more years of life. She would have felt good until, one day, she didn't. She would have lived until, one day, she died.

After she was diagnosed with lung cancer in 2006, every cough, rash, or stomach pain of my own had me convinced I was dying. I joked that I could go from zero to cancer in thirty seconds. A doctor prescribed Xanax, but I was too anxious to take it. I feared ingesting anything I wasn't used to. Besides, my problem was sadness, not illness, and that seemed to require a spiritual rather than a medical intervention. I decided to talk to a priest. This approach had two apparent advantages over pills: it was free and, for me, unlikely to be habit forming.

I was not regularly attending church, but I knew a smart, reasonable Episcopal priest, an acquaintance of my mother. When we sat down together, I told her I tended to rely on books to help me through my problems, and she found one I could borrow. But the book wasn't the real takeaway that day. Instead, it was something she said: "You're not going to die when your mother dies."

At first, it sounded foolish—her suggestion that this was what I was worried about. After thinking about it, though, I realized she was right. I was so close to my mother that some part of me found it inconceivable that I wouldn't die alongside her. Not only inconceivable but disloyal. How could I let her go off without me? And for the first time, she was being disloyal, too: How could she leave me behind?

Roland Barthes, writing November 28, 1977: "To whom could I put this question (with any hope of an answer)? Does being able to live without someone you loved mean you loved her less than you thought . . . ?"

In February 2010, the forty-year-old clothing designer Alexander McQueen committed suicide on the day before his mother's funeral. I habitually dress in yoga pants, yet I'm a devoted *Vogue* reader, and for some years, I'd been intrigued by McQueen's controversial designs, by turns romantic and menacing, full of historical references—bustles, cowls, veils, chain mail. Among his infamous couture collections was "Highland Rape," which featured lace and "tartans cut deep or torn to expose the breasts"; he also invented the Bumster, a pant that shows butt cleavage, on purpose. McQueen was famous for his meticulous cutting and tailoring, as well as for his inventive powers, and his shows were nothing short of theater, complete with elaborate storylines and special effects. Though he was acknowledged as a genius, it was said after his death that he had become disenchanted with the fashion world. He'd been depressed following the suicide of his friend and mentor Isabella Blow a few years before, then depressed again after a breakup, and, finally, distraught after the death of his mother, to whom he was very close.

His death frightened me, as all such deaths do. Here was an artist at the top of his form who had decided that art wasn't enough to sustain him.

For my fortieth birthday, my oldest friend, my high school BFF, gave me a locket. When I opened it, I had to laugh.

"Only you would give me a locket with a picture of my dead dog in it."

Whenever I wear that locket, I open it before putting it on and look at Rudy's dear gray face, his soulful eyes uplifted, alert for the treat the photographer was promising. Adopted when I was twenty-four and newly married, he was my first dog, a rescued Weimaraner-pit-bull mix with beautiful blue-gray fur and a distinguished white blaze down his chest. At home, he would try to climb into my lap. Out on the street, he lunged to attack anybody he considered a threat to me.

Looking at Rudy's picture, I remember how his warm body curled against me on the sofa, how he cut his eyes at me (as though he disapproved) when I made a dumb joke, how he licked my tears when I cried or put his ear against my belly when I was pregnant. I forget all the times he shat in the house or ate tampons out of the trash. I don't care that he destroyed a loveseat and shredded library books and chewed the shoe molding off the walls. Looking at his face, I don't think about how, given the chance, he'd run off down the road and not come back until his tongue was lolling out and he smelled like something fecal or dead.

I had this dream a few weeks after my mother died: We're in eastern North Carolina at the old homeplace, where she was just buried. My grandparents (long dead) are helping us decide what to do with the furniture and pictures and other objects in the house. William Faulkner comes in carrying a CD. There's tension between us—we've had a fling in the past but are now just friends. As my dad, whose memory is going, tries to identify the jazz songs on the CD, I say, "I gotta get out of here, Bill. Let's just take a walk."

Then I wake up.

Here's how I imagine things would have gone had the dream continued.

I ride off with Bill to a motel where we go on a three-day bender, during which we engage in enjoyable sex, a lot of high-flying love talk, and then, once the alcohol situation has become dire and confusing, a blow-out fight. After that, there's more sex, but it's the literary kind, not much fun and all dirtied up with madness and regret. Afterward, we part ways again.

But *before* that, before we even get in the car to go to the motel, we stroll around the yard of my family home, wandering among the oaks and the dogwoods, azaleas and myrtle. He says he's mighty sorry about my mother, and I let him take my hand, even though I'm still mad at him about our affair, the way he acted, the way it ended. We walk without talking to the far corner of the yard, almost to one of the red brick gateposts by the road. We stop and look across the furrowed field to where my people lie out there in our graveyard, and Bill says that thing he said: "Between grief and nothing, I will take grief."

In 2011, there are no limners around to paint my mother's face on ivory. I have no memorial of her that I can affix to myself and carry, other than the Rebecca Wilkinson miniature, which is too old and fragile to wear, and besides, the stick pin on the back is so thick it would leave permanent holes in any garment I pierced with it. Instead of one compact item like this, my parents have left behind thousands. As my brother and I sort, I make my own memento mori, using the only medium at all comfortable for me. "Use your words," we tell little children, and I feel like one of them, learning to use my words again, not yet convinced that it will do more good than hitting and kicking and crying in frustration.

When I try to conjure my mother this way, through writing, it's similar to how she occasionally comes to me in dreams. She's dead and alive at the same time, and real things from the past mix with imagined things that can never be. Together it all makes a scene that seems for a moment more real than anything that happens when I'm awake.

What is this writing but a feeble, belated, lapidary attempt to contain my wild, wild grief? It's like trying to stuff a wolf into a tiny golden cage. But writing is the only art I have for creating my own kind of miniature.

Compact, neat, a miniature can go with you everywhere. You can use it, like a key, to open the vault of memory whenever you wish. It's appealing to believe that you could be satisfied with a miniature as your only memento of your lost beloved. It would be nice if it could be the only badge of your sorrow that you had to carry.

So here's one for the road: It's spring, and I'm standing next to the weeping cherry tree that I love, out front of the house where I live now, a house Mama drove by hundreds of times without knowing it would be mine one day. I imagine she is coming to visit me. The ground around my feet is littered with pink blossoms, and when she drives up, she thinks of the Japanese woodblock prints she loves, in which cherry blossoms are always falling, reminding us how fleet is our time. She stops her van—the big blue Ford—no, the one before that, the ugly one she had when I was a kid, the one I was so ashamed of, the army-green van with the rounded engine cover that thrust between the two front seats like a table, where we put our Cokes and roadmaps and napkins and the plaid beanbag ashtray spilling butts.

I climb in. Her left arm is bent at the elbow, hanging out the rolled-down window. She's smoking a Salem Ultra Light 100—everything about her is superlative, ultra—but that's not why the window's open. It's open because there's no air-conditioning in this van, or else it's broken. She tells me to find some money in her purse so we can hit a drive-through for a sausage biscuit or a hamburger. I rifle through the crumpled Kleenexes, her glasses case, her tape measure, her red lipstick, her black vinyl daybook jammed with flyers advertising antiques shows, fast-food coupons, business cards, and torn envelopes with to-do lists scribbled on them. Finally, I find the wallet, the leather worn through in spots, the change spilling out, receipts and paper money stuffed in haphazardly, and the cracked photo sleeve, dirty with tobacco flecks and filled to breaking with me and my brother at every awkward age, and my father glowering at a thing in the distance. I hold the money and sit back, listening to Mama talk, ready to go with her anywhere.

Legs

My father had been dead about ten months when, in fall 2012, I called his prosthetics company and explained that I wanted to donate his legs to an organization that could reuse them. The lady on the phone was flummoxed. Maybe I could try a church, or the Veterans Administration? The VA receptionist put me on hold. The song: "Another One Bites the Dust." I was hoping the next one would be "She's Got Legs" when the receptionist came back on and gave me a number for the donations department. I hung up and called the new number, but they couldn't help either.

Had I not inherited from my mother a strain of doggedness that regards frustration as fuel and obstacles as things to be smashed, I might have chucked the legs in the trash. Instead, I searched online and found Physicians for Peace, a group that accepts donated prosthetics—which cannot be reused in the litigious United States—and sends them to medical missions in third-world countries. I emailed their gifts-in-kind manager, who invited me to call him.

And then, just as I was on the cusp of success, my fervor to be rid of the legs died. The email settled to the bottom of my inbox, and I put off calling. The holidays were coming—my first Thanksgiving and Christmas without both my parents—and it seemed too hard to let go of anything that had been part of them.

On the morning of Daddy's first amputation, in the fall of 2002, he insisted on driving to the hospital. He seldom got behind the wheel anymore. For several years his doctor had been paring away the mortifying flesh of his feet, and Daddy mostly used a wheelchair to get around. Besides this impairment, his eyesight was poor and his reflex time glacial. Riding as his passenger was a nerve-racking ordeal, but Mama and I knew it might be the last time he ever drove. I was in my late twenties by then, married, and feeling quite mature for not trying to argue with him. After all, he was sixty-four and had been diabetic for more than fifty years, and the awful thing that had been threatening for so long was finally coming to pass.

Along the way, he chuckled and said, "It's a good thing we don't live in England." It took me a minute to understand: he was attempting a joke about the cars being on the other side of the road and drivers powering the gas with the left foot—the one he was having amputated—instead of the right. I wasn't sure the joke made any sense. Weren't the pedals in the same position, just on the other side of the car? But I laughed anyway, cheered and heartbroken by his trying to have a sense of humor about the whole thing. This mood was a welcome change from the days leading up to the amputation, when he'd brooded about a distant cousin who had lost a limb, the subtext of his talk a self-pity that stretched my mother's patience. Nobody asked, out loud, why he couldn't just admit he was scared. For as long as I'd known my father, he'd rarely shown any vulnerability, and I saw him then as a man with a range of feeling as limited as the row of faces—smile to grimace—on those hospital-room signs patients are supposed to use to indicate the level of their discomfort.

A day or two after the surgery, he said all he needed for the pain was Tylenol. Was he that stoic, or did he just want us to think so? Most likely, he had studied his previous hospital bills and, ever parsimonious, couldn't bear the thought of what each dose of narcotic would cost him.

The circulation to the stump wasn't strong enough to heal it. The surgeon had to cut again, this time above the knee.

Five years later, his right foot and calf had to go. I had a son now, almost four years old, named for my grandfather who had died in a boating accident when my father was a boy. We went to visit Daddy, and they made a game together, laughing as they stretched and snapped the green rehabilitation bands tied to the bedrail.

The first time my brother's eldest son saw my father stand up on his prosthetic legs, he was amazed. At eight years old, he had only seen his grandfather in a bed or a wheelchair, and to behold him for the first time at his full height of six feet, three inches, was a revelation. Looking at the child's face, so lit up with shocked delight, I realized that he'd never been scared of my father's looming figure and unpredictable temper. I envied him.

The left prosthetic fitted onto his thigh; the right below his natural knee. First, you had to roll a rubbery, tight-fitting sleeve onto the stump. At the end of the sleeve was a threaded metal protrusion, about four inches long, called the pin, which resembled a big screw without a point. (It sounds like something my mother might have said: *Life*: a big screw without a point. Or a definition from Flaubert's *Dictionary of Received Ideas*, the sort of amusing trifle she used to put in my Christmas stocking.) Over this sleeve went a cotton sock with a hole in the end where the pin poked through. Last you attached the prosthetic, fitting the peachy-colored plastic cup over the dressed stump and pushing it until you heard the pin lock into place.

At the tip of each size-eleven plastic foot were grooves suggesting neat, rounded nails like those of my first baby doll, Boo-Boo, whose tiny toes were nearly chewed off by a dog one summer at the beach. Perhaps these new feet were an improvement over Daddy's own—high-arched, bony, with dry, mottled skin. His wildly crooked big toes sported thick yellow nails, and the smaller toes curled under—hammertoes, my mother said. Other than his ogre feet, he was good-looking: tall, slim, with high cheekbones, a square jaw, thick dark hair. In photos of him as a young man, he gives off a tense, smoldering air. You can see why he appealed to my mother. In those days, she said, people thought he resembled Clint Eastwood. A bit of swagger. Something dangerous about the eyes. Itching for a fight.

When the first stump healed enough to allow him to put on the prosthetic he'd been prescribed, Mama started driving him to physical therapy to learn how to use it. By then it was his habit to sleep well past noon, and there was the prolonged breakfast-and-shot routine, and then he had to be helped to dress. By the time she pushed him down their treacherous-when-wet, not-to-code ramp and assisted him into the not-wheelchair-accessible minivan, they were late for his appointment and cussing each other.

When they came home, she'd help him remove the leg and get back into his pajamas. Often when I visited, I'd find him in his recliner watching TV, Mama stretched out reading a *Newsweek*, her right leg thrown up over the back of the sofa. Every chair in the den was stacked with the newspapers Daddy hoarded, except the armchair that held his leg, knee bent so that the plastic cup took up the seat and the shoe's sole rested flat on the floor. A pair of slacks was scrunched down around the ankle, as though the wearer had been raptured, naked, while watching the evening news.

"Jesus," I'd say. "There's nowhere for me to sit. Does the leg have to have its own chair?"

"You can move it," Mama would say, waving her cigarette.

"It's like something out of Flannery O'Connor."

She'd laugh. "It'll be good material for you one day."

From Thomas Hardy, *Far from the Madding Crowd*: "Indeed he seemed to approach the grave as a hyperbolic curve approaches a straight line—less directly as he got nearer, till it was doubtful he would ever reach it at all."

When my parents were still living at home and before we'd thought about assisted living, there was one part-time helper—I'll call her Rose—that Daddy actually liked. He even let her help him practice walking on his prosthetics. She'd hold the straps of his gait belt and follow as he slowly made his way across the kitchen, encouraging him as he went.

One afternoon while they were walking, Mama and I came in from the hospital, where I'd just taken her for a PET scan. She was nauseated from the barium solution. (If you drank it fast, she said, you could fool yourself that it was a bad piña colada.) As I was getting her settled on the sofa, Rose yelled from the other room to call 911. I grabbed the cordless and ran into the kitchen. Daddy lay on the floor, eyes closed, Rose calling his name and trying CPR. I knew instantly the problem must be his faulty heart, with its long-ago by-passed blockages. When the ambulance arrived a few minutes later, he was motionless, his hands drawn and clawlike. Urine puddled beneath him as his breaths grew farther apart—sudden deep gasps that the EMS tech reported to his dispatcher as "agonal breathing," called so after the death struggle, known as "the agony," a term associated with the sufferings of Christ in the last hours before his crucifixion.

They got a pulse and prepared to put him on the stretcher. Mama, pacing, clutched my arm.

"Get his legs off! Don't let them go off with him."

She'd had enough experience of hospitals by then to know how easily those expensive prosthetics could be lost in the chaos.

I can't remember now whether the EMTs removed Daddy's legs or I did. All I know is that it was his last day at home. He never lived there again.

Whenever the doctor upset my mother with bad news about her condition, she said I would have to be the one to tell my father. At first I thought it was because she could not bear to hurt him. But then I wondered if it was because she knew he would think mostly about what the bad news meant for him—all the things she now could not do for him. Failing to understand my explanation of her diagnosis and the treatment options, he would ask questions he thought sounded smart but only revealed his lack of scientific knowledge and his growing short-term memory loss. Hearing the bad news, he'd feel sorry for himself, a sick man with a sick wife.

Once, when they'd been fighting, I fussed at him, begging him to have more patience, to give her the leeway for cranky behavior that she had so long given him.

"She's not used to being sick," I said.

Furious, he took his short stump in both hands and held it up as an exhibit—an action I found, even in the moment, at once terrifying, pitiful, ridiculous. (Pathos or bathos, I might debate, were the detail in a story someone else had written.) His exact words are lost to me now, but they were something like, "And what about me? Am I used to it?"

Time and again, there was bad news for my mother. You'll have to tell him, she'd say, every time. My heart would sink, then bob up. My writerly fascination with watching other human beings unfold, crumple, and unfold again kept me afloat. While my mother lay on the sofa in another room, I told my father the bad news, hating what I had to say, ashamed at how I relished the power of my telling and what it could do to him.

Even as Mom, tired and in pain, spent the summer of 2011 writing her own obituary and telling us what food to serve after her funeral, none of us believed she'd die. Judging by his shock when we told him she'd finally done it one August morning, Daddy had believed it least of anybody. They'd been married fifty years, since she was nineteen and he was twenty-two. The old folks' home (their words) where they ended up was half a mile from the garage apartment where they'd started out in 1961, where she'd wept those first nights, she said, because he snored so loud she feared she'd never sleep again. In assisted living, apart for most of the day and night, they got along better. After dinner every night, my father would bring her an orange and hold her hand for a few minutes before he went back to his room. After he'd go, my mother would tell me how crazy about him she'd always been—she didn't know why, she said. He could've been nicer. By then I'd taken to summing up their marriage as *Who's Afraid of Virginia Woolf?*, minus the alcohol. They drove each other crazy but were crazy about each other.

The day she died, we wheeled him down to her room to see her body before the undertaker came. My brother pushed him up to the side of the bed where she lay in her red plaid pajamas, so small now without her sly looks and tireless talk. Daddy leaned forward to kiss her but couldn't quite reach, so my brother tipped the chair to help him. When Daddy sat back, he took her hand, looked at her face, and said, "I wish I'd done more. I have so many regrets."

After her funeral at her family homeplace in eastern North

Carolina, where she was laid out in the parlor to be viewed by the mourners who streamed through the house drinking and eating and loudly telling stories in the late-summer heat, I stayed furious with him for weeks, my anger a convenient blind against my sadness. Why hadn't he been nicer to her, if he'd known all along that he ought to be? I was too angry to console my father, and he, in turn, had no comfort to spare anybody else. His own grief was too consuming, his habit of self-absorption too long-standing. It didn't surprise me—he'd always been so hamstrung by his own inexpressible emotions that he couldn't worry about anybody else's—but it hurt. I told myself that I ought to be kind because he was old, sick, and alone, and because *she* would have wanted me to be. Often, when I was a girl and they'd argued and the house had descended into a tense, silent gloom, she'd urge me to venture into the room where he was brooding and kiss him. I seldom wanted to, but she always insisted, and I always did it, even after I became aware that I was being used in those moments as a pontoon bridge, a way for one combatant to get to the other and extend a temporary truce before attacking again.

After she died, I visited him several times a week, and struggled to be kind. Once, he complained about a sympathy card from one of her friends; he was disappointed that she hadn't written more. Annoyed, I asked him how many condolence letters he'd ever written.

"Not many," he admitted.

Of course not. My mother would have been the one to write such notes, just as she'd been the one to buy gifts for Christmas, birthdays, graduations, for his side of the family as well as hers.

"They're not easy things to write," I told him. "It's hard to know what to say. Sometimes that's even more true when you're close to the person who died." And sometimes, I thought but didn't say, it's even harder when you found the deceased so loveable and the surviving spouse not so much.

Months later, after he'd died and I was going through his things, I discovered a newspaper clipping describing the boating accident that had resulted in the deaths of my grandfather and three other men on Easter weekend, 1950. Along with the clippings were a handful of letters assuring my grandmother that the Lord would sustain her in His own good time and in His own way. Amid these platitudes, someone had also written to my then-eleven-year-old father: "You're the man of the house now. Take care of your mother." What an ass, I thought. I pitied the bereft boy my father had been, the angry man he'd become. His life had been, like all lives, one long lesson in how little control we are given, and I wished I'd found a way after my mother's death to be more generous to him, more forgiving. I didn't yet understand what seems plain to me now—that my wish was the same one he'd expressed the day she died. Both of us wished we'd known better how to go easy on the people we loved.

He died not quite six months after she did, in January. True to form, he'd asked for an inexpensive burial, so my brother called a direct crematory service he found online. Within a couple of hours, a soberly dressed man and woman arrived, hands folded, faces professionally sympathetic. We waited outside the room while they zipped him up in their bag, then followed them down the halls of the nursing home and out the back door, where their minivan waited. They unfolded a carpet remnant, laid it over the rear bumper, and slid the body bag over the carpet into the van. They shook our hands and said again how sorry they were for our loss. We thanked them. It all seemed very appropriate until they drove away, windows down, and then, suddenly, the whole thing felt strange. I said to my brother, "Is it okay that we just let two complete strangers take our father's body away in a minivan?"

I thought of the time Mama took us to the dollar theater to see *Weekend at Bernie's*, in which two idiots have to take a dead guy around with them everywhere and try to make people believe he's alive. The plot doesn't matter because the movie's all about the gags—prop humor with a most unwieldy prop. They put sunglasses on Bernie and sit him up in chairs; they put Bernie between them and make it look like he's walking; they fix it so he appears to be waving or enjoying his lunch. My mother found this movie hilarious and referred to it often.

The morning after Daddy died, my brother and I sat in my living room, drinking coffee and eating the muffins a kind neighbor had dropped off. As we made our list—write the obituary, cancel his cable, plan a memorial service—we joked about what we could do with his prosthetics. We could film ourselves, I suggested, Candid Camera fashion, going around public places, each with a leg casually tucked under an arm, asking people if they'd seen our dad—an older man, gray hair, beige windbreaker? We could have them made into lamps, one for each of us, inspired by the movie *A Christmas Story*. Or, Daddy loved wine: maybe we could stand the leg up, put ice in the plastic cup part, and use it as a wine cooler.

The crematory was out an industrial road on the edge of town. Going there, we passed the discount bakery store where Daddy used to buy bread past its sell-by date for twenty-five cents a loaf. He'd buy six or eight loaves at a time, and half of it always went bad. "Just cut off the green parts," he'd say when we protested. (When I heard, as an adult, the theory that ergot poisoning from contaminated grain had caused the Salem witch trial hysteria, I thought, oh lord, between our dramatic tendencies and all that moldy bread we ate, it's a wonder we survived.)

At the crematory, my brother and I filled out forms in a sterile meeting room. The woman who assisted us was one of the owners, an African American woman in her twenties, touchingly proud of her business and eager to explain the limited options available to us. A basic cremation in a simple cardboard box was $895. If we wanted a small reception (ten mourners, max), we could pay a few hundred more for our father to be laid out in a fancier cardboard box, suitable for viewing. We checked off that we'd like that. There could be no metal on him, nothing that might explode; we checked off that he had no metal plates in his head, no pins in his remaining knee. Fillings were okay, but his pacemaker would be excised and discarded. We were to leave his dentures and prosthetic legs at home.

We were given a tour. We saw the small room equipped with sofa and chairs where we could welcome our few fellow mourners, the air-freshened bathroom and the coffeemaker and the small counter where we could put our snacks, and the dimly lit room where our loved one would be laid out in his upgraded box. We were led through a pair of curtained French doors into a large, bright, warehouse-like space with a concrete floor. In one corner was a metal box a bit taller than I—the freezer. In the other corner was something that resembled the trailer of a tractor-trailer truck. This was the oven, the crematory owner said, with none of the funeral-parlor euphemism I expected. Out here on the industrial road, the oven was the oven. Its door worked like a garage door, and the space inside was big enough that I could have walked around in it without stooping. She showed us the gauges and explained that the oven had to get to fifteen hundred degrees and stay at that temperature for three or four hours to fully incinerate a grown man's body.

Next to the oven was the metal table for cooling the hot cremains. It was about the size of a small desk, with a hole on one side. A wide-mouthed funnel led from the hole to a can underneath. On the table sat various lumps of brownish-looking material, some as big as my fist. A client, she said. When the pieces were cool, they'd be raked down through the funnel into the can, where a mechanism would pulverize them into the rough powder we call ashes.

The day after the viewing, when my brother and I came back for the cremation, Daddy appeared more sunken—even more dead somehow—than he had the night before. His body was doing what a corpse naturally does: his cheeks had grown hollower, his nose sharper, his eye sockets more concave. I was glad he hadn't been embalmed like my mother, who had looked waxen and uncharacteristically grumpy in her coffin. People have tried so many ways of preserving bodies, trying to give an impression of life in death, hinting at a possibility of return. Mummification. Pickling. Airtight glass coffins. Cryogenics. Embalming. But all these efforts at preservation do is make a creepy thing more creepy, a dead thing more dead.

He lay in a thin box lined with cheap white fabric and covered with a blue material like the scratchy stuff used on office cubicle panels. The night before, we'd stood around this box, listening to music he'd requested—classical guitar and Pavarotti singing "Nessun Dorma." We drank red wine and ate peanuts, because those were things he enjoyed, and we put pipe tobacco and a few nuts in with him because that was our family custom, to send off our dead surrounded by things they favored. Now, looking at the wine stains on his shirt (we'd poured out a little for him) and the nuts right where we'd left them, it struck me as a silly thing to have done. I saw afresh just how far beyond all our doings the dead are. I saw that this was how it was going to be from now on. Each day was carrying my parents farther away from me. For the rest of my life, any attempts to include them would be one-sided, and whatever I offered them, they wouldn't be able to take.

We said, *Good-bye, Daddy*, and they put the top on the box. We patted it gently and said *Good-bye* again. Then they wheeled the gurney to the lip of the oven and pressed the button that raised the door. Inside, I was relieved to see no flames, just that bare, brick-lined space. Still, my mind couldn't help shuffling a series of horrific associations—Holocaust ovens, suttee pyres, the burning stakes of martyrs. I reminded myself that there was no living victim here, that this was a traditional, reasonable way of disposing of our dead, the way our father had requested.

Just inside the door were several rows of metal rollers. Leaning into their effort, the crematory owners shoved the box off the gurney, across the rollers, and onto the oven's brick floor, almost running as they did it, pushing hard, and I remembered that even though my father was thin and legless and that cardboard box couldn't have weighed much, a corpse is still a heavy thing.

The door came down. My brother and I each put a finger on the big red button. We looked at each other, counted to three, and pushed. We knew we couldn't hurt him, nor he us; we were all free of that now. And it was surely the right thing to do, to be there with our father at the last, to send him on his way. But I'd be lying if I said that pushing that button didn't feel vaguely naughty, even slightly pleasurable, as pushing a button always does.

Daddy loved to recount this bit of dialogue from a TV show he'd seen:

Son: Mom, do you want to be buried or cremated?

Elderly mother: Surprise me!

I agree: Surprise me. As bad as burial seems—it's dark, it's airless, *you can't get out!*—I can't abide the idea of being burned. When it comes to thinking of myself without a body or of my body as a thing without me in it, I admit I suffer a complete breakdown of imagination. Perhaps the loss of your body is less frightening to contemplate if it has failed you so many times, as my father's had. Maybe then it's a comfort to think of being free of it forever.

We declined to buy an urn, preferring for both aesthetics and thrift to use a lidded pottery jar that Mama had bought for Daddy's pipe tobacco. When the crematory returned it to us, his three or four pounds worth of ashes contained in a thick plastic bag inside, I found it incredible that his body—the body that hugged me, the body that spanked me, the body whose ills caused so much trouble—was now reduced to something that fit inside a jar. The last time I'd seen a pottery jar used this way, it had been a smaller one, made by a close friend for the ashes of her five-month-old daughter. At the child's funeral, as the priest said his words, I watched my friend, milk tingling in her breasts, weep over the dug hole where in a minute she would have to put that jar, and I yearned for my own little son, healthy at home with his grandmother, and thought about what it would be like to have to put his body, so late of my body, into the ground.

At Easter, we drove Daddy's ashes out east to our family graveyard, which sits inside a chain-link half-acre square in the middle of a big field planted, depending on the year, with cotton, soybeans, or peanuts. Mom's grave still didn't have a stone.

"If he goes before me," she'd said before she died, "we'll keep the ashes, and you can put them in my coffin after I die. If I go first, bury his ashes on top of me. Make sure you put them at my feet."

We did what she asked. My brother's irrepressible younger son, then seven, squatted down to peer into the hole, eager to see what the ashes looked like. They looked like dirt, lying in a hole. We said the Lord's Prayer, and then the few who had gathered went away, and my brother and I leaned against the chain-link fence, passing a bottle of Daddy's red wine between us until it was empty.

The summer after my father died, the South African runner Oscar Pistorius competed in the Olympics. Born without fibulas, Pistorius raced on two carbonite prosthetics, springy black contraptions that looked nothing like legs, more like misshapen crowbars or commas rendered in a particularly angular font. The media gushed: he was handsome, he was gracious, he had overcome incredible odds. I had a little crush on him. Everybody did.

Watching Pistorius, I recalled how, after my father lost his legs, he'd talk enthusiastically about young athletes he'd seen on television, running on prosthetics, playing basketball, swimming. He talked as though if he were younger, he'd do the same. That he'd never been athletic—or even energetic—didn't matter. That he refused to practice the basic exercises physical therapists gave him to do, that he wouldn't quit eating ice cream or drinking alcohol, wouldn't follow the insulin regimen his doctor recommended—none of it mattered. What mattered was that all things were possible. He'd say, "When I can walk . . . ," and my mother and brother and I would think, *Yeah, right.*

We called his belief delusion; had we been kinder, we might have called it faith. He probably wouldn't have called it that, though. He was suspicious of faith, especially the religious sort. Yet, like many people, he tended to prefer stories in which those who suffer are redeemed. Don't we all like to be assured that the reward for being hurt or tormented or deprived is, ultimately, that we become noble and good and strong? That's why we love characters who keep standing up when they're beaten. We hope that is exactly what we will do when the time comes. Even if part of us gets broken, we want desperately to believe that what's essential will be left intact. Because we want to be better than we are—all of us—and we want others to be better. "The indomitable human spirit," the book and movie reviews say. But eventually we all are domitable, aren't we? Many of us much sooner than eventually.

In February 2013, I saw in the news that Pistorius had been arrested for murdering his girlfriend on Valentine's Day. South Africa is a crime-ridden place, went his defense, so when he heard what he thought was an intruder in the bathroom, he put on his prosthetics, got his gun, and shot four times through the bathroom door. Right away, it sounded like a bullshit story. I read that he'd been involved in domestic disputes before, that he might have been on drugs, that he was given to daredevilry and risky behavior. Over the next few days, numerous articles appeared—all on the theme of the golden boy tarnished. The inspiring story of an afflicted person triumphing over the odds had been ruined, and I was ashamed to find myself susceptible to disappointment when I knew full well that the real victim in this latest story was, as in every story like it, the woman lying dead on that bathroom floor, killed by a man whose body she had both desired and feared.

And what a timeless story it is. Reading Al Rose's 1978 book *Storyville, New Orleans: Being an Authentic, Illustrated Account of the Notorious Red-Light District*, I came across this: "One-Legged Duffy (née Mary Rich) did not fare so well. Her boyfriend not only stabbed her but bashed out her brains with her own wooden leg. The mid-nineteenth-century New Orleans underworld was not distinguished for gallantry." The grotesque violence of this tale made me think of Flannery O'Connor's work, especially her short story "Good Country People," in which a traveling Bible salesman steals a young woman's wooden leg while attempting to seduce her in a hayloft. The woman, Joy, is not a believer, and her existential despair is exacerbated by having to live with her mother, who says things like "a smile never hurt anyone," and who is a bit of a snob, disapproving of "trash" but fond and trusting of "good country people." Joy considers herself the only smart person in her world, the only one not deluded by Christianity or the stories people like her mother tell themselves about those with less. But look what happens when she realizes the Bible salesman has fooled her: "Her voice when she spoke had an almost pleading sound. 'Aren't you,' she murmured, 'aren't you just good country people?'"

A week before my father died, I was visiting him in the nursing home when he surprised me by saying that he'd been reading a book, David McCullough's *The Greater Journey: Americans in Paris*. His progress was painstakingly slow, made with a magnifying glass as he fought drowsiness, so he hadn't gotten too far, but he was excited to share what he was learning about expatriate artists and intellectuals in the nineteenth century. It was the first time in years that I'd seen him attempt to read a book, the first time since my mother's death that he'd shown enthusiasm for anything.

When I told him it was time for me to go, he said he hoped I'd come back soon.

"I always enjoy your visits so much. I think we have good times together, don't we? We've always been able to talk to each other."

I thought of all the upsetting things I'd never had the courage or the cruelty to say to him, and I thought of all our good talks about how much music and art and literature meant to us. I recalled my mother telling me once, "I think your father wanted to be a writer, but he never wrote anything."

I nodded. Yes, it had been true, sometimes: we could talk to each other.

He squeezed my hand. "It's what I always wanted, since the day you were born."

I have a few pictures from that last December, the first Christmas without my mother, the last time we took photos of my father. There are several with the grandchildren, and then there's this one, my favorite. Daddy's sitting in his wheelchair, wearing his old Black Watch plaid bathrobe, grinning as he holds up what the well-meaning nursing-home volunteers have given him for Christmas: a box of chocolates and a pair of socks.

It wasn't until after Christmas the following year that I finally called the gifts-in-kind manager at Physicians for Peace. From him I learned that there was a prosthetics company in my city that would accept my father's legs. A couple days later, I drove along a dreary road lined with office complexes, searching for the right address. By the time I found the low windowless brick building, few cars were left in the parking lot. It was late in the day and everybody was going home. My nine-year-old son looked up from his book to ask what we were doing. I explained, but he didn't follow.

"You're giving them his legs that were cut off?"

"No," I said. "His fake legs. You don't ever remember him wearing them?"

I showed him the prosthetics sticking out of the shopping bags. He frowned, shook his head, said he wanted to stay in the car. Inside, a young man and woman sat behind a sliding window looking out into the small lobby. The woman came around to see what I'd brought.

"Wow," she said, rummaging in the bags.

"This one has a joint," I said, with a kind of dumb pride.

The man said they might give the unused stump socks to local people, and what couldn't be used in the United States would likely go to Haiti. I walked out, feeling charitable, do-goodey, relieved of a burden. But a moment later, I felt a flash of the panic that was becoming all too familiar to me in those days. The legs were the closest thing to a body of his left on Earth, and I had given them away.

A couple months later, I met an artist who told me about a film she'd watched about Afghans living under Taliban rule. She described a scene in which prosthetic limbs are dropped by helicopters because conditions are too unsafe for aid workers to come in on the ground. English was not the artist's first language, and she was so passionate as she talked, so not-American in her willingness to use a frank vocabulary of emotion and aesthetic wonder, that it was hard for me to imagine how the film could be any more moving than her telling of it.

She described the prosthetics falling, each with its own parachute opening above it. As the limbs float down through the sky, a man on crutches moves toward them as fast as he can. A legless man crawls.

"The cripples," she said, and though I bristled at the word, I didn't interrupt. "It's amazing. How they struggle and fight with each other over these prostheses."

In another scene, she said, a man goes to a clinic to get prostheses for his wife, but what he is offered won't do. The artist described how the man puts one next to his own leg to show that it would be too big even for him.

"It's his tenderness," she marveled, "how tenderly he says, when he touches the thick, ugly prostheses, *But these are not the legs of my wife*."

The receipt came in the mail. I was listed as the donor. The approximate value of the donation: $780. I cried, just a little, over the gift description: UNOPENED LINERS, GENTLY USED KNEE, GENTLY USED FOOT ×2, OTHER MISCELLANEOUS GENTLY USED MATERIAL.

It was that "gently used" and the "×2" that got me. Why doesn't the loss of our loved ones break us completely? All I can think is that our selfishness, like brine, preserves us.

Horror Vacui

RELINQUISH:
Nothing

I'm five, maybe six. The Atlantic Ocean is right where I left it last summer. I'm happy to see that nothing has changed on the beach. Same wooden houses, same sunburned people. The ocean dazzles. For the last hour, driving here, this water called like a siren, singing a salty promise of thrilling rides on the waves. The first one knocks me to my knees. Water shoots up my nose, into my mouth. I sputter, struggle to my feet, dig in my heels, determined not to let the next wave overpower me. Pushing my wet hair back from my face, I suddenly realize: my plastic headband isn't there. I look down into the swirling froth, desperate to spy a flash of red. No luck.

The vast sea is indifferent. I reproach myself for losing my favorite headband, the only one I owned that didn't pinch my sizable head. My mother warned me not to wear something important to me into that unpredictable water. Now, because of my thoughtlessness, because I forgot what the ocean really is—in short, because I'm a fool—my headband is gone forever, separated from the only person who loved it.

In the summer of 2013, Moreland and I finally got serious about sorting out our parents' house. We hadn't cleaned it often or well during the two years Mom and Dad were in assisted living, nor during the nearly two years since Mom's death. Dust coated everything. Mice and spiders had left evidence of themselves in the corners, and mildew spotted the furniture because the failing HVAC system left the house humid and airless.

To clean seemed futile—the place was such a mess—and besides, who had the time? My brother showed no inclination to clean, and I certainly wasn't going to do it by myself. I began to be careful where I set down my drink and my purse, lest they get dirty. It disgusted me to eat there, so lunch breaks had to be taken elsewhere. Moreland, who had worked amid all kinds of filth at tag sales, thought I was being finicky and peculiar. He showed no sign of feeling the hot waves of unease that surged through me more and more often as the house began to empty.

When I took an object home to keep, I made sure to clean it thoroughly. That was reasonable enough; anybody might have done the same. But I didn't tell anybody the real reason these things had to be cleaned. My parents' house was a place of disease, doom, death, and I had an increasingly powerful sense that anything that came from it was tainted. If I didn't remove the taint, it would somehow make me and my family sick, disastrously so. And that catastrophe would be all my fault.

Soon my fear of contamination spread beyond the house. The whole world felt dangerous in ways it never had before. Later, amid the global Covid-19 pandemic, many people would come to consider such fear rational, but at the time, my response seemed paranoid. Nearly everywhere I turned, dirtiness threatened—in the air, on the kitchen counter, on the door handles of restaurants and the keypads at cash registers. On toilets and floors, obviously, but also on the dog, the car, my son's bookbag. *Germaphobia* was what I reluctantly called my new condition, when forced to call it anything, but my writer brain protested that the word wasn't precisely right. It was too particular, not all-encompassing enough. For while it certainly was true that I feared bacteria and viruses, insects and vermin, I also was wary of dust, mold, chemicals, smoke, fumes, vapors, and stale air. It was important to avoid places where I might be confronted with any of these, as well as places where people might not accommodate my anxiety. As you can imagine, my need for such special conditions considerably limited my ambit.

Because any environment, new or familiar, promised danger, I must always be vigilant. A rule of weird logic took shape in my mind. If a thing I wanted to eat fell on any surface other than my clean plate, I had to throw it away. If my hand brushed anything I considered threatening, I needed to wash it. Actual dirt that I could see was better than contamination I couldn't identify because at least I'd be able to see if I'd managed to wash it away. Garden soil on my hands was tolerable, but sitting in a coffee shop chair with vaguely stained upholstery was not.

My husband and I go for lunch at a restaurant where we've eaten several times before. When the meal arrives, it occurs to me that there *could* be rat poison on a shelf in the kitchen, and it *could* have fallen into my food. I tell myself that this is very unlikely, that the health inspectors surely advise restaurateurs not to put rat poison where it might inadvertently garnish a meal. I tell myself that restaurant owners don't want to kill their customers, since that's not so good for business.

But maybe, says my nervous mind, this restaurateur is a psychopath. Maybe he *wants* to kill people. It *could* happen.

Unlikely, I counter.

But not *impossible*, says my mind.

Come on, Laws of Probability, I beg, help me convince myself!

No dice. I cannot eat.

In tears, I confess my disturbing thoughts to my husband. He tries briefly to reassure me, then sees it can't be done. Without making me feel any more foolish than I already feel, he takes me home.

I drive to Chapel Hill to meet a friend for dinner. I've been looking forward to seeing him, as we always have great conversations. We meet at a hip, expensive restaurant where the meats and vegetables are locally sourced, and the other ingredients on the menu make you feel sophisticated if you know what they are, adventurous if you don't. When I ate there once before, the food was delicious.

This time, when the dishes appear, all I can think is that the beef smells *exactly* like my father's urine. Not wanting to betray to my friend that something is wrong, I continue to make pleasant conversation while privately analyzing my disturbing thought. Perhaps there's a logical scientific explanation. Naturally, I have an olfactory memory of my father's pee because I emptied his urinals so often. Perhaps the meat smells similar to me because it's protein, and Daddy, who was often dehydrated, probably spilled a lot of protein in his pee.

I pick at my dinner, smile at my friend, and mentally plead with Science to give me a plausible reason why my brain is making this disgusting association.

But Science offers no help. I can't eat.

We're invited to our neighbors' house for dinner. I stand beside the grill chatting with the husband as he cooks peppers and chicken. Sprinkles of pollen or leaf dust fall on the grill and the serving platter. He brushes it off, but my stomach falls. I remind myself of all the times I've eaten food from this very grill, or any food cooked outside. Food *grows* outside, it's part of nature, leaves and pollen fall on it all the time. I tell myself that my friends are going to eat this food, are going to feed it to their children, that I'm going to let my own child eat it.

And yet. Friendship, habit, Nature, maternal instinct—nothing helps. I can't eat.

Embarrassed, frustrated, I begin to cry. My puzzled friends try to comfort me and kindly do not call me what I fear I've become: crazy.

As illogical as I knew my "logic" was, the danger in these situations felt as real as a strong hand pushing my back, and my reactions were visceral—queasy stomach, racing heart, halted breath. My fears might have been unfounded, but there was no denying that my body was responding to them in uncomfortable and damaging ways.

Along with suffering these obsessions about food and germs, dirt and chemicals, I was doing a lot of compulsive checking. I'd put a paper in the trash and pull it out again, nervous that it might be important. This cycle would repeat several times—put it in the trash, worry, pull it out, unfold it, read it; put it in the trash again, worry, pull it out, etc.—before I could be satisfied. It got so I couldn't throw anything away in a public place, for fear that I might be so worried afterward that I'd have to decide whether to go through a trash can in a park or a movie theater bathroom, exposing myself to God knows what filth in order to check that my discarded item was safe to throw away. I learned to stuff my used napkins and Kleenexes in my pockets until I could get home to my own garbage can and enact my checking cycle in my own safe space.

Safety, of course, was relative. Even at home, there was plenty to worry about. I'd check and recheck the stove, the lights, the locks. Paying bills, I'd write a check, seal the envelope, then worry I'd written the numbers wrong or forgotten to sign the check. I'd have to open the envelope, make sure everything was okay, address a new envelope. With emails, I'd read and reread before sending them, anxious to be extra sure that I hadn't made any errors and that nothing in my words or tone could be misconstrued.

One afternoon, I went back into an office supply store where I'd just turned in a used printer cartridge to be recycled. I asked the clerk if I could check the box to be sure I hadn't left anything in it. She looked at me as though I was odd but located the box. Mercifully, there was an old receipt in the bottom of it, which I pretended was what I'd been looking for, and I scurried out, humiliated.

My need to check everything over and over was making it difficult to get rid of anything—a real problem when you're trying to empty a full house. Moreland and I would decide to get rid of stuff, but then it sat in piles for weeks before we actually got rid of it. He had even less time and inclination to deal with the problem than I did, so I was the one always pushing to get stuff out the door. Yet when the time came to let things go, I wanted to check the boxes again, worried we were letting go of something we shouldn't.

More than once, I traded in boxes of books at the used bookstore and afterward had a panic attack—a full-on, heart-racing, rapid-breathing, convinced-I-was-going-to-die panic attack. Had there been something important in the box, a book I didn't mean to get rid of, a book with a precious inscription from my mother? What if, interleaved between pages, there had been an old letter alluding to a family secret? Or a list of all our birthdates, bank accounts, and Social Security numbers? What if a nefarious person got hold of that paper and used those numbers to steal my identity?

This fear of having my identity stolen kept popping up in my more paranoid fantasies. One night, after we got home from a rare movie date, my husband realized that his cell phone had slipped out of his pocket in the theater. The phone had no security lock on it, so anybody might get into his email or whatever else he had on there. Naturally, I imagined a stranger stealing all our money through internet trickery, running credit cards up in our name, or coming straight to our house to murder us.

Once I spit an Altoid out my car window and a minute later reckoned that an evil genius *could* pick it up out of the middle of the road, harvest my DNA from my spit, and use it to clone me . . . thus stealing my identity.

Thinking about it now, I tell myself that I simply have a writer's overactive imagination. I can laugh at how far-fetched my scenarios were. Back then I knew they were outlandish, even funny, but all I could feel was shame and horror as the observer part of myself watched the nervous, active part. Why was I so afraid?

Italo Calvino, in a lecture called "Lightness," discusses the first-century, long poem *De Rerum Natura* (*On the Nature of Things*) by the Epicurean philosopher Lucretius: "[He] set out to write the poem of physical matter, but he warns us at the outset that this matter is made up of *invisible particles*. . . . Lucretius' chief concern is to prevent the weight of matter from crushing us."

In 1947 the weight of matter quite literally crushed Langley Collyer, who died after an avalanche of his own belongings trapped him in the notoriously overstuffed Harlem brownstone he shared with his blind brother, Homer. Any modern story of hoarding or extreme mess is obliged to mention these reclusive, pathologically retentive brothers. Indeed, whenever things got too piled up at home, Mom joked about the Collyers. Back then, I had no idea what she meant. We didn't yet have the opportunity to peer into people's homes via television reality shows, and I don't remember people using the word *hoarder* the way they do now. The more commonly used word was *packrat*, and everybody in my family certainly could have been described as one. We stuffed every available nook and cranny with the sentimental archive of our lives: papers, photos, baby clothes, family heirlooms. My mother kept a file, labeled "too good to throw away," which held an assortment of funny stories clipped from the newspaper, along with our childhood artwork and letters.

Each of us also kept collections. For my dad, it was pipes and record albums. My mother collected Chinese, Japanese, and Korean porcelain and eighteenth- and nineteenth-century baby caps. My brother squirreled away rocks, coins, stamps, tangles of rope and string, and odd bits of hardware. I filled my room with books and figurines of animals.

In *Stuff: Compulsive Hoarding and the Meaning of Things*, psychologists Randy O. Frost and Gail Steketee distinguish collecting from hoarding: "Most scholars who study collecting seem to agree that a collection must be a set of objects, meaning more than one, and that the items must be related in some way—they must have some kind of cohesive theme. They also must be actively acquired, meaning there must be some kind of passion or fire to seek out and obtain them. Someone who simply receives gifts that otherwise fit the definition is not a collector." In other words, a collection possesses a coherence that a hoard does not. Its boundaries are clear and discrete: a few items with special qualities belong within the collection; everything else is outside it. It is created according to specific criteria that purposely exclude the majority of things from entering the collection. Even a large collection has limits.

A hoard, however, can be boundless. This boundlessness is due in part to the owner's ability to envision possibility. According to *Stuff*, hoarders are often highly intelligent, creative, divergent thinkers who can dream up potential uses for any object. (Frost and Steketee give the example of a woman who kept caps of lost ballpoint pens because the caps might be useful as substitutes for missing game pieces.) They are often perfectionists, and because they fear making mistakes and have trouble making decisions, they find it hard to throw things out. Although they might realize that the volume of objects in their home is out of control, efforts to clean up result in an ineffectual shuffling, known in the hoarding literature as "churning." Objects move around the house, but they don't leave.

Part of the trouble for people with hoarding tendencies is their penchant for magical thinking. Not only do they develop emotional connections to objects, but some hoarders attribute the capacity of feeling to the objects themselves and believe that, if thrown away, the objects will feel bad. Even if their thinking doesn't go quite that far, they often believe that objects acquire unusual significance by virtue of their past association with loved ones. A perfectly common—and perhaps even faulty or useless—object seems important because it once belonged to a person beloved or famous. If your mother and your friend's mother both owned identical sweaters, for instance, the one that belonged to your mother would seem more special than the other and, thus, more valuable to you. That's normal, you might say—everybody's sentimental about certain things. True, but for a person with hoarding tendencies, even insignificant possessions are tied to emotions.

As I read *Stuff*, I realized that all of my immediate family members fit the hoarder profile; we all displayed "perfectionism, indecision, and powerful beliefs about and attachment to objects." The authors describe a typical hoarder they call Irene: "Possessions played a role in her identity, leading her to preserve her history in things. She felt responsible for the well-being of objects, and they gave her a sense of comfort and safety. In addition, things represented opportunity and a chance to experience all that life had to offer." Yes, to all that, for me, mother, father, and brother. Plus, dealing in stuff had been my parents' lifework, and their personal values were tied to the historical and aesthetic value of the old and sometimes very unusual things they'd collected.

Their house never came close to resembling the Collyers'—the floors in most of the rooms remained clear. But, the signs were there, and had Mom not tried so hard to combat the piles with regular purges, the stuff problem easily could have gotten out of hand. Daddy saved more newspapers, and Mom more books and magazines, than they could ever read. They'd kept items that once had been helpful or interesting—state roadmaps, brochures to scenic attractions, advertisements for stereo systems, obituaries. They were unlikely to consult those things again, but why discard them? Only an ignoramus throws away *knowledge*. They'd stockpiled more toiletries and office supplies than they could ever use. Those things had been on sale, a bargain, and it wasn't as though shampoo or manila folders expired. Only a spendthrift throws away something *useful*. They'd preserved memorabilia and heirlooms. Who dishonors their family by tossing out *memories*? They'd collected beautiful furniture, porcelain, art. You'd have to be a rube not to want to hold onto *antiques*, which are beautiful to look at and only increase in value over time.

As Moreland and I tried to move forward with emptying the house, I heard our parents haranguing from the grave. How does a person who professes to be intelligent, thrifty, honorable, and cultured throw away all these things that offer such *potential*? What kind of person does that? Did we raise you that way? Who are you?

I didn't know anymore. My childhood home had become a mire of confusion. Whenever I went there, my multiple selves battled for primacy. I had to be an executor, efficiently dealing with estate matters, but I was also a daughter in mourning. I was a younger child provoking her older brother, but also a wife and mother who wanted to be more available to her husband and son. I was a writer, observing, taking notes, but seldom finding time enough to write.

As we churned the contents of the house, I realized that my problem wasn't acquisitive hoarding (except for when it came to books). Instead, I had the opposite problem, called "reverse hoarding," where you can't get rid of anything because you're afraid of making a mistake. I'd always had an intense fear of screwing up. The idea that something might go wrong and it be my fault was intolerable. Maybe it was because my parents always overreacted whenever I spilled a drink or told a lie or lost my pocketbook, or Moreland didn't finish a school project on time and got a bad grade. Maybe I'm just unusually sensitive and cautious. I don't know.

What I did know was that every action I took to get rid of things only compounded my fear and guilt. Every time I talked with an auctioneer or antique dealer about selling my parents' things, they'd offer a perfunctory condolence, then launch into a tirade about how antiques had become devalued because people my age didn't want them anymore. Feebly I protested that I liked antiques, I just had limited space. They ignored me, griping on about my generation's lack of taste, and our disregard for craftsmanship and tradition, before coming to what was, for them, the crux of the matter: their own collections of antiques, which they'd seen as a smart investment, now were not worth as much as they'd expected. They were nearing retirement and dismayed that their nest egg had shriveled.

What could I say? It wasn't my job to go out evangelizing to convince my peers to covet antiques. All I wanted to do was clear out the fucking house. Could they help me or not?

Of course, I asked politely, not betraying my irritation. Because I'm a goddamn lady. They'd then tell me, grudgingly, that they could *try* to sell our stuff, they just wanted to make sure my brother and I understood that it wasn't going to bring us as much money as we probably hoped. They named the percentage they'd take from the sale and then added, in an especially callous parting shot, that it was a good thing my mother couldn't see what the antiques market had come to.

I wanted to tell them that in no way did I consider it a blessing that my mother was gone. And as far as the market went, she knew perfectly well that any investment made in the hope of financial gain always carries risk. She wouldn't have liked the market downturn, as it would have meant a reduced income for her, but she believed that the primary reason for collecting was because it gave you pleasure. The potential increase in objects' value over time was—or ought to be—gravy. In high times, you could sell your antiques if you needed cash. In low times, they proved a better investment than stocks because at the end of the day, she said, at least you had something to sit on.

My parent's house had not been my home for a long time. I'd left for boarding school at fourteen and had only come home for four more summers. My sophomore year of college, I rented a house with friends and never again lived with my parents. I'd always wanted to be independent, had always chafed under my parents' rule. Why was I now wishing they'd just come back and tell me what to do next?

⌇

From Dante's *Inferno*: "In the middle of the journey of our life, I came to / myself in a dark wood, for the straight way was lost."

⌇

I was forty when my dread of the unknown and the unknowable overpowered me so that I could not do the simplest things without anxiety. Checking, double-checking, avoiding, fasting, washing, worrying. These had become my occupations. Also, crying. I knew my hypervigilance was unhealthy, but I couldn't stop constantly sounding the alarm, asking bewildered friends and family: What is that spot? That white, brown, black, damp, dry, powdery, weird spot? Did you open this? Close that? Wash it? Wash it twice? Did you lock the door?

I was addicted to crisis, and like all addicts, I hit a bottom. July 2013: my husband, Glenn, was headed off to Japan for ten days. It wasn't an ideal time for him to go away. Along with cleaning out my parents' house, we were in the middle of buying a slightly larger house for ourselves, so that he could have a home office in which to do his freelance work and so that we could accommodate the things I'd inherited. We had a million things to do and I wasn't in good shape, but this trip was a rare treat for him, as well as an honor— most of his expenses were being paid by a fellowship he'd been awarded. I convinced him and myself that I was okay, dropped him off at the airport, cried, went home, and felt relieved that I'd managed to let him go. But then his flight was canceled, and he had to wait another day to leave. I drove back to the airport to pick him up, happy to have him home for a few more hours but wondering how I'd summon the courage to leave him there again the next day.

That evening, it rained. Water seeped, then poured, through

our bathroom ceiling. My panic overflowed. I couldn't handle everything. Or anything. I was terrified of being left alone. I begged Glenn not to go away. After a long night, we finally slept a bit, and the next morning, he made the necessary phone calls to delay his departure by a few days. Neither of us wanted him to cancel altogether, but I needed him to help me get on a stable footing before he left. I was deeply ashamed that my anxiety was circumscribing his life as well as mine. We've always encouraged each other to go off on solo adventures, and this mutual permission to roam independently is an important part of how we've defined our relationship.

While Glenn made his arrangements, a friend came over to sit with me. I sat on the sofa, depleted from weeping. All morning she handed me tissues and gently encouraged me to ring the therapist whose number I held in my hand.

Calling for help felt like a momentous decision. My parents had always seemed to regard psychiatry as a pseudoscience, and its practitioners as charlatans who enriched themselves by preying on desperate people. (Other suspect groups: chiropractors, sociologists, evangelists.) Paying someone to help you with your problems was a weak, dumb move, especially given that the person you'd wind up consulting probably wasn't going to tell you anything you didn't already know. Tolstoy and Dostoevsky, my mother said, contained all the psychology anybody needed to understand their fellow human beings. Emotional problems were best addressed at home through quarreling and sulking, insomnia or napping, eating junk food, drinking and smoking, and making jokes. For adults, happiness and anger were the only acceptable emotions to display; for children, happiness. Sadness or fear ought to be taken to one's room until it had subsided enough for you to come out with it all tucked in and hidden.

In my first session, I was quick to say that therapy was not what people in my family did. It was not what southern people did, not how girls—women—brought up to be strong southern ladies dealt with their problems. "My nice lady" (in a rare fit of euphemism, this is what I called my therapist when mentioning her to others) assured me that she knew what I meant. But she could tell me from professional experience that plenty of southern people did therapy, and lots of it. When I told her that I was accustomed to exploring existential questions through literature, my nice lady allowed that she'd been an English major. And when I said I wasn't sure I could make her understand what a force my mother had been, my nice lady revealed that she'd bought a few things from my parents' shop, and had been impressed by my mother's intelligence and wit.

I'd run out of caveats. Disarmed, I settled into a soft chair (it seemed too cliché to sit on the couch) and described the mental dissonance I was experiencing. Intellectually, I understood that grief for my parents had made me afraid of losing more people I loved, and that this fear was manifesting itself as obsessions and compulsions designed to avoid disease and danger. What I didn't understand was why, knowing all this, I still couldn't defuse my outsized reactions.

My nice lady explained how executive function, which lives in the front of our brains and guides our decision making, is separate from the impulses sent from the amygdala at the back of our brains. These impulses are what is popularly called the fight-or-flight response. I remembered some of this information from high-school biology, back when it seemed like just another thing to know for a test. Our amygdala is programmed from our infanthood to fear abandonment, because abandonment when we are helpless babies means certain death. My amygdala was acting according to its original programming. It was instinct to fear abandonment, said my nice lady, and my executive function was not having any luck in its efforts to change that.

How can I get better, then?

You can change the unhelpful things you're telling yourself, she said.

Tell myself new stories, then. That sounded doable, even simple. I knew a lot about stories. I was eager to start on this new project.

It was going to take time, my nice lady warned. Meanwhile, would I like to take medication, to quell the panic attacks?

I would not. I'd managed to scrounge a few low-dose Xanax in the first panicky days after the canceled flight, and I wasn't sure that I liked the feeling of disconnection they gave me. Plus, I was afraid of becoming addicted.

So, no, let's do this the long, hard way.

It made sense that I feared losing any more people I loved. But what about my problem with the house, the stuff? What about my conviction that if I made bad decisions about what to do with my parents' belongings, I'd get in trouble . . . *with my parents . . . who were dead!*

Over the years as they deteriorated, we'd grown to expect Death. We sat together in the valley, watching Death wend its way toward us. At times its shadow fell quite close, at times it was barely more than a dot on the horizon. I'd spent so long waiting that I'd become used to the more distant vantage point. Then, in what seemed an instant, Death arrived and claimed my parents, and it was hard to believe that I was free to move along now. Until I fully swallowed that irrevocable, indisputable, terrible, wonderful fact—that how I lived now was up to me, not my parents—I was bound to continue suffering in ways that made a good new life impossible.

To survive, I must leave the valley of the shadow of Death and pass through Dante's wood until I found my way again. My nice lady told me to write each of my parents a letter, telling them whatever I still needed to say to them, including good-bye. I cringed at this self-helpy, cheesy-sounding exercise. It was bound to yield pages of horrible writing, which gave me an aesthetic pain even to think about. But I did it. I put aside my writerly vanity and wrote two letters in which I told my folks how much I missed them. I thanked them for raising me and told them off for a few things. I said I needed to start making my own decisions and my own mistakes. I said, *I love you.* I said *good-bye.*

Despite my initial skepticism, writing those letters actually helped me begin to feel better. I stopped trying to hide my OCD behaviors. I felt a little ridiculous telling friends why I couldn't eat their cooking or sit on their porch furniture or walk past discarded mattresses on the sidewalk, but over time I found that admitting my vulnerability deepened most of my friendships. Apparently I'd chosen my friends well. Most of them didn't tease me, and many opened up about their own anxieties. In this humbling, stumbling way I came to know just how surrounded each of us is, all the time, by people who are also afraid.

⌁

Eula Biss's book *On Immunity* reminded me that our bodies live in symbiosis with the world; they are not separate entities embattled with outside forces. Her reaffirmation of this knowledge didn't solve my germaphobia right away, but it provided a useful way to talk back to the overcautious voice in my head that didn't want me to eat. As far as the checking went, I'd always done it, just not so intensively. When younger, I thought of myself as carefree and trusting. In college, to my housemates' dismay, I brought home to sleep on our couches a pair of unwashed hippies who were hitching around the country following magnetic lines deep in the earth. Back then, I wanted to believe people's stories long past the point when other folks called bullshit. Yet I also had a rigid side. I didn't like it when people sat in "my" chair at the table. Each night, I checked that the doors were locked against thieves and rapists and ax murderers.

Though the anxious tendency had always lurked within me, I'd never before been confronted with anything that scared me as much as losing my mother and father. I'd been incredibly fortunate to have loving parents who provided a safety net; when they were alive, I felt that nothing truly bad could happen to me. With their deaths came the realization that I'd depended on that illusion of security, and now I needed to learn to live without it.

I thought it might help to view my parents' house and its contents as one of Winnicott's transitional objects—as, collectively, the object that would help me separate from my mother and father. But that idea could only be helpful if I actually did separate, if I actually got rid of the transitional object. If I was going to overcome my anxiety, it was crucial that I not settle into keeping the hoard as my new safety net. If I did that, we'd never get the house emptied out, and it would continue to be a financial and psychological burden. Worst of all, I'd never be free of my obsessive-compulsive behaviors.

The introspection I was engaged in during this period of my life was necessary but deeply annoying. Not since I was a teenager had I spent so much time examining my own feelings. I felt selfish and narcissistic. But if I didn't figure out what this great fear was all about, and if I didn't figure out how to turn it way, way down until it was manageable, then I was either going to starve and/or drink myself into a bad state, have to be committed to a mental institution, or kill myself. I wasn't actively considering suicide, but I was beginning to remind myself with worrisome frequency that it was always an option.

Before she got sick, Mom and I used to go to yoga class together. At the end, we'd lie in Savasana, eyes closed. Using a dozy bedtime voice, the instructor told us to empty our minds, and I imagined that the question running through Mom's head at that moment mirrored my own thoughts: *How the fuck am I supposed to do that?* And then, *Why would I want to?* Emptying one's mind seemed not only an impossible task but a bad idea.

The instructor told us to notice our thoughts, then let them go. Silently, I laughed. My mother's mind, like my own, was never empty. She never let anything go. If your mind is empty, we figured, you must be stupid. Or dead. How horrible.

Poet and memoirist Nick Flynn writes:

In medieval times monks spent their days, their lives, transcribing the Bible into illuminated manuscripts. . . . at times there was not even any space between the words, the result being a solid block of text, often framed by illustrations—dragons, antelopes, angels. . . . Beautiful, yet the text—no white space, no hesitation, no delay—it was as if they'd forgotten poetry. This was deliberate, arising from what is known as *horror vacui*—the fear of empty space. The fear was—is—that the Devil will flow into any empty space, which is essentially the fear of thought, or of meditation, or of simply allowing the mind to wander.

The horror vacui. Fearing empty mind, we stuff ourselves with information. Fearing empty space, we surround ourselves with stuff. Flynn points to how gaps—"white space . . . hesitation . . . delay"— are the stuff of poetry itself. My parents understood the concept of negative space—even admired it. Didn't my father, lying in bed, admire the spare beauty of his three Chinese bronzes lined up atop the bookshelf? What about his beloved jazz—crescendo and diminuendo, yes, but also repetition, rest.

A pause, a gap, an empty space signifies that beauty is on its way, but you have to wait for it. You need a breath to get ready. Half the pleasure is in the waiting.

My mother knew that the better part of elegance is restraint, but restraint was not in her nature. She kept bringing things into the house, moving chairs or vases into any available space—what she referred to as "holes." Her defense: "Nature abhors a vacuum."

Advice about reducing clutter often suggests that taking pictures of what you want to discard will help you let go of the actual objects. I find this exercise unsatisfying. A photograph of an object denies the third dimension of space, so when I look at it, I see only a flat image and can get no sense of the *thingness* of the thing. Conversely, when I have no photograph of something I want to remember, I must conjure a mental image of it. In the memory palace, I can walk around the object, pick it up, touch the surface, open it, smell it—the memory becomes sensory. Certainly a photograph can trigger memory, but if it's a picture I took solely as an aide-mémoire, there's a whiff of postmortem about the whole thing. The pictured object is inert and, well, *objectified*. In other words, looking at an object in a picture I took for the purpose of not forgetting is very different from looking at a picture in which the object happens to appear, say, a picture of the family assembled before the fireplace at Christmas or a shot of us gathered around the table watching one of the children blow out candles on a birthday cake. In those pictures, the objects are never the focus; they are not bearing the strain of scrutiny. They are simply being themselves, taking up the amount of space they normally take up and no more.

I don't know if the strain of scrutiny was what broke the hold my parents' possessions had on me, or whether time was simply doing its work, but gradually it became clear that no one object or group of objects could answer all my questions or quell all my fears. Over the course of the two years when we were actively cleaning out the house, I came to feel that it hardly mattered what was in those boxes I took to the bookstore, the bags that went to Goodwill. My conception of myself as dutiful daughter diminished every time another carload of crap went away, and I asked myself again and again what, who, I was going to be now that my parents were gone. I wasn't sure yet, but I hoped the new me wasn't going to be so attached to stuff. I was heartily sick of it.

I'd been so afraid to throw out the keys to memory, and now I was finding that much of what was in my parents' house actually held no personal significance for me. The things I most associated with my parents—their smudgy eyeglasses, a star-shaped ashtray, Daddy's black-watch plaid bathrobe, a single clip-on earring from a pair Mom wore daily during my childhood—all these bits were valueless to anyone else, and mostly could not be useful or decorative even to me. I chose a few to save and let the rest go.

꒰ ꒱

Moreland and I found in Daddy's office a cigar box heavy with old keys of various sizes. We compared their teeth and grooves to the keys on our rings. We tried a few in desk drawers, file cabinet locks, doorknobs. No success. Ultimately, we agreed that regardless of these mysterious keys' potential, there was no point in keeping them. At this point they were nothing but metaphor.

Moreland carried the box to the kitchen, flipped up the cardboard top, and turned out the contents into the trash can. For a brief moment, all those unknowns jangled violently.

And then it was quiet.

NEXT

The Quilt

DONATE:

Nineteenth-century family quilt

Late on a clear spring morning, I drive to meet the curators at the Museum of Early Southern Decorative Arts. There I'll hand over a nearly 170-year-old quilt that's come down through the Ridleys—to Granny, then Mom, then me.

Every day, Mom sat on old chairs and pulled her underwear out of an antique chest of drawers, but she wouldn't have dreamed of using the Ridley quilt. Knowing how fragile old textiles are, how vulnerable to light, insects, vermin, and humidity, she shrouded the quilt in raw muslin, laid it in an archival, acid-free box, and shelved it in the guest-room closet. Periodically she refolded it to prevent fabric breakdown along the crease lines. It was always her plan to donate this family heirloom to a museum able to care for it better than she could, yet she never got around to actually doing it.

As I coast along the dull patch of interstate between Greensboro and Winston-Salem, I want to ask her why she held on to the Ridley quilt for so long. Well into the third year of her absence, I still want to ask her so many things. My current riding companion, the boxed mute quilt in the backseat, makes a poor substitute for my garrulous mother. How many times she and I made this drive together, bitching about road construction on the way over, then talking all the way back about the play we'd seen (Romeo wooing Juliet; Lady Macbeth crying, "Out, out damn spot") or the museum lecture she'd dragged me to. We'd last visited the museum several years before she died. She wanted to take my small son to see a dimly lit, deliciously creepy collection of antique toys. Together, we three sat close on a bench, mesmerized by Ray and Charles Eames's 1957 short film of toy trains, shot from the vantage of miniature people living in a toy world.

Now the toys are gone, replaced by the museum's newly expanded research center, bright and sterile as a doctor's office. When I arrive, several longtime employees greet me warmly, sharing their memories of my mother, whom they knew from historic preservation and antiques circles. They're excited to see what I've brought.

We unfold as much of the quilt as can lie flat on the table. At 99 by 118 ½ inches long, it's wider than today's queen-size sheet and longer than a king. The curators exclaim over its condition. Remarkably free of stains or damage, the calico colors remain vibrant, the white ground fresh. I realize this might be the first time I've seen the whole quilt spread out; I can't recall ever having glimpsed more than a corner. The pattern's complexity is dizzying, the skill of its makers stunning. I catch the curators' interest, and my sadness recedes.

Inside each of the forty-two fifteen-inch cotton squares is a pieced circle in the Kansas Sunflower pattern. A line of diamonds borders each square; these lines compose the orderly grid containing the sunflowers' kaleidoscopic geometries—small triangles and diamonds working together to make circles within circles, circles within squares. Green, pink, red, blue, and brown dominate; an oak-leaf pattern is quietly stitched into the squares' white ground. Near the middle, in one white circle, are words handwritten in ink: *Presented to Nathaniel Thomas Ridley By his Mother May 2, 1846.*

On that date Nathaniel was not yet two years old, and the next baby in the family, my grandmother's grandmother, Emma Wright, was almost two months. Their mother, Margaret Ann Bynum Jordan Ridley, had borne six children in nine years and would have two more. How did a woman with so many young children find the time to piece together more than 3,700 bits of chintz and calico and then quilt such an enormous bedcover? In a report written for an antiques appraisers' course, my mother speculated that Margaret Ridley might have held a quilting bee in order to "assemble all the blocks" she'd pieced together while pregnant with my great-great-grandmother. Mom liked imagining, as I do, what a sense of accomplishment her namesake must have felt as she and her friends completed this work. But envisioning these white women at their quilting bee is just an educated guess. What is certain is that Margaret had plenty of help from the African American women living at Bonnie Doon, the plantation where she lived with her husband, Thomas Ridley III, one of the largest slaveholders in Southampton County, Virginia. If enslaved women didn't work directly on the quilt, they surely performed the child minding and other domestic work that freed Margaret to sit and sew.

It's easy to picture camaraderie among Margaret and her neighbors, stitching as they exchanged confidences, gossip, laughter. It's also not hard to imagine their shared heartaches. In the antebellum South, the perils of childbirth took one mother out of two, and diseases now preventable by vaccine regularly killed infants and young children. The white women might have discussed these terrible yet common losses around the quilting frame; meanwhile, black women and children moved in and out of the room, thinking about their own losses and fears as they waited on the "ladies," tended the white children, asked Margaret Ridley what she wanted done about the supper.

I consider how the presence of black people in the room would have shaped the conversation among the whites. Would they have mentioned the horrific local event whose fifteenth anniversary was approaching as they pieced the quilt? Or did they avoid talking about it, even when enslaved people weren't listening? Had they already turned that unspeakable event into something of which they refused to speak?

⁓

At home in the hallway leading to the bedrooms, seven black-and-white photographs hung on the wall, arranged under glass and framed by a specially cut mat on which someone had written "Ridley Homes in Southampton County Virginia." Every day of my childhood I passed these old houses, seldom paying them any mind but liking to see my middle name displayed on the wall. What were these places to me? I'd never visited them; I didn't know or care who lived in them now; I could never feel as warmly about them as I did about my grandparents' Oaklana.

Beneath each white house was inscribed its name and that of a paterfamilias who participated in a major military action—American Revolution, War of 1812, Civil War. The usual history: men and wars. A small eighteenth-century house with a shed porch and three dormers was the least impressive structure pictured, yet its image boasted the longest caption: "Belmont. Here it was that Nat Turner's Insurrection was stopped by Major Ridley and his faithful slaves."

As a child I had no idea who Nat Turner was, even though plantations were the setting of much of my mother's family lore. Anecdotes about the intelligent, stubborn, humorous, and sometimes dreadfully ill-tempered people from whom I was descended—these were plentiful. But stories about the men and women they'd enslaved were few.

One rare tale concerned a black man who'd escaped from a neighboring plantation with a master known for his cruelty. In those days, my grandfather said, if a white man thought he could capture a runaway, he could offer to buy him from the owner while the runaway was still at large—at a cheaper price than usual but at his own financial risk.

"The runaway was hiding in the woods around Oaklana, and he

sent word by way of other slaves that if my great-grandfather Tyler would buy him, he would come out. So Mr. Tyler paid for him, and the man came right out of the woods."

What a relief for that poor man, my child self thought, *to be preserved from the mean master. What a nice guy our ancestor must have been.* I had no clue that this story—whatever its truth—was like so many handed down in old, white southern families, a story repeated to assure ourselves that *our* people had been benevolent: a narrative balm for guilt.

Even this self-congratulatory tale was a rare mention of "the peculiar institution." Slaves in the family history I heard then were nameless property, part of the landscape, just as they were in the history I was being taught in school. In 1980s North Carolina, social studies textbooks and teachers focused on white, powerful men, their governments and wars, their elaborate laws and treaties. It was a history of domination, told from the perspective of the masters, who claimed that American slavery had not been as bad as it was painted by Yankees, black radicals, and other unnamed enemies of the (white) South. Slaves were too economically valuable to be mistreated, and they'd had every need supplied: food, shelter, clothing. Therefore, the claim went, living a slave's life had not actually been *that bad*. And those rare owners and overseers who whipped, raped, and killed black people, or broke up families by selling parents and children separately? Well, they had not been *nice people*.

In school we were given to understand that "black history" was separate and not equal to, or even much a part of, (white) history. The little we did learn about African Americans was limited to a few broad strokes, constrained by the tensions of our times: Frederick Douglass ran an abolitionist newspaper, the Civil War freed the slaves, mighty steel-driving John Henry hammered on the railroad until he fell over dead. Dr. King had a dream. All of that seemed long ago and far away.

Closer to home, four students from the historically black NC A&T State University had protested segregation in 1960 by sitting in at the lunch counter at the Woolworth downtown, a few miles from the Woman's College (now UNC Greensboro), where my mother was then a student. In November 1979, the month before I turned seven and received for Christmas a Nancy Drew diary, members of the Ku Klux Klan and the American Nazi Party shot and killed five protesters at a Death to the Klan rally. Did anybody talk to me about what I must have seen on the front page of the newspaper? It's unlikely. Racial animosity was too recent, too ongoing, too perpetual—a subject to avoid.

But there was the library. In a biography of Harriet Tubman for children, I found a new heroine to admire. I marveled at her trips guiding others to freedom on the Underground Railroad, and despised the overseer who threw a metal weight that hit her head, causing her throughout her life to experience headaches, seizures, and visions. How could such extremes of courage and cruelty exist in human beings? Truly our variety was astonishing. I tried to fathom how you could be brave enough to act according to your moral principles even if it meant you might be killed. Conversely, I wrestled with the idea that you might use what you called your principles to justify the oppression, torture, or killing of other people.

Although I could not yet see that my ancestors and their cohort—*nice people, people like us*—had always had a choice about participating in the slavocracy, I was beginning to question the contradictions and silences in my schoolbooks and in my family stories. My parents taught my brother and me never to use racist language or act superior just because we were white. At the same time, however, they warned us not to risk offending other white people by being *too* outspoken about our views and opinions. They encouraged us away from prejudice, and yet those plantation pictures continued hanging in the hallway. Over the years, as I walked past them, I began asking myself, "Faithful slaves?"

In 2001, a few years after our first round of graduate school, my husband and I moved into Oaklana. Daddy-Jack had recently died, right around the time I'd quit my full-time job and become a free-lancer. Living rent-free at Oaklana, where we only had to pay the utilities, meant that Glenn and I could make ends meet with contract work. We'd copyedit for university presses and write book and art reviews for various papers. I'd have time to work on a novel.

I was the sixth generation of my family to live at Oaklana, and though the most valuable of my grandparents' furnishings had been sold or divided among my mother and her siblings, plenty of stuff remained. When Glenn and I first mingled our belongings with family pieces, the rooms felt like an awkward party where people from different parts of my life were coming together for the first time. Some groupings just didn't mesh. The framed print of Robert E. Lee in the den had to go, as did a handful of other Confederacy-related items. I wasn't trying to deny my history, but these things didn't represent my values or who I believed I was, and they certainly weren't what I wanted to display to any friends who might make the long journey to visit us out in the country.

I'd never lived anywhere so remote. Our nearest neighbors could not be seen or heard. On clear nights the stars were brighter than I'd ever seen them. Glenn was often away, pursuing another graduate degree in Greensboro, and whole days would go by without my speaking to another human being. Rarely did I feel lonely. I relished the solitude that gave me so much time to write, to think, to read.

In my copyediting work, I happened to be assigned manuscript after manuscript about slavery, abolition, Jim Crow, civil rights, and African American literature and culture. The more I learned, the more I realized the extent of my ignorance. Wanting to fill in the gaps in my knowledge, I set out to reeducate myself, learning about nineteenth-century black rebels Denmark Vesey and Toussaint L'Ouverture, and about southern-born white abolitionists, the Grimké sisters. Richard Wright, Toni Morrison, and James Baldwin were writers I'd encountered in college; now I followed up with W. E. B. Du Bois, Nella Larsen, Charles Johnson, and others. When Henry Louis Gates Jr. published Hannah Crafts's novel *The Bondwoman's Narrative*, I ordered a copy, fascinated by the story of the manuscript's discovery as well as by its connections to eastern North Carolina. Also connected to my home state, and to a city where my ancestors once lived, was Charles Chesnutt's *The Marrow of Tradition*, a novel about the 1898 massacre of black people by white supremacists in Wilmington.

Histories and novels by black writers shifted and deepened my understanding of the world in which I lived and the role of my people in it. Now, when I drove along the empty roads through the flat empty land, what I'd seen all my life looked different to me. Equipped with my new knowledge, I saw how slavery and its legacy had marked the place—the tobacco barns falling in on themselves, the neglected graveyards in the middle of peanut fields, the contrast of many poor, ramshackle dwellings with a few grand ones like Oaklana. The indigenous past was there, too, if you knew where to look, down in Indian Woods and lingering in the names of towns, creeks, and pocosins, and of the rivers winding through the counties—Chowan, Meherrin, Roanoke.

Sometimes it seemed as though I no longer lived in the modern world. Cell-phone service dropped on the backroads, and our dial-up internet operated on what some white people in the area cheerfully referred to as "colored people time," their casual racism as abundant as the tomatoes and yellow squash of their summer gardens. When people said such things, I froze in embarrassed silence, ashamed that the old politeness lessons about avoiding conflict were still trumping my urge to say what was right.

My discomfort with my own silence grew as I researched the nineteenth-century South for a novel I was attempting to write. One of the novel's main characters was inspired by Ida B. Wells-Barnett, the journalist and anti-lynching crusader who in 1895 published *The Red Record: Tabulated Statistics and Alleged Causes of Lynching in the United States*. Like Harriet Tubman, Wells-Barnett pursued what she knew to be morally correct, despite death threats. Her pen was her true sword, but while working as a newspaper editor in Memphis, she bought a pistol after friends of hers were lynched. "I expected some cowardly retaliation from the lynchers," she later wrote in her autobiography. "I felt that one had better die fighting against injustice than to die like a dog or a rat in a trap."

I kept reading, wanting to know what had endowed such women with the kind of courage my forebears—and I myself—lacked.

Looking back on the intellectual searching I've done throughout my life, I can't resist a quilt metaphor. What is a quilt, after all, but a patchwork document, written in scraps and stitches, and stuffed with matter that, although we cannot see it, gives the thing its weight? Through-lines of sewing hold it all together, connecting the pieces but also creating divisions as the lines crowd the batting to either side of the stitches.

Flipping the metaphor to study its obverse, we can ask, What is a piece of writing but a quilt? For her class report, my mother studied Margaret Ridley's handiwork, meticulously counting fabrics and shapes, before turning to her library to research quilting as far back as the "time of King Solomon," when "the funeral tent of an Egyptian queen was made from multicolored, dyed, gazelle hydes patchworked together." Reading my mother's typescript, with her scrawled annotations and painstaking diagram of the quilt's pattern, I miss her afresh. I love her afresh, too, for showing me what thoughtful work looks like, for teaching me how to piece together information and ideas, knowing as she did so that she was initiating me into the pricking, confusing pleasures and dangers that arise when you confront the borders of what you can learn.

At Oaklana one day, perusing the library's tomes about the South, I discovered William Drewry's *The Southampton Insurrection* (1900) and a first edition of William Styron's *The Confessions of Nat Turner*, inscribed by my mother to her mother in 1967. My relatives had been reading about Nat Turner, even if they weren't talking to me about him. When I asked an older cousin if she remembered her elders ever mentioning him, she recalled only that, by the 1940s and 1950s, Turner had become a sort of bogeyman, a threat to naughty children: "You'd better behave, or ole Nat'll get you."

Nat Turner was born on October 2, 1800. By the time he was five years old, it was said that he "surely would be a prophet." Endowed with the gift of sight, he told of things that had happened before he was born, saw things in books that had already been revealed to him. He learned to read before being sent into the fields at age nine. Adults, free and bound, remarked that Nat had "too much sense" to "be of any service to any one as a slave." As he grew older, he experimented with making things, including paper and gunpowder, and became known throughout his community as a sober young man who preached the Gospel.

From an early age, Nat Turner felt destined for a "great purpose." In his twenties, he began to hear the voice of "the Spirit that spoke to the prophets in former days." Visions sometimes accompanied the voice; in one, "white spirits and black spirits engaged in battle, and the sun was darkened—the thunder rolled in the Heavens and blood flowed in streams." The Spirit told him to prepare for a "great work." He was to wait for the "signs in the heavens," he reported later, then "arise and prepare myself and slay my enemies with their own weapons."

The signs appeared in 1831: a solar eclipse in February and, in August, a phenomenon witnessed all along the Eastern Seaboard—the sun turned green, then silver, then blue. After sunset, the sky glowed red, as though a mighty fire burned below.

Our human nature is alert to pattern; we seek it, construct it, take it for our guide. From my mother's report: "Although at first glance there appears to be no pattern to the way in which the different fabric scraps are placed in each sunflower, closer examination reveals that the mind of the quilter imposed a very subtle and unusual order to the placement of each patterned fabric. The sunflowers all have the same soft pink and gold striped centers, except for the one inscribed circle which is white. The main pattern comes from the varied combinations of the twenty-three printed fabrics in the quilt. The sashes and borders utilize a dark green with red and gold floral stripe fabric. The binding is a blue, brown, and white vermicular and striped fabric."

On Sunday, August 21, Nat Turner convened with six men in the woods not far from the farm where he lived. Among them was Hark, short for Hercules, described by a contemporary source as "one of the most perfectly framed men he ever saw—a regular black Apollo." The men roasted a pig and partook of brandy while their abstemious leader outlined his plan. They should "commence at home," then continue on to chosen houses in the vicinity, killing white families and picking up black recruits as they made their way toward Jerusalem, the county seat of Southampton. As they gained numbers and strength, their movement for freedom would spread throughout the countryside, ultimately resulting in the abolition of slavery.

Around 1 a.m., Nat Turner set a ladder against the side of Joseph Travis's house and let himself in through an attic window. Within a few minutes, he and his men dispatched Travis, his wife, ten-year-old Putnam Moore (Nat's owner), and a teenage boy. As the group proceeded toward the next house, somebody remembered "a little infant sleeping in a cradle," and after a moment of deliberation, two men returned to the Travis house to kill it. They left its decapitated body in the fireplace.

Over a twelve-hour period, Nat Turner's growing band shot, bludgeoned, or hacked to death twenty-four children, nineteen women, and twelve men at fourteen houses. A few survivors managed to hide or run away, but no white person caught was permitted to live. By midday on Monday, August 21, the band was making its way toward Jerusalem, which they hoped to capture. Their number had grown to thirty or more by the time they encountered the first white men prepared to fight back—a posse of eighteen. The factions skirmished, and when a second group of white men arrived to help the first, Nat Turner's men retreated.

Word spread fast throughout the county. By evening hundreds of white people had taken refuge in Jerusalem and the surrounding plantation houses, where armed men stood ready. These fortified houses included Major Thomas Ridley's Rock Spring and the nearby Bonnie Doon, later the home of Major Ridley's son, Thomas III, and his wife, Margaret. Both houses lay west of Jerusalem and not far from "Buckhorn Quarter, home . . . to a portion of Major Thomas Ridley's 145 slaves."

On Monday evening, Turner and his men camped at Buckhorn. The overseer had fled, and four of the quarter's residents had joined the rebels: Curtis, Stephen, Matt, and another male whose name is not recorded. The next morning, Turner's band attacked a nearby plantation called Belmont. Its owner, Dr. Samuel Blunt, "fifty-five and suffering from gout," defended the house along with his teenaged son, his overseer, and two neighbors. "They armed (with weapons unspecified) trusted slaves . . . and positioned them in front of the house." Thus were enslaved people forced to stand between the guns of their oppressors and the guns of their fellow bondsmen.

In the ensuing melee, one of the enslaved defenders, Frank Blunt, captured rebel Moses Barrow, who had dismounted to chase a servant girl trying to carry a white child to safety. Turner's right-hand man, Hark, was shot and fell from his horse. As the rebels retreated southwest, their leader sent Curtis and Stephen in a different direction to gather recruits. They were soon arrested. The remainder of the band encountered a contingent of white cavalry, and by Tuesday night the rebels had separated. Nat Turner hid in the woods and fields not far from where he'd grown up. It was nine weeks and four days before he was caught by a hunter out looking for game.

Take a hasty glance at the photograph of Bonnie Doon that used to hang in my parents' hall, and it could be a picture of Oaklana—five windows across the second story, wood siding, brick chimneys on either end. Intimate as I became with Oaklana in the years I lived there, it's not hard for me to picture what Bonnie Doon might have been like inside.

For several years after I moved into my grandparents' house, I nursed the idea that I'd never live anywhere else. The plumbing plagued us, the drafts in winter were vicious, but I loved the high ceilings and soft pine floors, the odds and ends I came across in closets. I cherished the rural quiet, the dark nights, the solitude. And yet, as I researched and wrote about southern history, learning more hard truths about the sources of my advantages and privileges, the less possible it became to enjoy Oaklana blindly. No longer could I focus solely on the personal, familial associations the place and its furnishings evoked for me. The full story was so much bigger than what I'd been told, and I wasn't sure what the past ought to mean for my future.

Soon after Nat Turner was jailed, a young lawyer published a thirty-one-page pamphlet, *The Confessions of Nat Turner, as told to Thomas A. Gray*. In the document, Gray paints his subject as a religious fanatic and a sociopath, thus trying to reassure the white southerners who would buy his pamphlet that the "insurrection" was an anomaly rather than part of a wider conspiracy.

For decades, critics have doubted this document's trustworthiness, rightly pointing to Gray's bias as a white man of the slaveholding class. Many have questioned the elevated language used by the confession's Nat Turner, while others assert that the historical Nat Turner may very well have spoken in eloquent phrases, given that he was a preacher, captured with a well-read Bible on his person.

Problematic as this document is, however, it's still regarded as important source material. Scholar and activist Vincent Harding says in Charles Burnett's 2003 film, *Nat Turner: A Troublesome Property*, "It is very clear by now that we cannot take Nat Turner's confessions at face value, but it is also very clear that we cannot cast it aside." Gray's *Confessions* is all we have that *might* give us something approximating Nat Turner's voice. Tellings of his story have largely drawn from the "confession" and a few other sources: early (often unreliable) newspaper accounts, trial records, the testimony of a few survivors, and oral history. From the very first day, "factual" accounts of the uprising have been riddled with inaccuracy and conjecture, rumor and exaggeration. And aside from the problem that white people wrote the only extant records, there's been the disagreement over what term to apply to the event.

Gray records Nat Turner as saying that he intended to conquer his oppressors "as the white people did in the *revolution*," and his admirers have sometimes referred to him as a general, leading a war for liberation (my italics). The seventh photograph in my parents' hallway was of an historical marker, erected in 1930 on Highway 58 in Virginia: "Buckhorn Quarters: One mile north was the estate of Major Thomas Ridley. In the servile *insurrection* of August, 1831, the houses were fortified by faithful slaves and made a place of refuge for fugitive whites. In this vicinity Nat Turner, the leader of the insurrection, spent the night after his defeat near Courtland, August 23, 1831" (my italics).

Although the dictionary labels *revolution* and *insurrection* as synonyms, the first suggests a substitution of one authority for another, whereas the second suggests a throwing-off of authority with no clear idea of what will come next. As citizens of a nation produced by revolution, we Americans like the self-determination implicit in that word. Rejecting the yoke of tyranny for a self-created free existence strikes us as morally legitimate: revolutionaries are justified in their actions because they fight back against an oppressive regime.

An insurrection, on the other hand, implies an unruly party pushing back against a legitimate government or authority; it suggests an act of faithlessness that deserves to be quelled. Slaveholding whites and their descendants called Nat Turner's uprising an insurrection because they could not bear to imagine what system would replace the status quo. They couldn't conceive of a new order in which black people were equal to white and were not forced to labor for their masters' enrichment. Nat had no trouble envisioning a new order, however. Gray records him as quoting the Bible on this point: "the last shall be first, and the first shall be last."

According to Gray, Nat Turner rejected the use of the term *insurrection* to describe his bid for freedom, no doubt because that word implies it wasn't legitimate for slaves to want to change their condition. *Uprising* seems fitting; so does *rebellion*, which includes defiance and resistance in its definition. The term is often applied to the action led by L'Ouverture in Haiti, the only slave rebellion that led to the creation of a modern independent state. Still, it's true that *insurrection*, in its second dictionary definition, aptly describes what Nat and his band committed: "an act or instance of rising up physically." Theirs was a physical assault, a sudden reversal of white brutalization of black people.

In a different context, Rebecca Solnit writes, "Revolutions are always politics made bodily, politics when actions become the usual form of speech." Denied a voice and power in the body politic, Nat Turner used the weapons at his disposal—his own physical body and the bodies of his compatriots, strengthened for action by the hard labor their oppressors had forced them to perform. Thus had the white stones sharpened the black blades that turned, inevitably, to strike them down.

Driving back to Greensboro after donating the quilt, I can't stop thinking about the Ridleys and Nat Turner. It's April 23, traditionally said to be Shakespeare's birthday as well as the anniversary of his death. It occurs to me that Nat Turner's rebellion is the stuff of Shakespearean tragedy: a complex central character who grapples with existential questions and the dangers of power amid warring factions; moral knots that tighten rather than unravel; copious bloodshed.

While the modern writer has yet to appear who can do full justice to the story in fiction, a number of thoughtful, well-researched histories have chronicled the events in detail. Reading them, I always search for mention of the Ridleys. What am I looking for?

First, perhaps, I'm looking for the moment when the Ridleys (and thus I) might have been wiped out as a result of their devil's bargain, the sin of slaveholding that made them rich. I find Major Ridley (quilt-making Margaret's father-in-law) on September 3, 1831, testifying in court that he witnessed Hark's arrest. Presumably this occurred soon after Hark was shot from his horse at Belmont, so Ridley may well have taken part in the skirmish there, as claimed by whoever captioned the photo in my parents' hall.

I wonder whether Major Ridley's two grown sons were armed and with him. Or did they stay home with the women and children? If there's a family document detailing the Ridleys' participation in the events of August 1831—a letter or diary—I've never heard about it or seen it referenced in the source material I've consulted. Perhaps such a document exists in another branch of the family and is a cherished relic. Or maybe it lies in an attic or under a bed, forgotten or suppressed. Or perhaps all mentions of the rebellion were burned out of the family long ago.

Second, I'm curious about the four men who left Buckhorn Quarter to join Nat Turner. The public record shows that one is thought to have been killed during the fighting and one was acquitted at trial. Curtis and Stephen were charged "with having feloniousley . . . consulted, advised and Conspired with each other and with Divers other Slaves to rebel and make insurrection and for making insurrection and taking the lives of divers free white persons of this Commonwealth." The testimony concerning their activities is brief: "Scipio a Slave Sworn on behalf of the prisoner" said "that he was at home when the insurgents came up—they took Curtis with them and he did not appear to go willingly. . . . Curtis the prisoner could not have escaped because the insurgents Surrounded him." When apprehended by the white men who brought them in, Curtis and Stephen apparently didn't fight or try to escape. Asked how they thought they could travel without interference to a distant slave quarter, they replied that Nat Turner had promised that the "white people were too much alarmed to interrupt them."

At this distance, I can only guess at Curtis's and Stephen's motivations. Doubtless they wanted to be free, and they might have joined Nat Turner whole-heartedly. It's also possible they were reluctant, as Scipio's testimony claims. Nat's actions were so audacious, and his followers so few, and the tide against them so strong, that success must have seemed impossible to most onlookers, even sympathetic ones. Maybe Curtis and Stephen went along because they feared to say no to men willing to kill infants in order to achieve their end. The record doesn't tell us. What it does say is that Curtis and Stephen were sentenced to hang and were valued at $400 and $450, respectively. These were the amounts for which Major Ridley could petition the government as recompense for the loss of his "troublesome property."

Reading about all these men with blood on their hands, I wonder about the women, white and black. Where are they? What did they think of the men's doings? Did they try to stop them? Did they support them? Aid and abet?

I must go by hints, brief mentions. The women can be glimpsed performing tasks, helping each other, hurting each other. There they are, the white mistresses, abusing the enslaved; there they lie, murdered with their children. There they are, the black women, trying to hide their own children, shield the white children in their care, secret their white mistress away from harm. There they are, trying to detain the white mistress so she can be killed. There they are, frightened in the big house, praying the bullets fly in the direction that will preserve them. There they are, frightened in the cabins, praying that the men know what they're doing.

There is Lucy Barrow, hung for "mak[ing] insurrection."

Occasionally, there is mention of Nat Turner's wife, an elusive figure. Was her name Cherry or Charity? Was her son with Nat called Riddick? Written records of black people's lives in those days are frustratingly sparse. Is it true that she was flogged in order to make her give up Nat's papers? What were those papers? Musings? A map? Plans for rebellion, for freedom?

A few years later, here comes Margaret Ann Bynum Jordan, "the belle and beauty of her age," marrying Thomas Ridley III, bearing all those children, making that quilt.

In 2012 the multimedia artist Sanford Biggers mounted an exhibition called *Codex*, comprised of antique quilts he'd painted and appliqued. The concept originated during a project in Philadelphia, where Biggers created installations at locations that were important sites in the Underground Railroad. Among his inspirations was the long-held tradition (contested by some historians) that antebellum black people used quilts as waymarks and warnings to their brothers and sisters escaping north. Whether it's true or not, handmade quilts functioning as signposts to guide people along the road to Freedom is a lovely idea.

For his various art projects, Biggers has developed an iconography that includes a red-lipped grin he calls "the Cheshire," after Lewis Carroll's famous cat, whose body disappears and reappears, leaving its unsettling smile hanging in the air. Biggers's "Cheshire" evokes the cartoonish, exaggerated grin of blackface minstrelsy and our national history involving the appearance of, and disappearing of, the bodies of black people. A second recurring image in Biggers's work is a flower design he calls "Lotus"; each petal depicts the cross section of an eighteenth-century slave ship, showing tiny dark figures chained and packed tightly into a cargo hold. The lotus is an important image in East Asian art, and Biggers's work has often referenced Buddhism and Japanese mandalas. Another spiritual tradition he considers is Vodun practice: to some of the quilt paintings, Biggers attached a paquet, a cloth-covered bundle containing objects of such spiritual power that they may not be seen by the naked eye.

Several years after I donated the Ridley quilt, I heard Biggers speak at Greensboro's Weatherspoon Art Museum in a gallery hung with his painted textiles. He talked about being a late collaborator on the work that went into the quilts, which he believes carry within their stitches something of the spirits of the women who made them. That the fabric arts are traditionally thought of as women's work, rather than as part of the high-art tradition, is important to him. He said he was blown away when he first saw the now well-known quilts by African American women from Gee's Bend, Alabama. They were displayed in the Whitney Museum in New York and, to him, were easily better art than many of the nearby paintings, mostly by European men, revered as part of the Western art historical canon. Along with the Gee's Bend artists, Biggers cited another important woman who inspired him: "Harriet Tubman was an astronaut," he has said, "traversing the south to the north by navigating the stars."

Listening to Biggers as I looked at his work, I experienced a feeling of kinship. He was thinking about things I've also been pondering for years—race and history, the importance of objects for carrying meaning, the ways different spiritual traditions guide us to think about transcending the corporeal. I knew some of my preservationist relatives might see Biggers's work as desecration—all that spray painting and appliqueing and stenciling on top of carefully worked and lovingly preserved family heirlooms. Part of me felt the same way. But another part wished I could undonate the Ridley quilt and hand it over to him, to see what he would make of it. I wondered what it might mean to him to work his vision atop a quilt connected to Nat Turner's story.

When your family history is well documented, studying it takes you down the proverbial rabbit hole. One person, one story, leads to more, and because they're all connected to you, they have the potential to be endlessly interesting—to you.

As much as the objects my parents left behind, these stories are my inheritance; each one a Kansas Sunflower of associations, colorful and pointed, dizzying. If I'm not careful, it's easy to let the story's twists and turns lead me away from facing the hot question at the center of it all: How could my ancestors have enslaved people simply because they wanted to enjoy material comforts and social status? And then there's the follow-up question, posed by Toni Morrison in *Playing in the Dark: Whiteness and the Literary Imagination*: "[What is] the impact of racism on those who perpetuate it?" She goes on: "The scholarship that looks into the mind, imagination, and behavior of slaves is valuable. But equally valuable is a serious intellectual effort to see what racial ideology does to the mind, imagination, and behavior of masters."

When I was younger, I suppose I hoped to find that my slaveholding forebears were indeed, as I'd been told, *nice people*, whose era's mores and systems prevented them from acting any other way. I wanted to think that somehow they just didn't know any better. But the more I studied, the less I could convince myself that they'd had no choice about living in the slavocracy. After all, in the slaveholding states, a minority of the population owned any slaves at all, and only a tiny fraction possessed more than a hundred. Some owners experienced moral conversions and decided to manumit; doing so did not render them destitute. There was always a choice, and my family made the wrong one.

In the months following Nat Turner's revolt, scores of black people were reported killed in Southampton County and surrounding areas; the number of these retributive murders has been estimated as high as two hundred. White voices in favor of emancipation or transportation lost out, and laws in the southern states grew more restrictive. In many places, "black codes" forbade enslaved people to assemble in groups and outlawed teaching them to read. White militia and patrols formed throughout the land.

Within a month of the uprising, William C. Parker of Southampton County "petitioned the governor to supply arms for seventy-five men." They asked the governor for "carbines, swords and pistols of the first order," as well as "the state's latest manual of cavalry tactics." The men adopted a uniform, "dark gray trimmed with black braid, gilt bullet buttons, etc.," and called themselves "the Southampton Greys." Theirs was to be a militarized local police force, ready to quash the least hint of rebellion.

On October 17, 1831, the Southampton County court record shows a Thomas Ridley accepting a commission as first lieutenant of Cavalry in the Fourth Regiment, Eighth Brigade, Fourth Division of the Virginia Militia.

When I first read about my ancestor becoming an officer in a militia formed to police black people, it is late summer, 2016. Police in Tulsa, Oklahoma, have recently killed Terence Crutcher, who was unarmed and had his hands in the air. Putting down my books on southern history, I turn on the television to see that protests in Charlotte, North Carolina, over the shooting death of Keith Lamont Scott have grown violent, and at least one protestor has been shot in the chaos. News footage shows unarmed protestors facing down rows of police in black riot gear: body armor, protective masks, shields, and clubs.

Four years later, in the annus horribilis that is 2020, countless people around the world fill the streets of their cities—amid a global pandemic—to protest the killings of George Floyd, Breonna Taylor, Ahmaud Arbery. Again we see police in riot gear, white supremacists toting guns, right-wing attempts to amplify the actions of looters and troublemakers in order to delegitimize the nonviolent protestors' legitimate grievance. Only one thing seems new: the presence of more white allies in the crowds led by black activists. Whether white allies will contribute anything meaningful to systemic change, we don't yet know.

In one early report of the Nat Turner rebellion, a newspaper editor described the murders at the Rebecca Vaughan house, then said: "When the work was done, they [Nat's men] called for drink, and food, and becoming nice, damned the brandy as vile stuff." In Middle English, *nice* meant foolish, wanton, derived (through Old French) from the Latin *nescius*, "ignorant." Other now obsolete meanings for the word are lewd, dissolute, coy, modest, diffident, reticent. In Nat's time, *nice* meant "showing fastidious, particular, or finical tastes." Only later did the word come to mean pleasant, satisfying, socially acceptable, benign, respectable, chaste.

How does one tiny word, over time, come to mean the opposite of its original definition? How does wanton become chaste? Discriminating become banal? Elite become everyday? Ignorant become socially acceptable? *Nescius* become *nice*?

If everything that Samuel Lemon and I know about our families is true, then we are very distant cousins. I've never met Lemon, but I purchased his *Go Stand upon the Rock*, a fictionalized family history based on his grandmother's stories. The book's central figure is Lemon's ancestor Cornelius, who escaped from Bonnie Doon and slavery in 1862. Cornelius claimed Thomas Ridley III as his father, and his pale skin helped him pass through Virginia and get north to Philadelphia.

In a chapter titled "Day the Sun Turned Blue," Lemon relates Nat Turner stories that came down in his family as well as in the wider African American oral tradition. By the time I read Lemon's chapter, I'd come to think of the faithful-slave narrative solely as a great white lie, but Lemon suggests another view of this narrative. Trapped in a terrible position, many enslaved people understandably decided the most sensible thing to do was avoid risky moves. If the goal was to avoid more immediate suffering, then presenting oneself to one's master or mistress as "faithful" was a smart, reasonable choice, and overt resistance a foolish one. As one of Lemon's characters puts it, "I ain't sayin' Nat was a bad *man*. I'm sayin' he had a bad *plan*."

Through his characters' dialogue, Lemon offers another rationale for the narrative of faithfulness: in describing the tenderness of black people's ministrations—nursing white children, nursing sick white people, feeding, dressing, cleaning white bodies, preparing them for the grave—this narrative points to the humanity and compassion of folk bound to care for people unlikely to do the same for them. Such compassion, and its accompanying capacity for forgiveness, are linked to religious principles, to the hope for eternal salvation implicit in the Christianity that has sustained many African Americans through hard times. Of course, this same religion supplied Nat Turner with his apocalyptic visions and bolstered his resolve to rebel. Abolitionists used the same Bible to decry slavery that slaveholders used to defend it.

It's not easy to make sense of how different people can use the same stories for such contradictory ends. It's hard to unfold and iron flat the complex narratives at the heart of our beliefs about who we are.

Shortly before my grandfather died at Oaklana, he told me the story of the runaway slave again. This time he happened to name the cruel owner from whom the man had run away. It was a Mr. Capehart, who was also my great-great-great grandfather—exactly the same degree of relation to me as the ancestor who ransomed the frightened slave. Suddenly, the story grew much more interesting—more troubling, more balanced, and, possibly, more true.

By 1853, Thomas Ridley III was the richest man in the Southampton County. That year, he commissioned oil portraits of himself, his wife, and their eight children, including Emma, my great-great grandmother. Oliver Perry Copeland, a failed innkeeper turned portraitist, likely stayed at Bonnie Doon for months in order to complete the work.

In Copeland's portrait of seven-year-old Emma, she wears a pink dress, coral necklace, and small black boots that match her dark hair. Her arm sweetly encircles a lamb. Her wide eyes are not looking into the past, when, on her father's twenty-second birthday, August 22, 1831, one of the largest slave rebellions in U.S. history took place. Nor is she looking into the future, when she marries George Pollok Burgwyn, the son of Anna, a Boston-born Unitarian who becomes a southern Episcopalian, and Henry, a landowner from Northampton County, North Carolina. Upon inheriting a vast tract of land and a quantity of enslaved people, Henry apparently struggled with a crisis of conscience and, perhaps at the urging of his northern bride, planned to manumit his slaves. However, after a failed experiment with paid Irish laborers (another exploited class in nineteenth-century America), he discarded the notion.

Little Emma in the painting doesn't yet know that her husband's brother, Henry King Burgwyn Jr., known as "Harry," will be part of the guard at John Brown's 1859 trial. In 1863 Harry will die at Gettysburg, leading the Twenty-Sixth North Carolina Infantry, which will sustain the heaviest losses of any regiment in the Civil War. Only twenty-two years old and the youngest colonel in the Confederate army, this son of a reluctant slaveholder and a northern woman will become known to Civil War buffs as "the boy Colonel." Harry will be buried in a gun box under a walnut tree, and Kinchen, the enslaved manservant who has accompanied him to war will *walk* home from Pennsylvania, in the opposite direction of freedom, carrying Harry's personal effects and leading his two horses. Kinchen will tell Anna Burgwyn where her son is buried, and a few years later she'll have his body brought back to North Carolina and buried in the Confederate soldiers' section at Oakwood Cemetery in Raleigh. A grand monument will be erected over his remains, full of praise for him.

Little Emma with her plump fists and rosy cheeks has not begun to think of her six children. The last two will be fraternal twins called Sumner and Maria (Minnie). When Emma dies of influenza (or maybe pneumonia), five-year-old Minnie will be sent off to boarding school, so young that a black nursemaid is sent to look after her. Five of Minnie's children will survive to adulthood, cared for by a black woman they call Aunt George. One of them will be christened Margaret Ridley, and she will also have a daughter named Margaret Ridley (cared for by Ms. Annie Gatling), who will have a daughter called Julia Ridley, me, the first girl in my maternal line in at least two hundred years not to be reared by or with the help of a black woman. Had I been a boy, my mother told me, my name would have been that of the child for whom the Ridley quilt was made: Nathaniel.

In 2016, I will receive an email from a distant cousin sharing the news that somebody has spray painted on the Boy Colonel's monument the words "He helped lead a war for slavery." That statement, despite its crude delivery, is true. The spray paint will remind me of Biggers's *Codex*. I will think about quilts and resistance, sewing and violence, houses and graves. I will think about all of this for a long time, then sit down to write at my dining room table, with Emma Wright Ridley's portrait on the wall behind me.

Rebecca Solnit again: "It is the nature of revolutions to subside, which is not the same thing as to fail. A revolution is a lightning bolt showing us new possibilities and illuminating the darkness of our old arrangements so that we will never see them quite the same way again."

Your people tell you things when you are young. You believe them because they are your people and without them you'd be lost. Their knowledge becomes your own, well before you understand there's such a thing as knowledge. There's no reason to question what your people say; there's not even a question. What you've been told, what you know and believe, is part of you, like your organs or your skin, integral and vital.

Believe, reason, knowledge, question—those come later, when you begin to wonder and doubt what you've been told. It's hard to hold those old stories up to the light, to withstand the exposure of it, until you begin to understand that you can separate yourself from the things you've been told to believe, if you want to.

For most of my youth I believed that aesthetics, history, and family sentiment were the only reasons we were holding on to all these relics of our family's past. The people who raised me were bright, charismatic, funny, intelligent, clever. From the stories they told, it seemed our ancestors were, too. But they were (we are) also stubborn, determined, intractable, and dominating, and nowadays, it doesn't seem so easy to compartmentalize the reasons why my family were (are) so proud of our ancestors, our big houses, our blood-stained acres.

How can we separate people's accomplishments from the system that allows them to succeed—a system they (we) made to their (our) own advantage? Didn't (don't) we celebrate our judges and statesmen, our soldiers and clerics because we were (are) proud of how they worked (work) that system? Proud of how they (we) kept (keep) order? Isn't that why we kept (keep) their stuff? Why else was (is) it all still hanging around?

Upon my mother's death, I inherited a quarter interest in Oaklana. At first I fantasized about returning there to write each spring, when the daffodils bloom. But then we went to bury my dad's ashes on top of my mother's grave in the big field, and I realized that, with my parents and grandparents gone, the whole place had become a graveyard, a ghost ship. To visit again would bring me nothing but sadness. The plantation legacy was nothing I took pride in, nothing my son would take pride in. Furthermore, Oaklana was a money pit, a financial burden that would keep me from doing more of what I wanted to be free to do: write.

I could see no good reason to hold on to the house. A lawyer drew up a quitclaim deed, and I signed away my portion.

There are nicer stories I could tell. I could repeat Lemon's claim that Margaret Ridley helped Cornelius escape Bonnie Doon. I could tell the story of how Daddy-Jack's lawyer father, Ernest, helped Godwin "Buddy" Bush get into safe custody after he was almost lynched in 1947, how Ernest then led the investigation of the perpetrators, for which he received hate mail, as well as letters of praise. There are many less dramatic stories, too, of charity and kindness, of friendships across the color line. It would be easy to remember only these stories and forget the others. But that would be disingenuous. I know there are more stories in the Red Record than I can ever know, and some of them cleave close to me. I know that I'm more like my ancestors than I care to admit, by which I mean: I've extended kindness to individual people but haven't done nearly enough to change the social systems that benefit me and oppress others. There's much work yet to do, and guilt and shame are not actions. They are indulgences we can't afford, a dead end.

⁓

Perhaps one day I'll get rid of every last thing that reminds me of my family's slaveholding legacy. But for now, I live with quite a few of them. I use and admire them. To return to Sherry Turkle's useful phrasing, I *think* with them.

In the old Boston secretary in my living room sits a small leather-bound Bible. Its tissue-thin pages are crammed with miniscule scripture. Engraved in gold on the cover: E. W. Ridley. No doubt it was given to Emma when she was a girl at Bonnie Doon.

Nat Turner is said to have carried his Bible through his "war." It languished in the Southampton County courthouse until the early twentieth century, when it was given to descendants of a family that lost many members to Nat's band. Now it belongs to the National Museum of African American History and Culture in Washington, D.C. The front and back covers are missing; the book of Revelation is torn out. It's a miracle it survived.

The Ridley quilt stays in another museum, farther south. It's too vulnerable to remain at home, and it's too late for it to become a different work of art altogether. I think about the quilt sometimes, but I don't wish it back. Google will show it to me anytime.

The photographs of the Ridley houses are put away in a drawer. I haven't been to Oaklana since Easter 2012. But every day, I eat with Emma Wright Ridley looking over my shoulder. In her portrait, she is forever a child holding a lamb, a picture of innocence. She doesn't know what stories she'll tell her children, what stories she won't tell. She can't imagine the world in which I live. She will never know she reminds me daily not to be too fragile to withstand the light, and to remember that the moral danger is nearest when we sit among our nice things and believe they make us nice.

Paper Chase, a Play of Desire

SHRED:
Unwanted papers

A paper chase is a version of a game called hare and hounds, in which the "hares" leave a trail of paper and then set off for a specific place, trying to get there before the "hounds" catch up. I can't say where exactly my parents set off to when they died—neither my theology nor my cosmology is firm enough for me to tell you that—but like the hares in the game, they left behind a lot of paper.

Figuring, rightly, that these papers would be time consuming to sort, Moreland and I kept setting them aside to deal with later. Eventually, we could postpone the task no longer. Out of drawers, bankers' boxes, and file cabinets spilled letters, postcards, photographs. The school essays, notebooks, and report cards of three generations. Road maps, brochures, business cards. Magazine and newspaper articles. Newsletters from various organizations. Daybooks, address books, bank books. Instruction manuals, receipts, product labels, price tags. Copies of every antiques appraisal my mother ever did. Bills. Decades of tax records. The inventory records back to 1971, the year they opened Tyler-Smith Antiques.

That so many of these documents were banal or useless made going through them a punishing test of endurance. Why didn't we just send it all straight to the shred truck? Mom had told us more than once about an unsuspecting person who discovered a copy of the Declaration of Independence in an attic. She'd frequently reminded us that today's mundane documents are tomorrow's archival treasures, crucial for revealing details of daily life in times gone by. To her, throwing away any record on its way to becoming historical bordered on a criminal act. I felt guilty even thinking about it.

Sifting through my parents' papers, I nursed a writerly hope of finding a jewel in the midden heap—juicy material I could use in a short story or novel. When I found a promising document, I'd carry it home and add it to my own growing archive. Mostly, though, I spent so much time with my parents' papers because it eased slightly the pain of missing them. The sight of their handwriting—hers large and vivacious, his tight, neat—reminded me of the mother and father I'd known before sickness changed them. All that paper formed more of a swamp than a trail, and as my brother and I hounded our way through it, we found ourselves vulnerable to the progress-arresting mire of reminiscence. We took pleasure in glimpsing the young woman and man Mom and Daddy had been before our births, before marriage and college, on back to their childhoods, before they'd met each other. Besides telling us about their past selves—the lives lived, the roads taken—the papers waved toward lost possibilities, other roads considered or imagined.

Every opened drawer revealed my parents' old wants as well as my own. With time, I came to see the papers as monuments not only to experience but to desire. Emptying the house was forcing me to grapple with the question of who I wanted to be now that my folks were gone. As I thought about the past, I pondered the future: Where did the two connect? Where must they diverge? How would I know I was on the right path now, without my parents to guide me? What did I *want*?

The hares are long gone, but I'm still playing hound. Come chase along with me.

The Playscript

Squirreled up in Mom's office, among my school awards and kindergarten drawings, is my rumpled photocopy of *The Glass Menagerie* from when I played Laura in ninth grade. The soft-edged pages, covered with my marginalia and doodles, transport me back to the dim auditorium at Western Guilford High School, where, aged thirteen, I played my first big part in a real play. The cute boy cast opposite me as the Gentleman Caller had recently moved to North Carolina from California, which made him exotic to me. He had short blond hair cut in a surfer style, twinkly blue eyes, and a rebellious attitude—a baby James Dean. By the time rehearsals started, we'd become friends, and I was nursing a swoony, sweaty crush. When I learned that the play called for us to kiss, that kiss became all I could think about.

I'd kissed a couple of boys by then, but the times were still countable on one hand. I struggle to recall now whether that hand had yet encountered a penis. I think maybe it had, just once, and in that moment, beneath my excitement and alarm and lust, I'd felt a twinge of surprised pity that such a soft-skinned thing was what boys had been given for expressing the power of their want. Nights, I kissed my pillow and pretended I was doing naughty things with my Gentleman Caller or movie star River Phoenix or the drummer from Duran Duran. I imagined making out with an imagined future boyfriend/lover/husband—handsome, sardonic, wildly romantic, a composite of characters from Georgette Heyer novels and episodes of *Fantasy Island*.

This activity, while arousing, was also deeply unsatisfying. I had no idea what was up with my body. Puberty had arrived with a vengeance, and everything was in overdrive. I was ravenous for food; my mind raced; I had too many feelings. I'd gotten my period at twelve and grown hips that made me feel fat and breasts that required, suddenly, a real bra. My nose, my legs, my butt were all too big; my thick hair too straight. My skin was oily no matter what I did. I begged for contacts instead of glasses. It didn't matter that my mother told me I was attractive; I knew the truth. She was just obligated to say that because she was my mom.

The only good part of the whole situation was that people often mistook me for being older than I was. That pleased me—I liked thinking I was mature for my age. But their mistake also made me nervous. I no longer felt sure of what anybody expected of me, and I wasn't even sure what I wanted myself, except a boyfriend to kiss, a real one. I tried to be attractive. Mom was forever sending me back to my room to change because my outfit was "too advanced." Still, boys at school showed nothing I could recognize as interest. I decided to practice acting sexier. Since we had no full-length mirror in the house, I'd go in the bathroom, stand on the flat edge of the tub as though it were a balance beam, and examine myself in the mirror covering the wall over the vanity. I checked to see how I looked with my stomach pulled in, wearing different clothes, dancing provocatively, or gesturing with a cigarette I'd taken from my mother's pack. Testing my balance on the tub's slippery rim, I posed, shimmied, pouted, practiced smoke rings, and tried out my best dialogue.

I danced alone in my room, the knob of the closet door serving for a partner's hand. My soundtrack that year was a dubbed cassette of *Nina Simone Sings the Blues*, a gift from my drama teacher. Ms. Locklear was a heavy woman with a choppy haircut and the faint scar of a repaired harelip. When she was angry—an occurrence that became more common as the school year wore on—her face screwed into one of the most scornful expressions I'd ever seen on a person. But she was also funny and down-to-earth, and she seemed to care about us students in a way the other teachers didn't.

At that time my favorite TV show was *Fame*, about teenagers at a performing arts school in New York City. Everything about this show appealed to me: the diverse cast, the dancing, the fashion, the snappy dialogue. I relished *Fame*'s depiction of artists as tough, hard-working people with big goals to accomplish. Oh, the youthful angst, the creative energy, the leg warmers. How cool it would be to go to school with a bunch of kids who wanted exactly what I wanted: to make art and to make out. I was still taking a lot of dance classes then, but it was in drama class that I finally found my people—the Gentleman Caller, as well as a handful of seniors who took me under their wing. Now that I had these friends, eighth period was the one part of the academically stupefying, socially humiliating school day I looked forward to.

Ms. Locklear took a special interest in my progress. Looking back, I think she recognized in me a fellow smart girl perplexed by society's demands and desperate for mental stimulation. When she introduced me to Nina Simone and Tennessee Williams, it was like pouring gasoline on a fire.

⌒⌒

In *The Glass Menagerie*, faded southern belle Amanda Wingfield craves success and security for her children, Tom and Laura. Their father—a telephone man who "fell in love with long distances"—has abandoned the scene, and it's not hard to see why. Amanda drives everybody who loves her crazy. She can't help it. Life has disappointed her, and keeping house in a shabby tenement is a bleak contrast to her romanticized memories of a carefree, well-dressed girlhood in which she once entertained seventeen gentleman callers in a single day. Her talk is by turns charming and grating, and beneath her hysterical effort to remain cheerful bubbles the dark threat of despair. Tom supports her and Laura by working a stultifying job under the fluorescent lights of a shoe factory, but he knows his dreams of the bigger world will lead him to leave and that his doing so will break all their hearts. "His nature is not remorseless," Williams's stage directions read, "but to escape from a trap he has to act without pity."

Shy, nervous Laura has dropped out of business school. She's burdened with a slight limp, emblematic of her incapacity to move through the world with ease. Worried for her daughter's future, Amanda begs Tom to find his sister a gentleman caller. The next evening he brings home his coworker Jim, whom Laura secretly admired in high school. Good-looking, conventional Jim is kind, and she grows comfortable enough with him to talk about her collection of glass animals, in particular, her prize unicorn.

JIM: Unicorns—aren't they extinct in the modern world?

LAURA: I know!

JIM: Poor little fellow, he must feel sort of lonesome.

LAURA [*smiling*]: Well, if he does, he doesn't complain about it. He stays on a shelf with some horses that don't have horns and all of them seem to get along nicely together.

JIM: How do you know?

LAURA [*lightly*]: I haven't heard any arguments among them.

Laura, of course, is intimately familiar with the sound of arguments and knows all about being the oddball left "on the shelf," that ugly old description of an unmarried woman.

Jim asks Laura to dance, and though she's embarrassed about her bum leg, she agrees. As they fumble about, they bump her unicorn off the table. Its horn breaks off, but Laura doesn't get upset. Jim, who's begun to see something special in her, kisses Laura with a sort of sweet regret, then tells her that he's engaged. Again, she doesn't seem especially upset. It's as though she's already resigned herself to the idea of never living as other people do, of never working or marrying or raising a family. Before Jim leaves, she gives him the broken figurine: "A—souvenir . . ."

In rehearsals, we kept skipping over the big moment . . . *And then you'll kiss*, Ms. Locklear would say, and each time, I longed for that magical future: *And then you'll kiss* . . . That stage kiss, I imagined, would be the first of many, the catalyst for a new, kissy phase of my life in which my Gentleman Caller and I would do lots and lots of kissing. Once our lips touched, the boy playing Jim would magically transform into my real-life gentleman caller, madly in love with me. It all hinged on that first kiss . . .

At home, waiting for this fairy-tale kiss, I played that Nina Simone tape over and over, singing the lyrics to "I Want a Little Sugar in My Bowl" as I danced behind the closed door of my room, learning by heart every word, every plaintive build and drop in the music.

The day came. On the grubby high-school auditorium stage, in front of the teacher and the other kids, my Gentleman Caller leaned in and pressed his lips softly against mine. It was embarrassing and awkward and totally thrilling.

We practiced the kiss maybe twice before he quit the play. Rehearsals conflicted with his cross-country track meets, and Ms. Locklear refused to work out a compromise. I agonized over whether he'd really quit because he found kissing me so repulsive, but the thought was so unbearable that I chose instead to direct my fury at Ms. Locklear, blaming her for not accommodating his schedule. By then, she was treating me too noticeably as a teacher's pet, a role I had no wish to play. She was jealous of my love for my Gentleman Caller, I figured, and didn't want me to pay attention to anybody but her.

My animosity eased a little when she conscripted a new gentleman caller, this one a senior, also cute, an affable clown-jock everybody liked. I thought he would be pretty fine to kiss, but sadly, he also was discharged on account of his athletic obligations.

And then Ms. Locklear managed to cast one of the few boys on the planet for whom I could drum up no erotic interest whatsoever. In my book, he was square, not cute, a total goober. To make matters even less sophisticated, he had a goofy girlfriend who kept telling me that when it came time for the actual show, she planned to cover her eyes so that she wouldn't have to watch her boyfriend kiss another girl. I coldly assured her that the prospect held no joy for me. My excitement for the mandatory kissing had been replaced with disgust.

No longer fixated on making out with a cute boy, I focused on the play and grew to understand what the interaction between Laura and Jim is about: his pity for her oddity and her refusal of that pity. I determined to give my Laura a quiet dignity. By opening night, the brief touching of lips had become a momentary nuisance, an actorly duty. Backstage, ignoring the graffiti a Rush fan had painted across the walls, I buttoned myself into a dusty-smelling gray dress and put a coin in one shoe to remind me not to limp on the wrong side. Dragging my leg, I crossed the stage with my ballet-trained back straight. The audience, invisible but audible in the dark patch under the blinding lights, waited to see what I would do. As I said my lines, I felt the audience settle and give me their attention; I tasted how delicious it was, to hold so many people this way.

The "unicorn" fell. I cradled a random glass animal in my hands and regarded it sadly. I accepted Jim's boneless kiss, his rejection and farewell. Stage right, on the fire escape, Tom delivered his final monologue.

> TOM: . . . Oh, Laura, Laura, I tried to leave you behind me, but I am more faithful than I intended to be!
> I reach for a cigarette, I cross the street, I run into the movies or a bar, I buy a drink, I speak to the nearest stranger— anything that can blow your candles out! [LAURA bends over the candles.]—for nowadays the world is lit by lightning! Blow out your candles, Laura—and so good-bye.

I blew out the candles. The lights went down to applause. Sweaty and grinning, we four actors took our bows. I no longer hated Ms. L. or the Gentleman Caller. Together we'd worked a magic that was, though fleeting, real.

A perfect Laura, a few people said afterward. I thanked them, pleased with the praise, but in the days after we struck the set, I realized that being called a perfect Laura didn't sit right. Though I'd done my best to give the character solidity, she still seemed to me all thin skin and no hard bones. In school I was quiet and obedient, and now I wondered if teachers and classmates saw me as like Laura— delicate, fearful, wounded. That was not the sort of girl I believed I was, nor the sort of woman I planned to become. Restless, curious, I was overflowing with visions and desires, ready to bust out, to grow up. One day, I planned to be the way Nina Simone sounded to me: smart, sexy, and not afraid of wanting.

_⌒_

Need versus want. It's a distinction parents are told they must teach their children, particularly when it comes to spending money. Needs are what must be met to ensure physical survival, while wants are the objects and experiences that supply pleasure or a sense of fulfillment. That pleasure and fulfillment are not necessary to sustain life is arguable, if not flat-out wrong, and most of us rightly dread the thought of a life in which we don't experience them. Even so, it's touted as a virtue always to know the difference between need and want, to meet the former consistently and safely, and to indulge the latter only occasionally, if at all.

While we're parsing, what about _desire_? Stronger than _fancy_ or _interest_, desire is exciting, dangerous. Desire is a force. It's a want that _feels_ like a need. It can come over us in an instant, and can disappear just as suddenly. Or it can grow slowly, become consuming, obsess us all our lives. Desire, even when met, is often not sated; in fact, a taste of what we desire may only make us hungrier for more. More food, sex, drink, or thrills. More money and fame. More rooms, and more stuff to fill them up.

As we grow older, it's not the fact of desire but its persistence that surprises. We wonder how we can still be desiring at our age, when we have seen what desire can do, the destruction it can leave in its wake. Although _The Glass Menagerie_ opened in 1944 to immediate critical and financial success, it was, for its author, "the saddest play I have ever written. It is full of pain." A few years earlier, Tennessee Williams had made his own escape from the shoe factory, leaving his family in St. Louis. He wasn't there when his mother agreed to have his troubled sister, Rose, undergo a prefrontal lobotomy. For the rest of his life, though he loved Rose dearly and paid for her care, Williams felt guilty that he hadn't done more to help her. But he knew, too, that getting away from his family had saved him from also being destroyed.

You don't have to go hunting in his plays for hidden meaning. It's all right there on the surface—*desire*. Not an undercurrent in his work, but a riptide. It was what pulled him so far from home, what pushed him to make a life for himself as a prolific writer and an active lover of men. He became an expert on desire, our greatest American dramatist of this force stronger than want, sweeter than need, and even, sometimes, more lasting than Death.

The Dossier

One morning in the early 2000s, my mother read in the *Greensboro News and Record* that a local couple had been arrested for running a prostitution ring. She soon realized they were Kim and Tim, the renters living two houses over from her. An expert navigator of the internet, which she'd learned to use for her appraisal work, Mom poked around online to see what she could learn about the neighbors. Quickly, willingly, she scampered down a specialized rabbit hole in which the words *rabbit* and *hole* have particular resonance. Sites selling sex listed the specific acts and durations available, the workers' hourly or base rates, travel charges, and à la carte prices for additional services. Some sites provided pictures, others only descriptions. While the content Mom turned up was salacious, what excited her were the intricacies of amateur sleuthing on the internet. The process of finding out things about a hitherto hidden world was as good as, or better than, the information itself, and she prided herself on her persistence, trying one search term after another.

Mom worked on a desktop and Daddy couldn't get his wheelchair into her office, so when she wanted to show him an email or web page, she'd print it. In the past, she'd shown him pictures of the grandchildren, or Republican-bashing jokes sent by friends, or antiques auction records from Christie's or Sotheby's. Now, she drained numerous ink-jet cartridges on information about Kim and

Tim and their associates. When the stack of printouts became too bulky for a file folder, she transferred the pages into a three-ring binder she took to calling "the dossier."

I wasn't sure what to make of my mother's new hobby. Sexual practices and mores in history, gossip about celebrity sex scandals, the affairs of relatives and acquaintances—it had long amused her to dish about these things. Make no mistake: these discussions always carried a hint of the anthropological; they were about studying other people, they weren't personal. She never talked to me about her own sex life (fine with me) and always made it clear she didn't want to hear about mine (even more fine with me). She gave me a children's book about the basics of reproduction when I was little and, as I got older, joked that I'd learn "the rest" on the school bus. When puberty struck, she handed me a dismal twenty-year-old booklet called *What Every Teen Wants to Know*. In my senior year of high school, when I finally had a boyfriend for a few months, she never mentioned birth control or gynecological care. And when I told her in college that I'd gone to the student health center because I'd read you were supposed to get a pap smear once you turned eighteen, she looked at me like I was crazy. She never went to the doctor if she could help it.

The only sex education her own parents had provided—or so she always claimed—consisted of a brief exchange during the car ride to Raleigh to install her at boarding school. It was 1956, and she was going into eleventh grade.

GRANNY: Ridley, you do know where babies come from?
MOM [*cringing*]: Yes.
GRANNY: Well. Don't.

⌐∿⌐

Investigating what the neighbors were doing with their bodies and those of their paying customers provided a welcome distraction during a period when my parents' own bodies were breaking down. As Daddy sat too long over his meals or clipped coupons, he watched, à la *Rear Window*, and reported who was coming and going from Kim and Tim's. Mom scoured the internet and talked with the other neighbors about what they'd observed. Whenever I visited, she insisted on showing me the dossier, and Daddy updated me on his latest surveillance.

I saw Kim and Tim in person only a few times, dressed in boring sweatshirts, getting out of their cars or planting flowers in their well-maintained yard. Tan, mustachioed Tim possessed the type of face my mother categorized as "Class rodentia"—pinched and pointed, with small, close-set eyes and prominent teeth. Kim lumbered down the driveway as though her joints ached. According to the dossier, they were willing to make calls together, offering their services to men who wanted to tryst with a couple, but mostly Kim worked alone, under aliases that sounded like the names of soap-opera characters. "Blair Winthrall" was pictured on one web page, her face fixed in a come-hither pout, the skin loose at her throat, breasts puddling atop her red bustier. Miss Winthrall, the text read, was a lady who liked flowers, satin, hearts, and champagne, and dreamed of a man who wanted true romance . . .

My own girlhood dreams of romance never included a honeymoon year on West 113th Street between Broadway and Riverside in New York City, but that was how things turned out. In the summer of 1996, after a wedding down home, Glenn and I left the apartment outside the city where we'd lived during our first year of graduate school to move into a tiny two-room apartment near Columbia University. He was studying Chinese literature; I was working on a master's degree in creative writing. That winter, for the first time in my life, I developed a solid writing routine. Each morning, I walked around the corner to my favorite café on Broadway to grab coffee and an almond scone. Then I headed a few blocks north to the reading room at Avery, Columbia's art library. Despite its lofty ceilings and heavy wooden tables, the room's grave, old-fashioned gloom felt cozy to me, and I could concentrate there.

I was supposed to be working on my master's thesis, a collection of linked short stories about a girl who was kinda sorta like me, except with anything remotely interesting stripped away. As best as I can recall, her family belonged to a country club (my parents loathed country clubs), her stern father was a lawyer (my stern father loathed lawyers), and her mother was a submissive housewife with no strong opinions (my unsubmissive mother . . .). One reason I made this fictional family so drippy was because my mother had warned me that if she ever recognized herself in my fiction, she'd sue me, and I wasn't entirely convinced she was joking.

Desperately bored with this project, I started playing around with a novel set in a made-up small town in rural eastern North Carolina. The plot followed two teenagers who sing at funerals, become rivals, then fall in love. I took the idea of funeral singers from a ninth-century Chinese story, "The Tale of Li Wa," assigned in one of my husband's seminars. Working on this novel manuscript, which I showed to nobody, provided a rich secret pleasure. Seated at my preferred library table, hard and dark as a pew in a Gothic cathedral, I wrote longhand in a spiral notebook, letting my imagination run loose in a way I didn't dare when typing stories for my graduate workshop.

I didn't worry about following the standard creative writing rules: write what you know, show don't tell, kill your darlings. I didn't have to avoid using southern turns of phrase that my Yankee classmates wouldn't understand. It didn't matter if my humor was too over the top or my coincidences too Dickensian. I could write whatever I wanted. And so, when I sat down to work in that library, I wrote myself into the state of entrancement all writers desire—a total immersion in which we forget to check the clock, or count pages or words, or distract ourselves with thoughts of supper or cocktails, fucking or chores; we forget the drags of the day, of the body, of time and the river; we forget the Sturm und Drang.

The mortal coil relaxes the iron tension of its grip, and we forget to worry whether our life has a point, or how soon it will end—we forget we have a life at all.

When I reached a stopping place and emerged from this enchantment, I was always amazed to see how much time had passed. Morning's writing done, I'd stop next door at the East Asian Library to see if Glenn wanted to go for lunch. One day, the library was conducting a sale of a former professor's book collection, mostly dry academic studies and literature in languages I couldn't read. We were about to leave when I spied an oversized volume with a pop-art-style jacket. A top-hatted Victorian gent stood in profile, holding a cheroot. He was done in black and blue; behind him, four silhouettes of his head graduated through the hot-pink ground surrounding the title—*MY SECRET LIFE.*

I recognized the title right away. Just a month earlier, I'd livened up the short, dreary January afternoons by reading Steven Marcus's *The Other Victorians: A Study of Sexuality and Pornography in Mid-Nineteenth-Century England.* Marcus mentions how rare copies of *My Secret Life* were, so I supposed it was a text I'd never see. Now, as luck would have it, this giant reprint became mine for a dollar. I lugged it back to our tiny overstuffed apartment to examine it in private.

From the jacket copy: "*My Secret Life* is the sexual memoir of a well-to-do gentleman of Victorian England, who began at an early age to keep a diary of his erotic behavior. He continued this record for over forty years, creating in the process a unique social and psychological document." The original octavo edition of six copies, which the author had privately printed in Amsterdam between 1882 and 1894, ran to more than four thousand pages. My 1960s reprint has 2,358 oversized pages filled with miniscule print. Its index begins with "Abortion" and ends with "Zora, French Harlot." Listed in between is every sexual act you can think of and some you might not have; see, for example, "Anus, toothbrush up a man's whilst he's gamahuched."

In the book's many chapters, the narrator, who refers to himself as Walter, chronicles adventures so plentiful, so vigorous, you wonder he had time for anything else.

> Looking thro diaries and memoranda, I find that I have had women of twenty-seven different empires, kingdoms, or countries, and eighty or more different nationalities, including every one in Europe except a Laplander. . . .

> I have probably fucked now—and I have tried carefully to ascertain it—something like twelve hundred women, and have felt the cunts of certainly three hundred others of whom I have seen a hundred and fifty naked.

Walter's documentary prowess keeps pace with his escapades. He is, in a word, tireless. He records encounters in a variety of locales, including a church, a game preserve, and a railway carriage. He and his partners copulate on beds and the floor; they fornicate on sofas, tables, chairs, and a carpenter's bench; they fuck on the ground. They do it against walls, fences, gates, and railings; against trees and windows, a kitchen dresser and a turnpike. The women are servants, prostitutes, working women—any woman he can seduce, coerce, or pay. Rarely, Walter manages to bed a woman of his own leisure class.

Most of his experience is with women, but he also fondles and fellates men and participates in orgies that include both sexes. Animated by the nineteenth century's coupled spirits of experimentation and classification, he exhibits the obsessive zeal of a true scientist or artist as he plays with positions, dildos, spanking. There is no orifice he shuns, no bodily fluid in which he does not delight. He can be aroused by nearly anything, and catalogs exhaustively the details of that arousal: what sight or smell or touch caused it, what it felt like, what he did next, how he felt afterward.

In his reflections, he considers the feelings of others, too, describing the fear and shame of the impoverished women he bribes for sex, of the virgins he deflowers, of the women he harasses and coerces so forcefully that today we would call his actions rape, though he doesn't. He sincerely believes that all women will enjoy sex with him, if only they will try it, and he happily reports the immense pleasure expressed by his consensual partners. Overall, he believes his level of sexual obsession is not unusual; he assumes that other men must feel and want to do—and probably *do* do—the same things he does, though perhaps not as frequently.

In the Victorian era, polite people could make no mention of sex in public, and Marcus discusses how *My Secret Life* is a shadow text to the era's novels. Scholars continue to argue whether the book is a work of fiction or the longest autobiography ever written, just as they continue to argue about Walter's real identity. Even if you don't read the entire thing—and I can no more make it through this book than I can get through *The Tale of Genji*—a few pages are enough to reveal the work's novelistic eye for detail and its propulsive narrative drive. The story, such as it is, begins with the twin foundational experiences of any British Victorian gentleman, or perhaps any gentleman of any time and place: a bout of pubescent peter-pulling with a male cousin, and a penchant for groping and molesting defenseless housemaids. These rites of passage expand for Walter into a career of unchecked fornication. His is a connoisseur's quest for novelty and variety. He seeks unusual experience, trying out any fantasy he can think up, as he tests his own ideas of perversion, pushing to see if, indeed, he has any limits at all.

Early readers of the first, six-copy edition of *My Secret Life* must have been affected by it much as we are when seduced by the internet today. The episodic nature of the Web and of pornography both is that one entry compels you to read/watch the next, and the next, and the next. First there's temptation, urge; then, pursuit and foreplay; build-up, then climax, then release, then collapse . . . and then here comes temptation again. What fascinates most about *My Secret Life* is its vastness, its sheer length—*it just keeps going*. Like the internet, it's a hoard of text that tests our credulity. We know, reading, that it may all be fantasy. But the book also feels, in a way, true. As in real life, one experience piles on top of another until their combined weight becomes bewildering, staggering, and we struggle to identify the thread we've tried to follow through the piles. We struggle to make sense of what any of it means.

For me, perhaps the most titillating part of all is Walter's profound lack of guilt as he celebrates his exploits. It's exhilarating to imagine a life in which one needn't feel guilty about one's desires.

My mother remained shameless in her pursuit of information about Kim and Tim. After their arrest, they weren't allowed to operate a business in North Carolina for a year, so they moved out of state. Mom continued to track them online. Besides keeping up with their sex work, she researched Kim's genealogy and her son's criminal record. The dossier thickened.

After the year away, they returned, renters again, two doors over. Tim's truck now advertised lawn-care services, and Craigslist ads appeared, offering an "erotic" housecleaning service. Young women came and went from the house. An older woman moved in—Kim's mother or aunt or grandmother. Each afternoon, a furious dog barked at their side door. Kim's grown son and his girlfriend took up residence. Another neighbor, who lived between them and my parents, agreed to give the son a ride to a shopping center and returned unnerved, talking about a drug deal in a parking lot, the boy flashing a gun.

At the time, I was juggling elder care, childcare, and work, and I wished these unsavory neighbors would go far away from my chronically ill and defenseless parents. Still, I couldn't help feeling bad for Kim, another working woman with too much on her plate, too many folks to care for.

Chance brings such different people to the same place. The working personas that Kim invented for herself suggest that she aspired to enter a white-collar milieu into which she had not been born, a class of people who lived in spacious houses with tidy yards on quiet streets. If that's true, then moving to my parents' cul-de-sac represented a step up for her. Conversely, for my mother, living on the circle was a step down. She'd grown up in the highest possible privilege in small-town eastern North Carolina in the 1940s and 1950s. When she married, she and my father weren't yet on a firm financial footing, so they moved to an area they considered affordable, with decent-enough schools and, mostly, decent-enough neighbors. After they opened the shop, their income was always unpredictable and never very high, and they stayed in their house once it was paid for. Mom didn't care about moving to a tonier zip code. She didn't worry about keeping up appearances. Raised to see herself as an aristocrat and an intellectual—roles that allow for eccentricity and carry an ingrained sense of superiority—she was free to decide which of bourgeois society's rules to follow and which to flout. A lady didn't need to strive because she'd already arrived. She was born that way.

One day, they were all gone: Kim, Tim, the grandma, the son, the girls, the dog. Workmen spent several months fixing up the house, and then it was sold. Mom and Daddy settled into assisted living, where they relished reporting the activities of the other "inmates."

> DADDY: You know that couple always holding hands on that bench?
> ME: Yes.
> DADDY [*leaning in with a conspiratorial air*]: The word is, they're sexually active.

And how about the old man, my mother laughed, who protested to the aide helping him undress: "But I can't *have* sex with you . . . I'm *old*."

Mom instructed me more than once that after her death I was to bequeath the dossier to the neighbors on the other side of Kim and Tim. It was a directive my brother and I agreed to ignore. As I threw the dossier's pages into a cardboard box marked "SHRED," I caught sight of a fading ink-jet image: Blair Winthrall, again in her favorite red, again displaying the squishy bosom, the glossy lips, the pink cheeks. A Santa hat, whitely trimmed, rode the dark roots of her yellow hair. Her squint seemed to say that delivering gifts was the last thing she felt like doing.

The Diary

Friday—December 12, 1958
The day was dull—nothing. Tonight I watched T-V for four hours. Mother and I watched one murder after another while Papa read the paper. Everybody is killing somebody. The three of us hardly spoke.

My father doesn't know what he should do with his life. He finds writing in his spiral-bound notebook soothing. His mother doesn't understand him. He has a girlfriend but is still lonely. Snow has fallen. He loves the snow. He ruminates for a dense page and a half in his neat, nun-trained script, then concludes, "There's nothing warm about the heat in the house; it's just hot. Hell is everywhere when I am alone and feel lost."

It was his freshman year at Chapel Hill. That same December: "Conformity has made senseless robots of the Human race." At the top of the page are two book titles, *1984* and *Organization Man*. Orwell's dystopian novel, of course, and a 1956 book by William Whyte describing how the rise of the corporation threatened individuality. Daddy was also reading Kerouac's *On the Road*, identifying himself with the late-fifties counterculture that rejected the churchgoing, TV-watching, flag-waving, tie-wearing ways of mainstream citizens. All his life, Daddy would despise country clubs, fraternities, organized religion, name brands, and nationalism. Suspicious of all things codified and popular, he would warn his children against trends and fads: *Think for yourself.*

My father stands next to a Mercedes sedan. He's smiling, wearing a white shirt. It's the late 1950s or early 1960s. He's young. Behind him is a wooden country fence of elongated Xs, painted white. I have no idea how he got the Mercedes or what it cost him, but he talked about it long after he'd had himself photographed next to it. The car was one more proof that he was an independent thinker, immune to the herd mentality.

"Now a Mercedes Benz is a status symbol," he'd say, "but back then, nobody in North Carolina drove one. Plus, it was diesel. Having a car like that was just plain *weird*."

On January 5, 1959, he recorded his impatience with college and disgust with "worldliness": "I would like to retreat to the forest, like Thoreau, with a menial income and just live as a free soul." In February, he drafted a letter to his mother explaining that he'd skipped his trigonometry exam because he was already failing the course. He couldn't force himself to study subjects in which he had no interest. (Like father, like daughter: thirty years after he wrote that, I hurled a trigonometry textbook across my dorm room, stomped screaming into the hall, and kicked a giant hole in the plaster wall.)

Daddy wrote to his mother that he craved her understanding even more than her love. I doubt he sent the letter; if he did, it didn't have the hoped-for effect. Elsewhere, he recorded her coming into the room and kissing him, something she hadn't done for a long time. They couldn't understand one another. Mimi grew up poor, with no opportunity to be educated, and owned few books beyond a handful of drugstore-rack prayer pamphlets. She'd striven to raise her only son in middle-class comfort, providing piano lessons and college tuition. To her, the point of getting a degree was that it enabled you to get a high-paying job. When my father dropped out after one year, she must have thought it one more proof he was "hard-headed."

On December 13, 1959, he wrote, "Today I went for a walk along the banks of the Potomac." After his terrible freshman year, he escaped to Washington, D.C., where he took a job in a drugstore. I have no idea how long he stayed or when he returned home, but getting out of North Carolina, even for a little while, made a difference to his frame of mind.

"Feb. 5, 1960 I have discarded this 'crank' that everything is futile and useless, and contend [*sic*] myself with the idea and purpose of 'setting out on the road of long search.'"

His disillusion and angst didn't subside entirely, but now he was seeking purpose. He grew fevered with the idea of being a writer. To train himself, he tried to read important books—history, philosophy, literature—and he experimented with style. Half a dozen handwritten and typed drafts of stories, and a few occasional musings on books, visual art, and music, are all that remain of his efforts. He wrote high-flying, philosophical purple prose, then switched to Hemingwayesque plain speak and scenes peppered with slang: *jive, sharp, cat*. Sick of the South's narrow attitudes about race, he attempted social critique. In an outline for an unwritten novel, he describes a young white man in love with a black woman—a scandalous, dangerous relationship in North Carolina at that time. The tenor of this proposed work was essentially romantic, like the rest of my father's stories. All his main characters long for love and connection with a special person as different from the rest of the crowd as the main character feels himself to be.

In 1960, shortly after "setting out on the road of long search," Daddy met my mother on a blind date. They embarked on a whirlwind romance and married less than a year later, in June 1961. They were both smart, rebellious, passionate. They both loved a joke. Her playfulness is evident even in her earliest photographs: her infant eyes challenge the camera. As she grew into a girl, and then a young woman, her boldness grew as well. Always she looked like she was up to something. She usually was. A woman who knew her in high school once delivered to me the verdict, "your mother was boy crazy." Another friend from college days recalled Mom as "our Elizabeth Taylor," and you can see what she means in photographs of Mom at nineteen, twenty: the thick, nearly black hair cut in a pixie style; the big blue eyes, pale skin, and hourglass figure; the fashionable clothes and poise beyond her years.

In *A Streetcar Named Desire*, Blanche DuBois comes to visit her sister, Stella, recently married to Stanley Kowalski. He's Polish and blue-collar, and Blanche finds him crude and common and altogether *beneath* herself and her sister. Stella knows Blanche is right, but her physical desire for Stanley is so strong that nothing, not even his violence toward her and Blanche, can make her want to give him up.

My brother found at a yard sale a large framed poster of Marlon Brando as a bare-chested Stanley in the movie version of *Streetcar*. He bought it for Mom, who hung it in her bathroom. It didn't go with the prints and paintings elsewhere in the house, of course, but it was also relegated to the bathroom because of its indisputable sexiness. There was another sexy picture—a portrait of a woman nude to the waist, painted by a college friend of my parents—in the bathroom my father and brother and I used. Her features are vague, outlined in loose black strokes, and I still remember my surprise the day I recognized her as my mother. I'd seen plenty of naked figures in art, but it made me uneasy to discover that my own mother had been willing to strip down, to be stared at and rendered on paper for anybody to see. Did she like being looked at naked? That the picture hung in my father's bathroom eventually made me think about whether he enjoyed looking at her naked, and—*eww*—suddenly I was contemplating my parents' sexual relationship, a thing I'd always strenuously avoided.

Mom's first sex talk with me when I was in kindergarten went like this:

MOM: When a mama and a daddy want to have a baby, they go to
bed and . . . [*explains intercourse*]
ME [*thinks hard for a minute. A look of disgust comes over her face*]:
Eww! You mean, you had to do *that* to get *me?*
MOM [*in a faux martyred tone*]: I wanted you so bad, I would have
done *anything.*

In pictures made just before their wedding, my parents' attraction is
plain. In one photo, she tilts her saucy head, teasing, while he looks
on amused, happy to let her and her big white dress take center
stage. In another, she stares adoringly at him; in a third, they gaze
at one another with serious, searching expressions. They only have
eyes for each other.

~~~

I imagine the parallels between my father and the character of Stanley did not escape my mother: sexy man from the working class
marries plantation daughter willing to come down in the world if
it means she can get her freak on. In marrying, my parents rebelled
against their own parents' expectations for them. Their defiance
was part of what bound them—that and their shared belief that intellectual compatibility was the best foundation for true companionship, a connection that could remain even if sex fell by the wayside.
They regarded their strife as the price: only stupid people could be
consistently agreeable, and household harmony wasn't worth being
shackled to a stupid person. From the beginning, the fighting was
part of the bargain.

Among my father's papers, I found no story drafts or diary en-
tries dated after their marriage. Given that he saved everything, the
absence of further drafts suggests that he gave up writing around
that time. Perhaps my mother truly filled the gap of his yearning,
and he no longer needed the outlet of writing. Possibly she criticized
his efforts, and he got mad, then grew discouraged. Maybe he ran
out of ideas, or writing just seemed an impractical thing to do, now

that he was a married man. Or perhaps he simply couldn't find the time. After the wedding, he briefly attended Guilford College before dropping out again, this time for good. My mother earned her BA, completed the coursework for a master's in English but didn't write her thesis, then taught high school for a year before working as a buyer at a department store. In 1967, seven years after declaring his compelling need to be a writer, Daddy took a correspondence course and became a stockbroker.

It was a rough time in their marriage. In those days, if you went over to my parents' house, and Daddy got tired of you, he'd tell you to leave. Just like that: *get out*. In 1968, he and my mother contemplated divorce. I found the abandoned separation papers in a pigeonhole: the one true surprise in our paper chase. The document was not clear about the cause of the rift, but I've heard a vague story about Daddy moving in with another woman for a week. This story upset me when I first heard it, in part because my parents were still alive, and I knew my mother wouldn't have wanted anyone to tell me such a thing. Now, however, the possibility that Daddy was unfaithful early in their fifty-year marriage no longer shocks me. What is more disturbing is how the separation document spoke of my mother—twenty-six years old in 1968—as though she were a child or mentally incompetent, with no volition or agency of her own. According to that document, she was a problem it was up to my father and my mother's father to solve.

The plan fell through; Mom and Daddy made up. My brother was born the next year, and I arrived three years after that. They moved to a neighborhood not unlike my grandmother's, to a house similar to the one my father in his teens had longed to escape. There Mom and Moreland and I would spend decades trying to predict Daddy's moods, working to divert or calm his anger.

I felt a little guilty reading my father's private writing after his death, knowing it was something he never meant anybody to see. But I was too fascinated to put the notebook down. Maybe I'd finally found a clue to why he'd spent so much of his life in a bad mood. Maybe he felt his early dreams of becoming a writer had been thwarted by having a wife and children, a mortgage and a business. If so, I could understand that feeling. By then I'd written several book manuscripts, published none of them, and was feeling resentful that so much of my time and energy had been spent caring for others. The difference was, while I've wanted to write longer than I've wanted anything else in my life, for Daddy, the ambition to be a writer seems to have been a passing phase. Music was the art form he truly loved, not literature. I rarely saw him reading a book. When I decided in high school to become a writer, Daddy never said that he'd once shared my ambition. And though he professed pride when I won an award or published a review or a story, I don't know if he ever read anything I wrote.

When I teach creative writing, I ask students to think about what their characters most want. It's important, I tell them, because desire causes conflict, which moves the story forward. *What* a character wants can be anything—a material object, the love of another person, a different mode of living or state of being. Maybe a second character doesn't want the first character to have the thing; maybe she wants it for herself. Or maybe she wants to get it for the first character but she messes up, goes about it all wrong. Maybe nobody gets the thing. Or they get it and lose it.

These gyrations of wanting and getting, missing and losing make a plot, but to have a full-fledged story, there must also be mystery. The mystery of desire is not just about the object; it's about the characters' complicated feeling that wanting that thing (or person) is dirty or holy or a bit of both. The mystery also is about how the dirty, holy desire persists in the face of humiliation and self-loathing, mutilation or exile, even death. It's about how we *keep* desiring, despite knowing that no lasting good will come of it. Even when we understand that everything is temporary, we keep on wanting moments of beauty, sweetness, transcendence. Fulfillment or forgetting. We want such moments—and will risk much to obtain them—because, as Blanche DuBois says, "Sometimes there's God so quickly." And when God, whatever that is, shows up, you want to be there for it.

Desire is at the center of *Streetcar*—right there in the title—just as it is at the heart of all of Williams's plays. Sexual desire in his dramas is not only metaphorical (although it is that, too): Sex is sex in Williams. He was not bashful about carnal pleasures, and the popularity of his work surely owed much to its forthrightness. His plays sold like hot pants in the 1960s; my mother owned them in Signet paperback. Hawked on drugstore racks for thirty-five cents, their pulp-fiction covers featured voluptuous women and hard-muscled men ready for action.

Ultimately, though, sex and its irresistible, often shame-inducing repetitions can't satisfy a character like Blanche. She seeks a sustaining, true, spiritual love. A pure love. If she can't find that, though, she'll take beautiful illusion, and risk the damnation that goes along with it.

> BLANCHE: I don't want realism. I want magic! [*Mitch laughs.*] Yes, yes, magic! I try to give that to people. I misrepresent things to them. I don't tell the truth, I tell what *ought* to be truth. And if that is sinful, then let me be damned for it!—*Don't turn the light on!*

She knows that if Mitch, her smitten date, looks at her in strong light, he'll realize she's lied about her age. A few moments later, as she describes nursing her mother back home on the family plantation, Belle Reve (beautiful dream), she says, "Death—I used to sit here and she used to sit over there and death was as close as you are. . . . We didn't dare even admit we had ever heard of it!" Outside, a passing Mexican vendor cries, "Flores para los muertos, flores—flores . . ." (Flowers for the dead, flowers—flowers). And Blanche goes on: "The opposite is desire. So do you wonder? How could you possibly wonder!"

If Blanche is right, if death and desire are opposites, and if desire is what makes us know we're alive, then what happens when desire isn't met? What happens when we accept a lesser fulfillment—a make-do relationship, ho-hum job, piles of material goods—as a substitute for what we can't get? And what happens when death and desire meet in the impossible situation we call grief, that condition when our strongest desire is to have our dead back with us and nothing else will suffice?

Desiderata, in Scraps

In Daddy's office—that catacomb of dead wishes—we find a stack of cheap date books with brown vinyl covers, each one dated with a year long gone. Customers' names and telephone numbers are written inside, next to descriptions of antiques they hoped to find.

> Doctor from Nashville
> Wants George Edwards (18th c) bird prints
> Canton (especially helmet pitcher)
> 10″ or larger dinner plates
> Cary maps, and other early maps
>
> wants paintings of animals
> $80–$250 cat or *dog*
>
> wants a pembroke—mahogany
> > height 28″
> > length 26″
> > leaves down 16″
> call her mother at local #
>
> wants a 30″ × 60″ writing table
> with 1 drawer on either side as
> you sit at it, no center drawer
> wants Chip. but will take Hepp.
>
> infatuated with boxes, especially lacquer
>
> interested in ivory
> dominos for him

Together, these notes compose a found poem about the collective (and collecting) human condition: a persistent state of longing for the perfect treasure, the thing that will satisfy us. Reading these lines, I'm touched by the optimism implicit in my father's gesture of writing down strangers' wishes. I like to imagine him promising that he would tell my mother to be vigilant on their behalf, that she would keep her eye out for the things they desired. This vision of him as a matchmaker is antithetical to how I saw him for much of his life: a man selfish and often dismissive of other people's wishes. Most days my father was a closed loop, so unsettled by change that he preferred to operate without input from the outside world. But those cheap date books testify that he *did* believe in being open to possibility. Occasionally, my mother *did* find on her rambles what a customer wanted, and uniting buyer and object must have provided rare satisfaction to all parties. More often, though, the strangers' wants my father recorded were met elsewhere or nowhere, or were forgotten altogether with the passage of time.

He also preserved thousands of index cards, one for each inventory item that passed through the shop in its thirty years. My mother wrote the majority of them, recording the stock number, a description of the item, the price, and details of its purchase and sale. The cards were shredded in the great purge, except for a few whose descriptions I liked, such as these lines in my father's tight script:

> watercolor of two children about to go
> into an embrace or the male child
> is indicating he wants to start
> something but she appears reluctant

In act 2 of *Cat on a Hot Tin Roof*, the patriarch Big Daddy complains about a miserable trip he took with his wife: "That Europe is nothin' on earth but a great big auction, that's all it is, that bunch of old worn-out places, it's just a big fire-sale the whole fuckin' thing, an' Big Mama wint [*sic*] wild in it. . . . Bought, bought, bought! . . . an' half that stuff is mildewin' in th' basement." It's Big Daddy's sixty-fifth birthday, and he's taking stock of his life. For him, the things Big Mama found so desirable have turned out to be worthless: "A man . . . can't buy back his life when his life is finished . . ."

He's ranting to his son, Brick, who can't get away because his leg is broken. Big Daddy brags and repeats himself; he's cruel to his wife and refuses to accept his own mortality. He's a prime example of his own claim that "the human animal is a beast that dies but the fact that he's dying don't give him pity for others, no, sir." When he finally hands Brick his crutch so he can go to the liquor cabinet to make himself the real crutch he's desperate for, Big Daddy says, "I think the reason he buys everything he can buy is that in the back of his mind he has the crazy hope that one of his purchases will be life everlasting!—Which it never can be. . . ."

All that worthless stuff—it's no more satisfying than sex but every bit as seductive. My mother loved twentieth-century American drama: Tennessee Williams, Eugene O'Neill, Edward Albee. A clear literary lineage of desire runs through their plays, in which characters wreck everything by chasing property and people that cannot and ought not belong to them. They drink and fornicate, throw fits and fight and hurl insults; their creators seemed to take it as gospel that cruelty leavens the bread of love. These writers dramatized how we pursue and hold the people we desire in such wrongheaded fashion that ultimately we drive them away or kill them. And how, when our beloveds are estranged or dead, we desire them afresh, even as we mourn all the ways we killed what was between us.

I begin to think I used to have it all wrong. Maybe Mom was Stanley, and Daddy was Blanche. He was the one who preferred romantic illusions, after all, and she was the one capable of turning on the harsh light to get at a truth you'd rather not see.

An iconic image from the most famous movie version of *Cat on a Hot Tin Roof*: Elizabeth Taylor in a white slip, trying to provoke pajama-clad Paul Newman. "I'm alive," she screams at him. "Maggie the Cat is alive!"

After seeing the film on television, I'd think of it whenever Mom wandered about our hot house in summer, smoking in a damp, white slip as she railed at Daddy for refusing to run the air-conditioning.

When my mother was alive, she reminded me of Maggie the Cat. Now, my mother is gone, and Maggie the Cat reminds me of her.

Hoping to keep us from repeating their mistakes, our parents urge us to want only what they think can't hurt or disappoint us. They try to steer us toward people or paths we don't want to follow, and we resist, just as they did their own parents, because desire has nothing to do with good sense.

Consider these lines from a slip of paper dated "1-27-61," a month after my mother and father, to my grandparents' profound displeasure, became engaged:

> *[in pen, Daddy's writing]*
> My love; my love of a thousand dreams
>   I will cherish you forever....

> *[in pencil, Mom's writing]*
> I am alone plus he is alone;
> And not because of a common enemy,
> We are together

During the years my brother and I were cleaning out the house, I tried to do what I thought my mother would've wanted me to do—

with her belongings, with my life—but the effort was making me miserable. Grief and stress had changed me from a playful, inquisitive, open-hearted person to someone who was prickly and ungenerous. I dreaded becoming like my father on his worst days—angry, self-pitying, blaming others for his losses and unpursued ambitions. It was time to be done with the house, time to quit moving stuff around. It had become clear to me that all I really desired was exactly what I'd wanted at thirteen: to make art and to make out. To write. To love and be loved. And so, no more shuffling papers. No more chasing hares I would never catch.

The Sum of Trifles

SELL:
Whatever's left

In August 2013, two years after my mother died, I moved with my husband and son into a house just around the block from where we'd been living. The portrait of Emma Wright Ridley took its position over the Capehart sideboard in the dining room. In my new parlor, we hung the golden Tale of Genji screen over Daddy's mid-century hi-fi. Mom's bonsai tree, with fragile leaves, flowers, and fruits carved from jade, had always sat on the coffee table in her own living room, surrounded by an aura of *don't touch*. Now I gave it a place on my mantel, where I hoped it would be safe from children.

In the fireplace, gas logs left no room for andirons. A good word, *andirons*, but homier is *firedogs*, which conjures for me hearths older and more picturesque than my own. My real dog liked nosing around this new fireplace, attracted by the swifts nesting in the chimney. Needing a barrier to keep her out of there, I found at my parents' the perfect thing: an early nineteenth-century wire fender, black and plain. A narrow metal band runs around the top, and a flat base stabilizes the fender and keeps it upright. It's a homely thing, the only hint of decoration a subtle wire swag repeating across the top—a curt nod to the neoclassicism popular at the time it was made.

That this fender sits now on my hearth owes as much to literary association as to practicality. Whenever the word *fender* comes up, I think of the auction scene in George Eliot's novel *Middlemarch*. I first read it as a teenager in a motel room in Raleigh or Charlotte, where I was staying with my mother and another antique dealer, a thin, brassy lady named Helen. We'd spent a long day minding the booth at an antiques show, then taken a greasy supper at a diner. Back at the hotel, we read on the double beds, grateful to have our feet up, and Helen, chain-smoking over her paperback, peppered my initial foray into Eliot's provincial Midlands society with lurid details about Lana Turner's teenage daughter stabbing her stepfather.

The second time I read *Middlemarch*, I was twenty-two, engaged, and enrolled in a graduate course on the nineteenth-century novel. For an assigned paper, I focused on a part in the novel in which a prosperous tradesman's household effects are sold. It's not hard to understand why I was drawn to this scene, having been dragged to auctions from my infancy. Among my earliest sound memories is the auctioneer's harsh gabble, with its worrisome, pushy cadence. The tension mounted as people twisted in their metal folding chairs to see who put up the final bid and captured the prize. The auctioneer's loud, urging voice alarmed me all the more because it was disembodied—I was too short to see over the seated crowd. When he shouted *Sold!*, there was a break, and then the whole thing started all over again.

The auction goers were generally in a jovial mood, and there was always junk food to be had, hot dogs, potato chips. It was not so different a scene from the one Eliot describes: "At Middlemarch in those times a large sale was regarded as a kind of festival. There was a table spread with the best cold eatables, as at a superior funeral; and facilities were offered for that generous drinking of cheerful glasses which might lead to generous and cheerful bidding for undesirable articles." The phrase "in those times" lulls the reader into feeling that such scenes are bygone, and in a strictly chronological sense, they are. They were at a remove even for their author; although Eliot published the novel serially in 1870–71, she places the action as beginning in 1829, when she was ten years old.

But Eliot's depiction of the public's thoughtless consumption of material goods remains as apropos today as it was 150 or 200 years ago. Because the author is female (George Eliot was the pseudonym of Mary Ann Evans) and the surface of the prose polite, readers might be tempted to dismiss Eliot's gentle raillery as toothless. Certainly, her good-natured satire operates on a human scale; nothing is outsized, fantastic, or grotesque. Her humor's modesty fits with the novel's realism and its setting, the middling town of Middlemarch, where no heroic feat occurs or deus ex machina appears to take us out of the realm of the everyday. Still, Eliot gets in her digs at human nature; we see them in "superior funeral" and the "cheerful bidding for undesirable articles," phrases meant to skewer by pointing at how we overvalue frills and trappings, how we covet what is base, and ignore what is truly golden.

In this scene, the prosaic items auctioned are of mediocre quality and not altogether necessary. Among them is a fender "of polished steel, with much lancet-shaped open-work and a sharp edge." Mr. Trumbull starts the bidding by praising the fender's "workmanship" and "antique style." A woman in the crowd complains, "Every blessed child's head that fell against it would be cut in two. The edge is like a knife."

"'Quite true,' rejoined Mr. Trumbull, quickly, 'and most uncommonly useful to have a fender at hand that will cut . . . Gentlemen, here's a fender that if you had the misfortune to hang yourselves would cut you down in no time—with astonishing celerity—four-and-sixpence—five—five-and-sixpence—an appropriate thing for a spare bedroom where there was a four-poster and a guest a little out of his mind—six shillings—thank you, Mr. Clintup—going at six shillings—going—gone!'"

The auctioneer's skill as a storyteller is what sells the old thing: "'It was worth six shillings to have a fender you could always tell that joke on,' said Mr. Clintup, laughing low and apologetically to his next neighbour. He . . . feared that the audience might regard his bid as a foolish one.'"

Making a sale so often depends on the story the seller tells about the object on offer. Information is part of the story, but only part. For a story to work, to stick, there must be a detail or anecdote that strikes the listener/buyer as unusual, or moves them in a personal way, sparking a memory or feeling. As a child, I didn't understand that a sale is an act of seduction. Listening to my parents talk to customers, I wondered how they could bear to part with things they thought so wonderful. I didn't know that once the customer is convinced, and the conquest is made, then the seller's job—and their interest in the object—is finished. Look at Mr. Trumbull, once he has secured the sale of the fender: "The auctioneer's glance, which had been searching round him with a preternatural susceptibility to all signs of bidding, here dropped on the paper before him, and his voice too dropped into a tone of indifferent despatch as he said, 'Mr. Clintup. Be handy, Joseph.'"

It's not only the seller who tells stories. When I worked the cashier table at the tag sales my brother conducted, customers often justified their purchases to me or their companions or even to the strangers in line behind them. Like Mr. Clintup, they seemed to think that others might judge their expenditure foolish, and they felt compelled to explain their attraction to the thing they were buying. Perhaps they had one or more just like it at home and "needed" another to match. They owned a collection of similar things but not one *exactly* like this. They'd had one once but it had gotten lost or broken. Their grandmother displayed in her curio cabinet one just like it, and not until now had they seen another. Never before had they encountered such an object; it was just so _____ (fill in the blank). Or maybe they'd seen such things before, but *this* one was superlative. So old. So big. So tiny. So cute. So weird.

Some customers wanted to be the expert and tell me all about what they were buying; others asked questions, hoping I had knowledge to share. Mothers bought for absent adult children they suspected might not even want the thing; children begged for objects their mothers didn't think they ought to have. Confessions abounded: They needed more things like they needed a hole in the head. Their families were going to kill them for bringing home more crap. I should see their overstuffed attics and barns, garages and storage spaces. Probably they ought to have tag sale of their own, but they couldn't bear to part with anything. Others had started an eBay business or rented a booth at the antiques mall—the justification and release valve for a portion of their junk.

The hard-core regulars showed up on sale mornings well before the advertised start time. A few were dealers whose bread and butter it was to buy low and sell higher, but the majority of the early birds were just folks who regarded each weekend as a new opportunity to discover treasure. They were eager to buy, and they knew the rules. They didn't try to peek in the sale-house windows, which we always curtained; nor did they bother begging to be let in before 8 o'clock, the way the uninitiated did. They knew that if you wanted a position at the front of the line for the 8 a.m. opening, you had to be holding one of the numbered index cards Moreland gave out just after dawn. The lower the number, the closer you were to the door, and that meant first dibs on the merch. And so, determined as children hunting Willy Wonka's Golden Tickets, the hopeful arrived before the sun rose, nursing fast-food coffees in the dark.

As opening time approached, the obedient crowd lined up by number order. They fidgeted with anticipation as Moreland gave his humorous, elaborate speech on sale etiquette. He explained the purpose of the holding area and the grave contractual implications of removing the bottom portion of a two-part tag from a large piece of furniture. If anybody wanted to negotiate, he said, they should come straight to him, "the meanest man in Greensboro." The regulars offered a few good-natured heckles; my brother cheerfully rebutted. It was all part of the game. Finally, at 8 o'clock on the dot, he announced, "Let's play." With a dramatic flourish, he opened the front door to let in the first twenty-five or fifty people—however many he thought the first rooms of the sale house could accommodate. The low-number holders rushed in, jostling one another as they made a beeline in whatever direction their instincts led them. Those left outside craned their necks to look through the open door and fretted that the good stuff would be gone by the time they were allowed in.

Astonishing how quickly the public could ravage all our neat displays! In the movie *Zorba the Greek*, villagers swarm into the room of a woman who's just died. Within a matter of minutes, they strip it bare of her belongings, leaving only her corpse on the naked bed. Mom laughed knowingly whenever she recounted this scene of violation. She'd witnessed too many times how opportunists and heirs fail to respect the dead as they hurry to claim the goods, the spirit of their last owner still rising off them like steam.

About an hour into the sale, the fluffers would begin to circulate. "Fluffing" was what we called the simple but important job of going around the house straightening and rearranging the merchandise to make sure it was showing to its best advantage. A critical part of fluffing was finding items customers had squirreled under tables or behind books in hopes they'd still be there after noon, when everything went half price. You couldn't blame anybody for wanting a bargain, but we also needed to make a profit, and anyway, what if they didn't come back, and that Wedgwood box or bag of Matchbox cars missed its chance of being sold? Back out onto the floor it went.

When the customers were especially avid, Mom would declare, "They've got the fire in their eyes today."

"I feel like a drug pusher," I told my brother once. "Selling people stuff that's obviously not good for them." He admitted he felt the same way, then wandered away to make another deal.

If I avoid sales and shopping now (and I do), it's because I know how easily I can be tempted to buy, lured by the beauty of objects and the stories I tell myself about them. The apartments and houses in which I've lived throughout my adult life have been furnished with things my mother gave me, but also with tag-sale finds and stuff my husband and I bought in thrift stores. When we were newly married, secondhand was how we came by our kitchenware, books, and wardrobe. We loved discovering vintage mixing bowls in candy colors, first editions in their original jackets, Brooks Brothers shirts, or glittering costume jewelry. At one sale I bought a Mission armchair and an early edition of Eudora Welty's *Delta Wedding*; at another, I snapped up restrikes of Dürer's woodcut scenes from the Book of Revelation and demitasse cups with devils on them. That we got it all cheap pleased us nearly as much as the things themselves.

Thrilled to finally be grown and independent, the state I'd always craved, I worked on putting together my first real house. I was nowhere close to achieving my *ideal* house—the beautiful one I fantasized about, situated in the right place and full of "the real thing." That house was where I'd raise my two children—a boy and a girl—and write genius books until my husband and I died peacefully at the exact same moment in our hundred-year-old sleep. That magic lay a long way off. For now, I was only making a start. And so, at the end of each sale, I carried home several boxes of stuff, hot to clean it all up and rearrange what I already had to accommodate my new purchases.

Presale, I vowed not to spend too much. At the sale, in the heat of the moment, I figured only a fool would pass up such bargains. Post-sale, euphoria gave way to buyer's remorse. I'd spent most of my day's pay (or more) on things I'd been getting along fine without just the day before. My purchases weren't even all that practical or interesting. I dwelled resentfully on what else I might have done with the money, which was by no means petty cash to me in those days when I lived small paycheck to paycheck, with scant savings in the bank. Building a nest egg with my tag-sale earnings would have been more sensible than buying things I mostly didn't need, but that was not how I thought back then. Like every other young person, I planned to live forever, and be rich before long.

My regret over what I spent at tag sales wasn't unique. As I added up tickets at the cashier table, anxious customers watched the adding machine tape spool out, then sighed with relief when I announced the total. "I wasn't as bad as I thought," they might say, as though the amount due was a light penance. Customers who couldn't believe the amazing deal they were getting happily forked over the money. Others, for whom the prices could never be low enough, insisted on haggling, and it was hard to have patience when they were carrying designer handbags or driving shiny, late-model cars, and asked for discounts just for sport. I much preferred the people who spent little but shopped with an air of purpose. They paid without fuss for their sweater or frying pan or nearly full bottle of shampoo. Then they left. They had more important things to do than hang around squabbling over the remnants of a stranger's life. They might be wearing uniforms or name tags from the jobs to which they were headed, or where they'd just gotten off third shift, jobs at hospitals or stores or fast-food restaurants, and likely bought things secondhand because that's what they could afford, not because they found it an entertaining way to spend a Saturday.

Occasionally, customers came up short and asked me to hold their pile while they borrowed a twenty from their shopping buddy or ran out to the bank machine or called their spouse to bring a checkbook. If their efforts failed, and they had to leave empty handed, I beckoned the fluffers to return the "spit-backs" to the sale. How quickly a thing could transform from merchandise to object of desire to mere merchandise again.

During the years when I was cleaning out my parents' house, the country was still feeling the effects of the 2008 recession and the mortgage crisis. Making do with less had become a necessity for people who'd seldom had to think about thrift, and minimalism was a trendy topic. A conversion narrative of ditching conspicuous consumption for a materially simpler, more personally fulfilling lifestyle grew in the cultural imagination, particularly for many of my Generation X peers. As I've watched this narrative evolve, I've been struck by how it resembles the racial conversion narrative of my parents' generation. White liberal thinkers who came of age during civil rights opposed the segregation their parents and grandparents upheld as the natural social order. Now, their children want (among other things) to give up our forebears' wasteful habits and stop destroying our imperiled planet. Concerned about climate change and dwindling natural resources, we know Earth can't survive current levels of consumption, and so we look around for ways to change our toxic relationship with throwaway material goods. We carry our reusable water bottles, we purchase stainless-steel straws, we wash cloth diapers and install solar panels. We click through tiny-house websites, oohing and aahing at those bitty kitchens and clever storage benches, even though we know there isn't enough Xanax and craft beer in the world to enable us to live in an eight-by-ten-foot box with our partners and kids and pets. Not to mention the books and vinyl records we can't give up, or the giant flat-screen TV.

The dream of minimalism is as much about casting off the duties stuff brings with it as it is about ceasing to need the stuff itself. It's a fantasy about having less responsibility. This fantasy assumes that you're starting out with too much and yearn to scale back, which can sound pretty privileged, except that disposable material goods are now so cheap. Today, even low-income Americans, those without enough ready cash to pay their bills, tend to have more material goods than the poor of earlier generations.

Another problem with today's simplification narrative is that it assumes everybody can afford to choose where to live—for instance, near farmer's markets and public transportation. It assumes that you're able to walk a long way or ride a bike, and that your body is one that feels safe to take out into any public space, day or night.

Still, while the quest for simplicity may be romanticized, there are practical ways most people can live more simply. You can choose to upcycle, recycle, and share; to fix and make and clean things yourself; to help your neighbors and accept their help. Doing any of these things can help you follow a vision of success or fulfillment that isn't based on acquisition.

All the world's major religious traditions teach that throwing off worldly attachments is key to reaching enlightenment. Yet you need not be religious, or even spiritual, to like the idea of going through the world with less baggage. Take the phrase "traveling light." I love the ease of movement it implies, the openness to serendipity. Saying it, I picture a body free to roam, a mind ready to let preconceptions go, to accept the invitation of whatever challenges or delights it, without knowing what might happen down the road. Traveling light, I imagine, you'd feel free to move unburdened, unfettered, through a world that seems to want nothing more than for you to discover it.

Of course, you can read the phrase another way. Traveling light: illumination on the move. Sun rising, stars shooting. Closer to the earth—a lantern or candle, flashlight or cellphone. Carrying such light, we follow the rays roving through darkness; they hit our path with momentary patches of radiance.

I want lightness. I want light. I like to think I'm moving toward both, gradually, learning that I don't need or even want all the things I once believed I couldn't stand to lose.

During Daddy's first few months in assisted living, he'd ask us to retrieve items from home. He described precisely where he thought they were: *On my dresser, on the left-hand side, toward the back, between the lamp and the tray where I used to put my wallet.* It didn't occur to him that change was ongoing even in that house where no-body lived, and we didn't dare tell him, because that would have meant saying what he didn't want anybody to say—that he'd never live at home again.

Mom only went back a few times, then stopped asking us to take her. I figured she found going home too painful, and I was relieved. I didn't want her to see the dust and mouse droppings, nor the hairy vine that had grown through the den wall and was snaking its way across the crown molding.

One day as we talked about what would become of Oaklana, she said it no longer mattered to her.

"It could burn down tomorrow." She put the flat of her hand over her heart. "Because Mama, Daddy, everything—it's all right here."

I was stunned. My mother, who'd spent her career thinking about and with objects, now was saying that the stories we think live inside objects actually live inside of us.

Objects need stories if they are to have meaning, but stories don't require objects to live. People are all they require. Faulty and forget-ful as we are, people make the best containers for stories. We write them down, print them, remember them. We persist in carrying them across geographical borders and through time, no matter how heavy they are. We safeguard our stories past those who refuse to hear them or let them be told. We tell them to the next generation. It's our way of keeping alive the people who have meant the world to us.

After the people we love die, we may mend, but we stay cracked. Mom admired *kintsugi*, the Japanese practice of mending damaged porcelain with golden lacquer. Instead of trying to hide the object's imperfect state, you call attention to it. In gilding the rifts, you as-cribe beauty to the brokenness, inviting anyone to see how, treated tenderly, it can shine.

Emptying the house slowly was a means of holding on to my mother and father, as was writing this book. And though I'm more than ready to complete this project, I'm reluctant to leave my parents behind. In a Borgesian parallel world, there's a version of this book that considers every one of their possessions. In that world, I go on making this thing, this book, forever. Such a volume is an impossibility, unwritable and unreadable. Thank goodness. The very idea of it is my mind's way of telling me to wrap it up. If I don't fight the compulsion to keep remembering, recounting, recording, then eventually I'll buckle under the weight of what can never be regained.

By the end of 2013, Moreland and I had chosen what we wanted and sent the rest of the better furniture, ceramics, and paintings off with the high-end auctioneer Mom recommended. Quite a lot still sat in the house: less valuable antiques and artwork, hundreds of books, and household items like Mom's worn Revere Ware and Daddy's cache of vintage office supplies. The market for common antiques had continued to decline since the 2008 recession, and one auctioneer advised that we'd make more money if we held a sale ourselves. While I hated the idea of watching strangers roam through my childhood home, grabbing my parents' things, Moreland was eager to try it. I said okay, so long as I didn't have to come.

Throughout the autumn and winter leading up to the sale, I'd start reading a novel, then put it back down. For perhaps the first time in my memory, fiction failed to satisfy me. This situation was nearly as worrying as my distrust of food. Desperate to find a book to sink into, I turned to nonfiction and found Rebecca Mead's *My Life in Middlemarch*, a memoir about what Eliot's novel meant to Mead at various moments in her life.

If you've ever in middle age reread a book you loved in your youth, then you know how different it can be the second time around. The book may not only fail to evoke the feelings your younger self experienced reading it for the first time, it may, like an ex-lover, make you wonder what you ever saw in it. Or, the book may move you on second reading in a new, deeper way, now that you've done more living. The words on the page haven't changed, but you have, and that makes all the difference.

Mead reminded me that "Virginia Woolf described *Middlemarch* as 'one of the few English novels written for grown-up people.'" Deciding I now fully qualified as grown up, I read *Middlemarch* a third time. Again, I paid special attention to that auction scene and even dug out my old grad-school paper to see what I'd said about this passage:

> Meanwhile Joseph had brought a trayful of small articles. "Now, ladies," said Mr. Trumbull, taking up one of the articles, "this tray contains a very recherchy lot—a collection of trifles for the drawing-room table—and trifles make the sum of human things—nothing more important than trifles—"

In my paper, I discussed Mr. Trumbull's use of "recherchy," his accented twist on *recherché* (from the French, meaning sought after, rare, possibly pretentious), and I talked about his focus on trifles. My own research did not, back then, turn up the source of the phrase "trifles make the sum of human things," which comes from "Sensibility," a 1782 poem by British writer and abolitionist Hannah More:

> Since trifles make the sum of human things,
> And half our mis'ry from our foibles springs;
> Since life's best joys consist in peace and ease,
> And few can save or serve, but all may please:
> Oh! let th' ungentle spirit learn from hence,
> A small unkindness is a great offence.

More's message is a variation on a line from the Gospel of Luke: "He that is faithful in that which is least is faithful also in much: and he that is unjust in the least is unjust also in much." In other words, how we behave in the large moments of our lives mirrors how we behave in the small moments.

Hannah More's "Sensibility" was quoted so frequently during the nineteenth century that the line "trifles make the sum of human things" became a well-known motto, a piece of conventional wisdom. In chapter 53 of Charles Dickens's *David Copperfield* (1850), for instance, when David's childlike first wife, Dora, lies dying, he regrets having been unkind to her when she did not satisfy him. He cherishes the innocent, happy moments of their time together: "I think of every little trifle between me and Dora, and feel the truth, that trifles make the sum of life."

In *Middlemarch*, Mr. Trumbull takes a maxim meant for moral instruction and applies it to stuff, rather than sensibility. There is no doubt Eliot is making fun, and by putting More's phrase in the auctioneer's mouth, she slyly mocks the undue importance we (mis)place on our possessions and points out what our attachment to trifles reveals about our character. This idea of small things adding up to a bigger whole is the theme of the entire novel, itself composed of small episodes in the lives of average people. Throughout the novel's eight hundred pages, Eliot is explicit about her theme, reminding us that most people, especially women, who nurse epic, noble yearnings to do great things are generally allotted but ordinary lives. Most of our actions are small and will be forgotten. Yet the book's fine last sentence asserts that it all matters, everything we little people do: "for the growing good of the world is partly dependent on unhistoric acts; and that things are not so ill with you and me as they might have been, is half owing to the number who lived faithfully a hidden life, and rest in unvisited tombs."

Another good word, *trifle*. Somebody who is trifling is no 'count. Useless. Somebody who is not to be trifled with is somebody you don't aggravate.

Trifle was my mother's favorite dessert. It hails from England and is traditionally made of sherry-soaked cake layered with jam, custard, fruit, and whipped cream. At our house, we knocked it together with grocery-store angel food, bourbon, vanilla pudding, strawberries, and Cool Whip. I have a photograph of Mom in a royal-blue dress and red lipstick, seated at the long table in my grandparents' formal dining room, eating trifle directly out of the big cut-glass serving bowl. She is elegant, mischievous, voracious. In another photo, taken a half-hour later, she's stretched out on the den sofa, shoes off, arms folded, napping. This is the mother I remember and resemble: a woman of appetites, a woman in need of respite.

Sale week, March 2014. Everything is cleaned, arranged, and priced, except the books in Mom's office, which we've closed and marked as off-limits. Everything is ready, except Moreland hasn't hired enough staff. He needs me to work the cashier table. I'm furious. It's the one thing I asked, that I wouldn't have to be there to watch it all go away. But there's no help for it. My brother needs me, and though I cry and fuss and cuss, part of me is curious to see the thing unfold. So I shove my stupid, inconvenient hurt feelings in the deep, ancient hole where I prefer to bury them, and do what has to be done, because that's how my mom taught me to roll.

On opening day, around 7:15, the old tag-sale crew arrives—Moreland and me, my husband, cousins, aunt, various friends. We stand around the kitchen eating sausage biscuits and donuts as we catch up on news of jobs and mates, parents and children. An ice storm struck Greensboro two nights before, so we swap complaints about road conditions and power outages. We worry the weather will discourage customers. Then we walk through the house, adjusting goods displayed on folding tables and taping up posterboard signs:

"Hardbacks: $2 / Paperbacks: $1 / Magazines .50."

"Holding Area"

"OFF-LIMITS"

As the start time draws closer, the person working the jewelry and small-items case takes up her position. The fluffers disperse through the rooms, ready to monitor the commotion and to fluff as needed. Cousin Margaret and I make sure our checkout table is stocked with calculators, sales-ticket pads, and cigar boxes full of change. Just before 8 a.m., Moreland steps outside and gives his speech about sale rules. Some old regulars are in line, grayer and more wrinkled, numbers in hand, heckles at the ready. They shift their frozen feet and shiver with anticipation as Moreland, in true showman fashion, holds up his phone to watch the last seconds elapse.

Precisely at 8 o'clock, he calls out, "Let's play," and opens the door.

In streams the public. Discomfited as I am by the surreal scene of my childhood home invaded by strangers, I feel a not entirely unpleasant sense of tag-sale déjà vu as I watch them rush through the rooms. Soon customers appear at the checkout table, and Margaret and I begin adding up purchases. In the lulls, we struggle to recall the names of the regulars who tell us how happy they are to see us back in the tag-sale business. Oh, no, I protest, this is a one-time deal. Like a Brady Bunch reunion show or a going-out-of-business sale.

I've forgotten how similar running a tag sale is to mounting a theatrical production. The stage must be set, roles cast, standard lines memorized, contingencies considered. Each sale morning, we take our places and wait for the door to open (*Let's play*). Once the thing is in motion, there's no stopping it. When things don't go to plan, we improvise, taking cues from each other and relying on cooperation to make the sale a success. Working with people I worked alongside twenty years earlier feels like revisiting a past life, and I'm surprised to find myself actually having fun.

On stretch breaks, I circle the house, fluffing and listening to my brother and aunt talk to customers. Telling the stories that end in deals, they are in their element, just as my parents were at their shop. Of all the occasions Moreland and I have planned to pay our respects to Mom and Daddy—the funerals and celebrations of life, the visitations and graveside rites—this tag sale is as fitting a memorial as any to the lives they led.

From Annie Dillard's *The Writing Life*: "How we spend our days is, of course, how we spend our lives."

In the *Middlemarch* auction scene, Will Ladislaw has been sent to buy a painting for wealthy, pious Mrs. Bulstrode. The painting is said to be by Guido Reni, an Italian Baroque artist whose work George Eliot found vulgar. The fictional painting's biblical subject is the Supper at Emmaus, a scene that takes place after Jesus has been crucified and placed in the tomb. Two disciples walking along the road to Emmaus are joined by the resurrected Jesus, whom they don't recognize. They *can't* recognize him because in their minds he's still dead. His identity is revealed as they break bread together; in that moment, Jesus's friends must wonder if they're in a dream. In our dreams, the dead walk and talk with us, behaving as though it's perfectly normal for the dead and the living to inhabit the same realm. When my parents come to me in my sleep now, I think, *But aren't you dead?*, and then we rearrange furniture and argue about who will ride in the backseat. Until I wake up, it's as though I'm young and middle-aged simultaneously; time has become a wide plane instead of a narrow line.

Purchasing the picture for Mrs. Bulstrode, Will doesn't yet know that he and she are linked by a secret. Nor does he know that the instrument for its revelation is the rough character lurking at the edge of the scene, a stranger "just turned in from the road." A blackmailing drunkard, Raffles holds an ugly secret that, when told, will humiliate and humble each person touched by it, as well as show how changeable social positions and wealth can be. Yet the unleashing of this secret will also prompt acts of empathy beyond what any of them might have imagined possible. A low, dirty character like Raffles may seem an unlikely agent for enlightenment, but by bringing him off the road and into the story at the same time that she describes the Supper at Emmaus, Eliot reminds her readers how Jesus, too, was doubted. We can seldom predict, she seems to be saying, what transformations a stranger may bring.

After much measuring and deliberating, a family carts off my grandmother's dining table. Mom's college friend buys back her husband's pottery—Mom purchased countless bowls and mugs to encourage him in his craft. A taciturn older man piles up country antiques—tools, ladderback chairs, woven coverlets—for his booth at a mall a few counties away. My kindergarten teacher ponders a set of silver flatware for her daughter. A down-the-street neighbor buys a stack of CDs and says somebody around here had great musical taste. A pale young woman closely examines the condition of drawings and prints she hopes to resell online, while my friend's brother takes a fancy to the big crazy painting that always hung over my parents' bed. As a girl, I couldn't fathom what they found appealing about its thick daubs of orange and blue. The menacing male figure at the center scared me. Near him stood a girl in a Harlequin dress whose wounded stare made me avert my own eyes whenever I came into the room. I'm glad to see the last of her.

When strangers ask whose things we're selling, and I tell them, reactions vary. A few people say "oh" and change the subject, whether
out of indifference or discomfort or some vein of private feeling,
I can't say. Perhaps they don't care much for their own mother or
father, or perhaps the idea of losing their parents is too much for
them to think about. Maybe they simply dislike discussing personal
matters. More often, though, people are quick to say they're sorry
for my loss, their sympathy a prelude to their own stories of other
sales, other parents and grandparents. I add up tickets and they
write checks, but in the moment, that mundane business seems only
a thing to occupy our hands while we discuss the agonies of losing
loved ones, the sorrows of missing the dead.

As the hours pass, one stranger after another tells me about their
own losses, then departs with objects that have long constituted part
of my picture of home. I begin to understand that my experience of
loss, which for more than two years has felt so painfully isolating, is
also painfully ordinary. Certain aspects of my relationship with my
parents, and our intense relationship to objects, might be uncom-
mon, but grief itself is not. Grief, I'm realizing, doesn't have to set
you apart forever. Eventually, it might become a thing—perhaps *the*
thing—that connects you to other people.

During a lull, I step into Mom's office and shut the doors. Moreland
and I have moved out the desk and chairs, and the room has become a catch-all for the photographs and letters we've so far resisted
carrying off to our own homes. But the office still feels like Mom's
sanctuary, the room of one's own she built for herself. The three
walls of bookcases still hold hundreds of volumes, arranged by subject and bristling with her makeshift torn-paper bookmarks. Soon,
I know, all these books will go away. Soon, the house will be sold,
and I'll never set foot in it again. I can't yet make sense of that fact.
I'm not sure I ever will.

I take a few deep breaths, then rejoin my cousin at the cashier table. Sitting where my parents used to watch television every evening, Margaret and I add up tickets, make change, wrap breakables in newspaper. A happy customer appears before us, holding out price tags on which Moreland has scrawled new lower prices. People track gray slush across the linoleum in the side hall and leave dirty fast-food cups on the kitchen counter. Talk and laughter echo in the rooms as they empty.

The unbearable sadness I expected fails to arrive. Instead, as stuff goes out the door, I grow lighter. Never before has the transitory nature of ownership been so apparent. No longer do I need to worry about caring for all these possessions, about where they should go and what will become of them. As I listen to people chat about their purchases, objects I've been regarding as burdensome again become interesting, evocative, beautiful, now that there are new eyes to admire them. My parents' things are not passing away by leaving me and changing owners. They are simply beginning new chapters of their long and storied lives.

Acknowledgments

Huge thanks to my fabulous agent Maggie Cooper at Aevitas Creative Management, who read multiple drafts; offered calm, cheerful, timely counsel; and worked so hard on my behalf.

Thank you, Bethany Snead, Jon Davies, and everyone at the University of Georgia Press for believing in this book and guiding it to publication. I am grateful to the anonymous readers whose insightful suggestions helped me refine the manuscript. Eagle-eyed copyeditor Deborah Oliver did a superb job, and Kaelin Chappell Broaddus and Elizabeth Alexander gave me a dream cover—thank you.

Selections from this book originally were published elsewhere. Parts of "Always Magic" were previously published as "First Things" in *Southern Cultures* 23, no. 3 (Fall 2017), southerncultures. org. "A Miniature for My Mother" was previously published (in slightly different form) in *New England Review* 38, no. 4 (December 2017), nereview.com. "Legs" first appeared (in slightly different form) in *Ecotone* 26, fall/winter 2018, ecotonemagazine.org. Thank-you to editors Beth Staples and Anna Lena Phillips Bell at *Ecotone*, Carolyn Kuebler at *New England Review*, and Ayse Erlinger at *Southern Cultures*. Thanks also to Robert Atwan for recognizing "Legs" as a notable essay in *Best American Essays 2019*.

I am grateful to the United Arts Council of Greater Greensboro for their generous support of this project.

Elizabeth Evitts Dickinson, thank you for your invaluable feedback on the first draft and for your friendship and commiseration. It was a happy day when I met you.

Thanks to Claudia Cabello Hutt and Emilia Phillips for reading chapters, and to Holly Goddard Jones for advising me on literary business and for telling me to just get on with it.

Various literary institutions have contributed mightily to my writing life. Virginia Center for the Creative Arts, where I wrote much of this book, has been my literary second home for twenty years. I'm forever grateful for the time I've spent and the friends I've made there. Thanks especially to staff Sheila Gulley Pleasants, Dana Jones, and Beatrice Booker. Thank you, Kevin Wilson and the staff of the Sewanee Writers Conference, Ben Shattuck and Tamalin Baumgartner at the Cuttyhunk Island Residency, Katrina Denza and the Weymouth Center for the Arts and Humanities, and the Millay Colony.

I have been fortunate to study with many wise writers who are also teachers of writing, including Tony Earley, Marianne Gingher, Kathleen Hill, Randall Kenan, Mary LaChapelle, Stephen O'Connor, Michael Parker, and the inimitable and unforgettable Doris Betts. Jill McCorkle and Margot Livesey have taught me so much, and encouraged and mentored me for so many years, in and out of workshop. Thank you for believing in me and my work.

Thanks to my UNC Greensboro English Department colleagues, for your support and camaraderie, especially Heather Adams, Xhenet Aliu, Risa Applegarth, Matt Carter, Emily Cinquemani, Tony Cuda, Stuart Dischell, Jen Feather, Ross Garrison, Terry Kennedy, Noelle Morrissette, Nancy Myers, Scott Romine, Jessie Van Rheenan, Karen Weyler, and Jennifer Whitaker.

For keeping me well supplied with books, thanks to Shannon Purdy Jones, Brian Lampkin, and Steve Mitchell at Scuppernong Books; Diarra "Crckt" Leggett at Boomerang Books; and Ben Mathews at the Browsery, which, though closed now, will always rate among my best-loved places. Thanks also to the librarians at the Greensboro Public Library and UNCG's Jackson Library.

Friends and family too numerous to name here enrich my life

and make it a lot more fun; I love and appreciate you all. In particular, I thank the kind friends who held me up and helped us out while we were caring for my parents and their stuff, especially Claire and Jeremy Aufrance, Saskia and Ben Barnard, Alicia Warrick Bouska, Thea DeLoreto, Ginny Gaylor and Joe Barvir, Jenna Gerber, Dorothy Hans, Cathy Jordan, Kathy Newsom, Rachel Richardson, David Roderick, and Sarah Martin Ward.

To my fellow orphans, Brandye Peterson, Anne Schroth, and Kara Wilson, thanks for including me just when I needed it most. It's always a joy to see your faces.

The following people, in various ways, helped me stay the course as I completed this book: Audra Abt, Julie Alpert, Christina Askounis, Carole Burns, Jaquira Díaz, Terri Dowell-Dennis, Robert Long Foreman, Bryan Giemza, Kathy Glenn, Bill Goldstein, Jane Gutsell, Mary Herbenick, Michael and Belinda McFee, Anne Ray, Nina Riggs, Laura Schmitt, Kathleen Sweeney, Felipe Troncoso, Stephanie Whetstone, Ross White, Sarah Williams, and Brandy Woodford. Thank you.

I'm fortunate in my family—blood kin, kindred spirits, and cherished inlaws and outlaws. Thank you, Ken and Lorraine Perkins, Julia Perkins and Gabriel Mejia, Carolyn Shankle, Vince Mason, Gregory Tyler and Billy Peacock, John and Marti Tyler, and Liz Urquhart. Special gold stars to my cousins Margaret Wade, Nicholas Reynolds, and Tyler Hand, who helped us take care of my parents. Thank you.

Loving gratitude to my sisters from other mothers: Heather Bachelder, Sarah White, and Lucy Yates.

To my parents, Ridley and James, thank you for showing me how humor can leaven our sorrows and art raise our spirits. To my brother, Moreland, thank you for enduring all this alongside me and not minding my telling the tale. To my son, Theo, kindhearted music maker, I love and admire you more than words can say.

And to gentle Glenn, my boon companion. Thanks for feeding me and praising every draft. Everything's better with you around. All my love.

Notes

Always Magic

Peter Menzel's *Material World: A Global Family Portrait* (Berkeley: Counterpoint, 1995) is the exhibition catalog for the *Material World* exhibit.

Donald Winnicott discusses the "transitional object" in chapter 1 of *Playing and Reality* (London: Routledge, 1997).

The 300,000-object statistic is cited in Mary MacVean, "For Many People, Gathering Possessions Is Just the Stuff of Life," *Los Angeles Times*, March 21, 2014.

Joan Didion's *The Year of Magical Thinking* (New York: Knopf, 2005) is a seminal autobiographical work on grief.

The Italo Calvino quotes are from his lecture "Quickness," published in *Six Memos for the Next Millennium* (New York: Vintage, 1993), pages 32 and 33.

For more on animism, see George Kerlin Park's entry at *Encyclopædia Britannica*, https://www.britannica.com/topic/animism, last updated October 29, 2020.

The quotes from Sherry Turkle's *Evocative Objects: Things We Think With* (Cambridge: MIT Press, 2007) are from pages 4–5.

The House Beautiful . . . or
the House Good Enough

For discussions of kanji, kana, and hiragana, as well as Japanese literary and pictorial conventions in the Heian period, see Masako Watanabe, *Storytelling in Japanese Art* (New Haven, Conn.: Yale University Press, 2011).

Donald Keene's "Tale of Genji" is reprinted in *Murasaki Shikibu's "The Tale of Genji,"* edited by Harold Bloom, Bloom's Modern Critical Interpretations (New York: Chelsea House, 2003), on pages 12–13, 39.

The "gentleman farmer" definition is from Merriam-Webster's Online, https://www.merriam-webster.com/dictionary/.

For the doings of the saints and the sinners, see Nathaniel Philbrick, *Mayflower: A Story of Courage, Community, and War* (New York: Viking, 2006). The internet offers many accounts of Stephen Hopkins's adventures. A succinct but informative one, "Stephen Hopkins, Jamestown Settler, Mayflower Pilgrim—and Shakespeare Character?," may be found on the New England Historical Society site: https://www.newenglandhistoricalsociety.com/stephen-hopkins-jamestown-settler-mayflower-pilgrim-shakespeare-character/.

The quotes from Richard Bushman, *The Refinement of America: Persons, Houses, Cities* (New York: Knopf, 1992), are on pages 19, xiii, and xiv.

The Art of Dying

The quotations from Atul Gawande are from his *Being Mortal: Medicine and What Matters in the End* (New York: Henry Holt, 2014), pages 239, 249.

Nina Riggs's *The Bright Hour: A Memoir of Living and Dying* (New York: Simon and Schuster) was published posthumously in 2017.

The *ars moriendi* quotation is in Pat Jalland, *Death in the Victorian Family* (New York: Oxford University Press, 1996), page 17.

Sherry Turkle's useful phrasing is from *Evocative Objects: Things We Think With* (Cambridge: MIT Press, 2007), page 5.

The quotations from *The Death of Ivan Ilyich* appear in Leo Tolstoy's *The Death of Ivan Ilyich and Other Stories*, translated by Richard Pevear and Larissa Volokhonsky (New York: Knopf, 2009), pages 39–91.

Vladimir Nabokov's comments about Tolstoy are from his *Lectures on Russian Literature*, edited by Fredson Bowers (New York: Harcourt, 1981), 237–38.

Oscar Wilde's "My wallpaper and I . . ." is quoted in Richard Ellman, *Oscar Wilde* (New York: Random House, 1988), page 546.

A Miniature for My Mother

For more on miniatures' role in mourning in the United States, see Robin Jaffee Frank, *Love and Loss: American Portrait and Mourning Miniatures* (New Haven, Conn.: Yale University Press, 2000).

Lou Taylor looks at mourning clothing in Europe and the United States in *Mourning Dress: A Costume and Social History* (London: George Allen and Unwin, 1983).

Other books I found helpful as I mourned and sorted out my parents' household included Paul Auster, *The Invention of Solitude*; Roz Chast, *Can't We Talk about Something More Pleasant?*; Edmund de Waal, *The Hare with the Amber Eyes*; C. S. Lewis, *A Grief Observed*; Helen MacDonald, *H Is for Hawk*; Peter Orner, *Am I Alone Here: Notes on Living to Read and Reading to Live*; and Rebecca Solnit, *The Faraway Nearby*.

Roland Barthes's notes on the death of his mother are in his *Mourning Diary*, translated by Richard Howard and annotated by Nathalie Léger (New York: Hill and Wang, 2010). Quotations are easily found by date.

"Violet" describes some of Alexander McQueen's shows in "The Alexander McQueen Archive," posted March 15, 2010, at *The Fashion Archive: London Fashion, Timeless Style* (blog), http://thefashionarchive.blogspot.com/2010/03/alexander-mcqueen-archive.html.

The oft-quoted line, "Between grief and nothing, I will take grief," comes from William Faulkner's *The Wild Palms* (New York: Vintage, 1995), page 273.

Legs

The quote from Thomas Hardy is in chapter 15 of *Far from the Madding Crowd*.

The sad tale of Mary Rich is one of many told in Al Rose, *Storyville, New Orleans: Being an Authentic, Illustrated Account of the Notorious Red-Light District* (Tuscaloosa: University of Alabama Press, 1978).

Flannery O'Connor's "Good Country People" is in *The Collected Stories* (New York: Farrar, Straus and Giroux, 1999).

Horror Vacui

Italo Calvino discusses the first-century poem in his lecture "Lightness," published in *Six Memos for the Next Millennium* (New York: Vintage, 1993), pages 8–9. My italics.

Randy O. Frost and Gail Steketee distinguish hoarding from collecting in *Stuff: Compulsive Hoarding and the Meaning of Things* (New York: Mariner, 2011), quotes on pages 52, 43.

The lines I quote from Dante's *Inferno* were translated by Robert M. Durling (New York: Oxford University Press, 1997), page 27.

Eula Biss's *On Immunity: An Inoculation* (Minneapolis: Graywolf, 2014) helped me grapple with my germaphobia.

The Nick Flynn quotation is from his memoir *The Reenactments* (New York: Norton, 2013), page 195.

The Quilt

For Ray and Charles Eames's 1957 short film, see "Toccata for Toy Trains," Eames Official Site, www.eamesoffice.com/the-work/toccata-for-toy-trains/.

Details and quotations about the quilt are from Margaret Ridley Tyler Smith, "The Ridley Quilt," September 26, 1991, an unpublished report in my possession.

Ida B. Wells discusses buying a pistol for protection in *Crusade for Justice: The Autobiography of Ida B. Wells*, edited by Alfreda M. Duster (Chicago: University of Chicago Press), page 62.

There are many studies of Nat Turner's rebellion. Unless otherwise noted, quotations and information on this topic come from David F. Allmendinger Jr., *Nat Turner and the Rising in Southampton County* (Baltimore, Md.: Johns Hopkins University Press, 2014). His account of Nat Turner's youth relies in part on Thomas R. Gray's *The Confessions of Nat Turner* (Baltimore: Lucas & Deaver, 1831), and some of the quoted material in my chapter are passages Allmendinger quotes from that document.

The town of Jerusalem was renamed Courtland later in the nineteenth century and remains the seat of Southampton County, Virginia.

A third of "Major Thomas Ridley's 145 slaves" in 1830 were children aged ten and under. Another third were males between the ages of ten and fifty-five—any of these could conceivably have been drafted by the insurgents (Allmendinger, *Nat Turner*, 195).

The definition of *insurrection* is from Merriam-Webster's Unabridged Dictionary online, https://unabridged.merriam-webster.com/.

Rebecca Solnit's quote regarding revolutions ("Revolutions are always politics made bodily") is from her *Wanderlust: A History of Walking* (New York: Penguin, 2000), page 220.

The quotations concerning Curtis's and Stephen's trials and Scipio's testimony may be found in Southampton County court documents available online at https://www.natturnerproject.org. The site also furnishes other interesting documents connected to Nat Turner's rebellion.

In her report, my mother quoted the "belle and beauty of her age" description of Margaret Ridley from the genealogy volume *Ridley of Southampton* (1992).

For the quilt makers of Gee's Bend, Alabama, see "Gee's Bend Quiltmakers," Souls Grown Deep, www.soulsgrowndeep.org/gees-bend-quiltmakers.

Sanford Biggers's comment that "Harriet Tubman was an astronaut" is noted in "Codex," Sanford Biggers, http://sanfordbiggers.com/archives/gallery/codex.

Toni Morrison's question about the impact of slavery on the perpetrators is in *Playing in the Dark: Whiteness and the Literary Imagination* (Cambridge, Mass.: Harvard University Press, 1992), pages 11–12.

The report on the murders at the Rebecca Vaughan house was included in John Hampden Pleasants, "Southampton Affair," *Richmond Whig*, September 3, 1831, reprinted in *Norfolk American Beacon*, September 6, 1831, and quoted in Allmendinger, *Nat Turner*, page 188.

The definition of *nice* is from Merriam-Webster's Unabridged Dictionary online, https://unabridged.merriam-webster.com/.

Samuel Michael Lemon's fictionalized account of his family's escape from slavery is *Go Stand upon the Rock: From Stories Handed Down by My Grandmother about How Our Ancestors Fought to Be Free* (N.p.: Buckhorn Press, 2012), pages 85–86.

Concerning Irish immigrants, Eula Biss writes, "In the South, they were hired for work that plantation owners considered too dangerous for slaves. They drained bogs and died by the hundreds digging canals" (*Notes from No Man's Land: American Essays* [Minneapolis, Minn.: Graywolf, 2009], 175). In another essay, "Relations," Biss contemplates the word *nice* in relation to race.

The second Rebecca Solnit quotation on revolutions ("It is the nature of revolutions") is also from *Wanderlust*, page 230.

Paper Chase, a Play of Desire

The lines quoted in "The Playscript" section are from Tennessee Williams, *The Glass Menagerie* (New York: New Directions, 2004). In his introduction to the play, Williams refers to it as "the saddest play I have ever written."

"Kim" and "Tim" are not the real names of my parents' former neighbors. Neither is Kim's alias real.

Steven Marcus's *The Other Victorians: A Study of Sexuality and Pornography in Mid-Nineteenth-Century England* (New York: Basic Books, 1966) presents a fascinating flip side to our image of the Victorians as prim and buttoned-up.

Quotes from the nineteenth-century tome *My Secret Life* are from the complete and unexpurgated edition, introduced by G. Legman (Secaucus, N.J.: Castle Books, 1966).

The Oxford online dictionary defines *gamahuche* as vulgar slang meaning fellatio or cunnilingus, and offers this curmudgeonly etymology: "Late 18th century. From French gamahucher, of unknown etymology (a suggested etymology from classical Latin gamma + ut, with metaphorical reference to a low position, is probably entirely fanciful)" (https://www.lexico.com/definition/gamahuche).

Blanche's and the flower vendor's lines are from Tennessee Williams's *A Streetcar Named Desire* (New York: New Directions, 2004).

My father's note "Wants Chip. but will take Hepp." refers to furniture styles named for renowned eighteenth-century English cabinetmakers Thomas Chippendale and George Hepplewhite.

The lines Big Daddy speaks are from Tennessee Williams's *Cat on a Hot Tin Roof* (New York: New Directions, 2004).

Elizabeth Taylor played "Maggie" opposite Paul Newman as "Brick" and Burl Ives as "Big Daddy" in *Cat on a Hot Tin Roof*, directed by Richard Brooks, written by Tennessee Williams, screenplay by Richard Brooks and James Poe (Culver City, Calif.: Metro-Goldwyn-Meyer, 1958).

The Sum of Trifles

Quotes from George Eliot's *Middlemarch* (New York: Modern Library, 1992) are on pages 573, 576–77, 799.

Rebecca Mead's *My Life in Middlemarch* (New York: Crown, 2014) mixes memoir with rumination on the pleasures of rereading. The quote from Virginia Woolf is on page 45.

Hannah More's 1782 poem "Sensibility" is reproduced at http://spenserians.cath.vt.edu.

The quotation from Luke 16:10 is from *The Bible: Authorized King James Version*, introduced by Robert Carroll and Stephen Prickett (Oxford: Oxford University Press, 1998).

David Copperfield's reference to the famous line from More's "Sensibility" is quoted from Charles Dickens, *David Copperfield* (Oxford: Oxford University Press, 1998), page 768.

The quotation from Annie Dillard's *The Writing Life* (New York: Harper and Row, 1989) is on page 32.

Crux, the Georgia Series in Literary Nonfiction